D1731655

Christian M. Stracke (Ed.)

The Future of Learning Innovations and Learning Quality

How do they fit together?

Christian M. Stracke

The Future of Learning Innovations and Learning Quality

How do they fit together?

Organized by the University of Duisburg-Essen, Germany (UDE)

Open-*Minded*

Christian M. Stracke (Ed.)

The Future of Learning Innovations and Learning Quality

How do they fit together?

Proceedings of the European Conference LINQ 2012,
held in Brussels, Belgium on 23rd of October 2012.

Bibliographic information published by the Deutsche Nationalbibliothek:

The German National Library (Deutsche Nationalbibliothek) lists this publication
in the German National Bibliography (Deutsche Nationalbibliografie);
detailed bibliographic data are available in the Internet at <http://dnb.d-nb.de> .

ISBN: 978-3-942183-86-4

Cover photo: © Sabine Dertinger, Bonn (Germany)

Published by GITO 2012
Detmolder Straße 62
10715 Berlin
Internet: <http://www.gito.de>

The digital copy of this version is online available: <http://www.learning-innovations.eu>.

Contact:
Christian M. Stracke
University of Duisburg-Essen, Campus Essen
Information Systems for Production and Operations Management
Universitaetsstr. 9 (FB WIWI: ICB)
D-45141 Essen (Germany)
christian.stracke@icb.uni-due.de

Information about LINQ 2012 online: <http://www.learning-innovations.eu>.

Information about Q-Cert-VET project online: < http://edu-certification.eu/>.

Information about the University of Duisburg-Essen online: <http://www.wip.uni-due.de>.

Table of Content

Learning Innovation and Quality - An Introduction

Learning Innovations and Learning Quality are crucial for learning processes and success: That is also discovered, addressed and reflected by many European policies and communication by the European Union, European Commission, European Parliament, as well as by the European experts and communities.

The articles on learning innovation and quality in this book try to give an overview over current developments in all learning, education and training sectors from different point of views. Therefore this book provides a basis for further discussions about improvements and current developments in the field of learning innovations and learning quality.

The presented articles are the result of the Open Call for Papers issued by the European Conference LINQ 2012:

LINQ is the leading European conference focusing Learning Innovations and Quality (LINQ) and addressing in particular Lifelong Learning (LLL), Technology-Enhanced Learning (TEL), quality standards and certification, human resources development, competences and skills, as well as learning, innovation and quality management systems. LINQ is organized by the University of Duisburg-Essen, Germany, and its Institute for Technology-Enhanced Learning and Innovations for Didactics and Quality (TELIT).

The motto of the LINQ conference 2012 that took place in Brussels on 23rd of October 2012 was: "Innovation and Quality: How do they fit together?".

Learning innovations and learning quality are hot topics but very often are discussed only solely: LINQ intends to bridge and to connect both important topics for the improvement of European learning, education and training.

LINQ 2012 explored the relation between learning innovations and learning quality for the first time: Often seen as contradictions, LINQ 2012 was focusing their common grounds and synergies. The LINQ conference opened the debate on the relationship of learning innovations and quality and facilitated the exchange of ideas between involved individuals and organizations in many diverse ways, bringing them together for a productive meeting.

The scientific articles published in this book are the selected papers of applicants from over 15 countries received upon the Open Call for Papers issued by the European Conference LINQ 2012: They were reviewed by the scientific Programme Committee of LINQ 2012 in double-blind peer reviews and selected according the review results. In addition all authors of the selected articles could present and discuss their papers at the LINQ conference in a speech.

In the introductory article **Christian M. Stracke** (Germany) presents an overview of the relations and interdependences between learning innovations and learning quality and focuses their future for the improvement of learning, education and training in Europe and beyond. The argumentation is based on the hypothesis that the unique focus on either learning innovations or learning quality is not helpful: In contrary, the learning quality requires learning innovations as well as well-proven and mature learning traditions from the history. And learning innovations are needed to improve future learning, education and training.

Florence Dujardin (United Kingdom) presents how an innovative pedagogy that focuses on participation and knowledge creation can address quality in learning experience and outcomes. She uses an auto-ethnographic action research approach and the context is in a year-long module in Reflective Practice offered on an online Master's program in professional communication (MAPPC) which introduced collective blogging. Literature review and pedagogical implications are discussed.

The relevance of competences for learning opportunities is addressed by **Charalampos Thanopoulos** (Greece), **Giannis Stoitsis** (Greece), **Jad Najjar** (Belgium) **and Yiannis Psochios** (Greece) by their analysis of a survey in the agricultural sector. Regarding these survey results, the agricultural competences are divided in different metadata elements and submitted to agricultural experts for rating.

Kenji Hirata (Japan), **Simone Laughton** (Canada), **Kazuhisa Seta** (Japan), **and Christian M. Stracke** (Germany) discuss the importance of proficiency levels for the definition and measurement of learning outcomes. They highlight the benefits and contributions by international standardization to learning, education, and training (LET). In a preliminary version they introduce the information model for representing proficiency levels (PLIM) for LET aiming at demonstrating its capacity to adequately represent the main elements characterizing proficiency in order to simplify management and interoperability between different LET systems. The European Qualification Framework is used as application example.

Achilles Kameas (Greece), **Ed Mahood** (Germany) and **Michael Negri** (Germany) present the processes adopted by ProInternet (PIN) network in order to assess and validate internet-related, employment-functional qualifications and profiles in SMEs. The effort consists in developing an approach toward labelisation, certification and normalisation of these qualifications by addressing knowledge, skill, and competence requirements, on the one hand, and education and training development and provision, on the other.

Hua-Hui Tseng (Taiwan) describes the 3P model (people, process, and products) to analyze and explore the process of learning and giving students tools in education that would lead them to become successful and responsible learners. The 3P model is presented in the context of the Taiwan University of Techology.

Boris Pozdneev, Yuri Kosulnikov and **Maxim Sutyagin** (all from Russia) focus on the deployment of a Quality Assurance Model in the e-learning system in Russia as basis for national and regional certification models for ICT based education. They present the Russian standardization policy and its achievements and impact for the Russian educational system.

Katie Goeman and **Stijn van Laer** (both from Belgium) provide the findings from year 1 of a 2 year project that seeks to combine online and offline courses for adult students. Describing the project objectives and outcomes, the authors focus on the development of a continuous quality improvement framework.

Marcel Berthold (Austria), **Ingo Dahn** (Germany), **Andreas Klefel** (Germany), **Pablo Lachmann** (Germany), **Alexander Nussbaumer** (Austria), and **Dietrich Albert** (Austria) focus on technology-enhanced learning and self-regulated learning and introduce a Learning Ontology for responsive open learning environments. The authors present the learning ontology building on a connection of learning phases of a Psycho-Pedagogical Integration Model to learning strategies, techniques and activities. In addition, two practical applications are presented.

Ju-Youn Song (Luxembourg) and **Katerina Zourou** (Greece) provide the results of their desktop research identifying how projects integrate social media to valorise project dissemination and communication activities and what kinds of social media applications are actually used in LLP projects. Focussing on the first analysis of 150 selected LLP projects, the authors provide a first step towards the establishment of a state-of-the art regarding practices developed in LLP projects and associated needs for further development of skills and competences.

Manfred Lohr (Austria) presents a new educational concept and learning activities for using iPads and Apps in the context of physics teaching. After describing the didactic approach and the implementation of e-learning sequences in teaching, the author give a short overview and assessment of the new experiences in Austrian schools.

M. Naeem Mohsin (Pakistan) focuses on using computer assisted learning (CALL) in teaching of English. He discusses the impact of CALL in helping 50 secondary school teachers to improve their English language pronunciation. The research results show meaningful pronunciation improvement. These results recommend the development of a specific CALL model for foreign language teaching in Pakistan.

New methods of adaptive technology literacy testing are presented by **Renata Danielienė** and **Eugenijus Telešius** (both from Lithuania). This innovative testing system is used according to people's occupations and area of activity. The authors propose this testing as an alternative to the computer fixed test approach which is based on pencil-and-paper test model.

Carol Priestley (United Kingdom) presents a project named EMPATIC. It claims to gather and prepare materials to influence practitioners and policy makers to enable them recognising information literacy as an essential skill for all citizens and to stimulate the use and adoption of information literacy training across all learning sectors. The background, activities and results of the EMPATIC are described.

Anca Cristina Colibaba (Romania), **Elza Gheorghiu** (Romania) and **Irina Gheorghiu** (Germany) are focusing on an innovative methodology (developed by the psycholinguistic faculty from the Sapientia University in Rome) in teaching foreign languages to very young learners. The authors present a project that claims to develop an innovative didactic approach on intergenerational family learning and claim that the affective relationship between the adult and children improves the foreign language learning process.

Sarah Land (Ireland) gives an overview of the European Netbox project which aims to leverage the benefits of social media in re-building capacity for learning and education in rural communities across Europe. After presenting the state's view on the project the model for the development and provision of community-based education is described.

Monika Nowakowska-Twaróg (Poland) presents in her short paper a project that claims to develop innovation with respect to the vocational language learning and to introduce standardization in the vocational language learning. The project focuses on language courses and e-learning platform as main products as well as on an effective model for teaching vocational languages, along with the tools and techniques to facilitate the process through an e-learning tool.

Paweł O. Nowak and **Jacek P. Zawistowski** (both from Poland) present in their short paper brief results of several Leonardo da Vinci projects (LdV CLOEMC I, II, III projects, LdV MAIN.CON project, LdV TRAIN-TO-CAP project, LdV SHANIME project), especially on life-long learning for construction personnel across the EU.

Finally sixteen European projects are briefly presented in this book. They were selected upon receipt contributions following an Open Call for European Projects that was issued in cooperation with the European Commission and its European Agency EACEA responsible for the management of European projects from the Lifelong Learning Programme. Every project description starts with the logo, name and acronym of the project. Then, the information about aims, objectives and main target groups of the project are given. Furthermore, the project description provides an answer on the question how every project contributes to learning innovations and learning quality. After that, the projects' main outcomes are presented. All project representatives have been asked to give a short quote on the question what is most important for learning innovations and quality today and could present their project at the LINQ conference in a short speech.

To summarize this book contributes to the current developments and debate on learning innovations and learning quality by offering different views and solutions on competence modeling and by giving suggestions for future improvements of learning opportunities and European educational and training systems in all sectors and levels from kindergarten and K-12 schools, vocational education and training, higher education up to adult and life-long learning:

For the best learning innovations and learning quality in Europe!

Christian M. Stracke and Tatiana Shamarina-Heidenreich

Learning Innovations and Learning Quality: Relations, Interdependences, and Future

Christian M. Stracke

University of Duisburg-Essen, Information Systems for Production and Operations Management,
Institute for Computer Science and Business Information Systems,
45141 Essen, Germany
ISO-Convener ISO/IEC JTC1 SC36/WG5 (www.sc36.org)
Chair CEN TC 353 (www.cen.eu/isss/TC_353)
Christian.Stracke@icb.uni-due.de

Abstract. Learning innovation and learning quality are very often addressed separately and solely. But in fact they are interdependent and have to be reflected both for achieving the best learning quality: This article discusses how to achieve the best appropriate learning quality as the core objective in learning, education and training by combining the three dimensions learning history, learning innovations and learning standards. Only their mix can ensure to meet the learners' needs and to provide the best and appropriate learning opportunities and learning quality fitting to the given situation and for a long-term and sustainable improvement across all sectors in learning, education and training, all communities, educational and training systems and societies in Europe and worldwide.

Keywords: Learning quality, learning innovations, learning history, learning standards, quality development, education and training systems, digital age

Learning innovations and learning quality are important and reflected topics for a very long time from the beginning of discussions and theories about learning processes: In Europe, Plato's Allegory of the Cave is one of the earliest examples. Their debate continued during the introduction of the first universities in the Middle Age and of the school systems in the 18th century. During the last years and the upcoming so called "digital age", many discussions took place in particular due to the two main changes covering all sectors, branches and levels of the society:

1. Globalisation and

2. worldwide internet establishment

These two factors are leading to global markets, worldwide networking, communication and competition, as well as to the digitalisation of services and systems with the introduction of internet-based services, hardware and software within all parts of our lifes.

The European Union has identified the challenges and opportunities by these global changes and published several communications and framework for the future European society and its learning, education and training: Based on the Lisbon Declaration, the vision of the Information Society called i2020 and the established Bologna Process (European Commission 2005), the European Commission and Council have have reviewed and analysed the impact of the globalisation, the internet and the information technologies in general leading to current new communications and policies: The Digital Age for Europe, EUROPE 2020 and Education and Training 2020 are reflecting these movements with speial emphasis on the potentials for the European citizens and communities (European Commission 2010a and 2010b, European Council 2009).

In the international discussions about the future learning, education and training from theory, research and politics but also from press, individuals and social communities, the main focus is currently on the technological innovations and their opportunities. Theories and experts are claiming brand new and extraordinary chances, sometimes promising new learning eras and paradigmas. Even the arrival of fundamental new ways of learning are promised under the label of learning 2.0 / 3.0 in analogy to the terms web 2.0 / 3.0.

It seems that learning innovations are the only path and road map for a better future education and training: The underlying (and often hidden) argument is that through them we are earning many new chances to learn, without them not fitting we are not fitting to the changing times of globalisation and worlwide internet as well as to the new digital generation, the so labelled "digital natives". We call this discussion the (learning) innovation strand.

On the other hand, there is a long-term discussion with huge tradition (since the beginning of our culture) about the learning quality covering a broad range of topics like quality of learning design, objectives, materials, input as well as learning processes, outcomes and the achieved knowledge, skills and built competences. Many theories were developed in the past dealing directly or implicitly with the question how to ensure or to improve the learning quality. We call this debate the (learning) history strand even if some of the topics like quality management for education and training are less than 100 years old.

Surprisingly, both discussion strands, the new innovation and the old history, are not interconnected and not reflecting each other. It seems that the supporters of learning innovations do not want to refer to theories of the past and that the authors of learning history do not want to recognise global changes vice versa. That leads us to an important question that requires urgently attention and an answer in our changing times: What is the relation between learning innovations and learning quality?

Our answer is based on three hypotheses of the current learning situation:

1.   Learning history should not and cannot be ignored.

2.   Learning innovations are mainly technology-driven.

3.   Learning is not completely changing.

First of all, it has to be stated clearly that the worldwide changes by globalisation and internet for all through world wide web and social media and communities do not justify to withdraw or ignore all theories from the past. They are resulting from many discussions across socities, cultures and centuries leading to learning experiments, evaluations, failures as well as successes and finally to the improvement of both, the learning opportunities as well as the learning theories themselves. Modern innovation theories ignoring this treasure of expertise from the history are losing a well-proven underground for basing their argumentation (even if contradictory) that is providing a huge variety of different concepts (e.g. cf. for extremes the theories of cognitive development by Piaget (1953) and the systems theories by Luhmann (1995 and 1998) and Maturana/Varela (1992)). Moreover they cannot convince by such ignorance because without definition of their relation to the historical strand they claim to jump out of nothing (see figure 2 below) and start from the scratch (what is evidently not the case).

Second, the currently claimed learning innovations based on the effects of new internet opportunities, services and social media are only dealing with technological changes and chances: Of course we can realize diverse learning scenarios and (digital) communities, services and systems today that were not available several years ago (like social communities, MOOCs, blogging). But these technological inventions and changes are offering only new options and preconditions. They cannot be successful by themselves, they still require an appropriate learning design and setting with an attractive and motivating learning environment.

Finally learning is not completely different and changing only due to the globalisation, new technologies and network opportunities. The new technologies and global changes are providing challenges and chances to establish new ways to base, present and integrate learning processes within education and training and learning groups including new options for self-regulated learning. But these new modes and types of access and interactions in learning processes do not change completely the way how people learn. The style how to use, consume and reflect learning opportunities and materials may change through increasing speed and multi-tasking and lower attention but that is only increasing the requirements for learning designers, educators and teachers.

What is most important for the success of learning processes is the learning quality. Learning opportunities have to meet the need of the learners and to provide the appropriate quality to fulfill their requirements. That can sometimes mean a simple learning course with teacher-centered education and sometimes a complex sophisticated learning environment with learner-oriented group work enriched facilitated by an educator as moderator, tutor or enabler and with new learning technologies and innovations including social media and communities. That means that learning quality cannot pre-defined but have to be adapted to the given situation and learners. In this sense, learning history and learning innovations are two different approaches and points of view that are interdependent and cannot be reflected solely but have to be analysed in conjunction for achieving the best and appropriate learning opportuniy and success. Next to them, standards are building the third source for planning and designing the best learning opportunity and quality (see figure 1) what will be explained more in detail below.

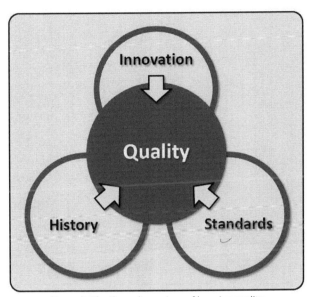

Figure 1: The three dimensions of learning quality

This overall objective for the continous improvement of learning quality can be called quality development: Quality development has to combine the relevant and appropriate approaches, concepts and elements from all three dimensions that are basing the learning quality: History (by learning theories and traditions), innovation (by new learning options) and standards (by consensus building on learning).

As shown in the following figure 2, there could be three alternatives and options in theory: To focus only on the learning innovations only (1.), to focus only on the history of learning traditions and theory (2.) or to arrange the mix between both approaches (3.). As already explained above, it is not possible to argue that the only focus on learning innovations can succeed by jumping out of nothing as it cannot be argued and proven how such a jump can take place by ignoring the learning experiences and theories. On the other hand, future learning opportunities have to reflect the changes in society and chances by innovations and would also fail by ignoring them. Therefore only the mix of learning innovations and history based on learning experiences and theories from the past is promising and convincing as shown in figure 2.

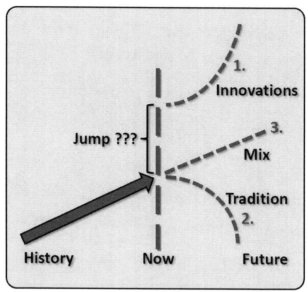

Figure 2: The potential three options for future learning quality

Thus, we can say: Quality development is the crucial task for learning, education and training.

In the past, a long-term debate has focussed the quality development in general regarding the different quality issues, aspects and approaches (cf. Deming 1982; Juran 1951 and 1992; and for an overview Stracke 2006a). Quality development in its broad sense can be defined as follows (cf. Stracke 2006b):

> Quality development covers every kind of strategy, analysis, design, realisation, evaluation, and continuous improvement of the quality within given systems.

Quality development can be described formally by the chosen scope. Quality is not a fixed characteristic belonging to subjects or systems but depends amongst others on the point of view and scope. The following differentiation of the scope into three quality dimensions has become widely accepted:

1. Potential dimension: What are the potentials for the quality development in the future?
2. Process dimension: How can the processes be described and optimized for the purpose of quality development?
3. Result dimension: How can the quality development be supported regarding given results and systems[1]?

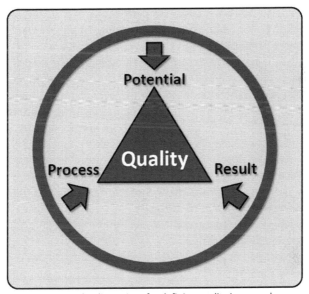

Figure 3: The dimensions for defining quality in general

Quality development requires a long process to be established and integrated throughout a whole organisation and in particular the society. Once started, it has to become a continuous improvement circle to be finally successful (Crosby 1980; Deming 1986). Quality cannot be described and fixed by a simple definition, because in itself quality is too abstract to have any impact. Therefore, quality has to be defined and specified according to the given context and situation considering the perspectives of stakeholders involved (Donabedian 1980). It is important to identify the relevant aspects and to specify the suitable criteria. It is necessary to find a consensus amongst the different views and

---

[1] Cf. Donabedian 1980, for the whole long-term debate on the quality issues, aspects and approaches cf. Deming (1982 and 1986) and Juran (1951 and 1992).

perspectives to gain a common understanding of quality for the given context and situation due to different and sometimes contradictory needs and definitions of quality by all stakeholders (for detailed explanations on context determinations cf. Crosby 1980; Deming 1986; Donabedian 1980).

In this way quality awareness is the basic requirement for the adoption of quality development by all stakeholders from any organisation. But quality awareness will also be raised by the implementation of quality development on the other hand. To come to a sustainable integration of quality development within the whole organisation and to ensure the involvement of all stakeholders it is crucial to build a quality strategy and to integrate the quality objectives into the educational and business processes. Also the stakeholders' needs and responsibilities need to be integrated into the overall quality development.

The process of the adoption, implementation and adaptation of quality development can roughly be divided into three steps based on three different levels that need to be covered and addressed for a sustainable and long-term quality development according to the concept of the introduction of quality development within organisations (see figure 4, for the three level concept of the introduction of quality development cf. Stracke 2006b and 2009):

1. Level of the individual persons
2. Level of the organisations, communities, education and training systems and societies
3. Integration of quality development involving all stakeholders

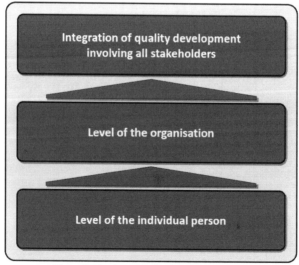

Figure 4: The three levels of quality in general

Currently, two major projects funded by the European Commission are focusing such a broad and sustainable introduction of quality development within learning, education and training across Europe[2]:

1. Open Discovery Space (ODS) with a focus on the school sector involving more then 2,000 schools and offering training for over 10,000 teachers in all 27 EU member states: ODS introduces innovative learning designs and scenarios into K-12 schools through the support by technology enhanced learning and social communities

2. ARISTOTELE addressing the learning processes within organisations with a specific focus on enterprises and the relation between working places and (organizational) learning

Finally, the following short section is focusing and highlighting the role of standards for learning, education and training as the dimension of standards is the most under-estimated one from the three sources and inputs for the learning quality (see above and figure 1). Quality standards are offering specific benefits for organizations, processes, and products. The quality standards themselves cannot guarantee high quality and success: it is always a question of the implementation and adaptation. Users of a quality standard will gain sustainable and significant advantages for their business if they are implementing and adapting the quality standard in a correct, appropriate, and long-term way that lives the idea of the quality standard.

Quality standards have got an impact in particular on seven main factors: The following figure lists these factors together with the main benefits of quality standards at a glance that can be identified in general related to these seven factors.[3]

---

[2] Both projects are presented more in detail in the chapter on European projects of this book, for further information see for ODS at: http://www.opendiscoveryspace.eu/ and for ARISTOTELE at: http://www.aristotele-ip.eu.

[3] For a detailed introduction of the seven factors and related benefits cf. Stracke 2009.

Figure 5: The seven main benefits of quality standards

In a short summary, quality standards have got the potential to improve the organizations, processes, and products leading to high quality and business excellence. The benefits of standards for learning, education and training could be characterised only in brief here.

A real first success story was proven by the first ISO quality standard for learning, education, and training (ISO/IEC 19796-1)[4] that was developed by the ISO standardization committee ISO/IEC JTC1 SC36/WG5[5] and approved and published in 2005. It has been adopted by the European standardization committee CEN TC 353 as European Norm (EN ISO/IEC 19796-1)[6] in 2009 as well

---

[4] For more details cf. Stracke 2009.

[5] The abbreviation stands for: "International Organisation for Standardization (ISO)/ International Electrotechnical Commission (IEC) Joint Technical Committee 1 (JTC1) - Information Technology - Subcommittee 36 (SC36) - Working Group 5 (WG5) Quality Assurance and Descriptive Frameworks"; cf. http://www.iso.org/jtc1/sc36 and http://www.sc36.org/. Members of SC36 are National Bodies, i. e. national delegations of appointed experts, and Liaisons Organizations without voting rights.

[6] The abbreviation stands for: "European Committee for Standardization (CEN) Technical Committee (TC) 353: Information and Communication Technologies for learning education and training", cf. http://www.cen.eu/isss/TC 353. Members of CEN TC 353 are National Bodies, i. e. national delegations of appointed experts, and Liaisons Organizations without voting rights.

as by more than 60 countries worldwide as national standard (including all EU member states, China, Russian Federation, Japan, Korea, Canada, and USA).

A similar success story can be expected from the new ISO metadata standard Metadata for Learning Resources (MLR = ISO/IEC 19788-1) that was developed by the ISO standardization committee ISO/IEC JTC1 SC36/WG4 and approved and published in 2011. It is compliant with the international metadata standards Dublin Core (ISO 15836) and OAI from the Open Archives Initiativea and will work as a successor of IEEE LOM (Learning Object Medata).

Finally a new Portuguese standard (NP 4512) was developed and published in 2012 by the National Body of Portugal IPQ with the support of the European consortium Q-Cert-VET. This Portuguese standard is now under submission to the international (SC36) and European (CEN TC 353) standardization committees. Q-Cert-VET deals with development and publication of such a quality standard and initiates the development of required tools for professional quality certification. In this context the Q-Cert-VET consortium hopes to contribute to the ongoing development in the area of learning innovation and quality.

Summary

Learning innovation and learning quality are very often addressed separately and solely. But in fact they are interdependent and have to be reflected both for achieving the best learning quality: The best appropriate learning quality remains the core objective in learning, education and training and can be achieved by combining the three dimensions learning history, learning innovations and learning standards. Learning innovations can increase the learning quality but require a basis provided by the learning experiences and theories from the past. On the other hand learning traditions have to enriched by innovations, in particular facing the current worldwide challenges of globalisation and worlwide internet establishment. Together with the third dimension, the learning standards, learning history and learning innovations are building the basis and potential inputs for planning and design learning opportunities. Only a mix of history from learning experiences and theories and current Innovations combined with international consensus on learning standards can ensure to meet the learners' needs and to provide the best and appropriate learning opportunities and learning quality fitting to the given situation and for a long-term and sustainable improvement across all sectors in learning, education and training, all communities, educational and training systems and societies in Europe and worldwide.

References

Crosby, P. B. (1980): Quality is Free. The art of making quality certain. McGraw-Hill, New York.

Deming, W. E. (1986): Out of the Crisis. MIT, Cambridge, MA.

Deming, W. E. (1982): Quality, productivity and competitive position. MIT, Cambridge MA.

Donabedian, A. (1980): The Definition of Quality and Approaches to Its Assessment [= Explorations in Quality Assessment and Monitoring, vol. 1]. Health Administration Press, Ann Arbor.

European Commission (2010a): A Digital Agenda for Europe [COM/2010/0245 final]; http://eur-lex.europa.eu/LexUriServ/LexUriServ.do?uri=CELEX:52010DC0245:EN:NOT.

European Commission (2010b): EUROPE 2020 - A strategy for smart, sustainable and inclusive growth [COM/2010/2020 final]; http://eur-lex.europa.eu/LexUriServ/LexUriServ.do?uri=CELEX:52010DC2020:EN:NOT.

European Commission (2005): i2010 – A European Information Society for growth and employment {SEC(2005) 717} [COM/2005/0229 final]; http://eur-lex.europa.eu/LexUriServ/LexUriServ.do?uri=CELEX:52005DC0229:EN:NOT.

European Council (2009): Education and Training 2020 (ET 2020); http://eur-lex.europa.eu/LexUriServ/LexUriServ.do?uri=CELEX:52009XG0528%2801%29:EN:NOT.

ISO/IEC 19796-1:2005: Information Technology - Learning, Education, and Training — Quality Management, Assurance and Metrics — Part 1: General Approach. International Organization for Standardization (ISO), Geneva (2005)

ISO/IEC 19788-1:2010 (2010): Information Technology - Learning, Education, and Training — Metadata for Learning Resources — Part 1: Framework. International Organization for Standardization (ISO), Geneva.

Juran, J. M. (1992): Juran on quality by design. The new steps for planning quality into goods and services. Free Press, New York.

Juran, J. (Ed.) (1951): Quality Control Handbook. McGraw-Hill, New York.

Luhmann, N. (1998): The Society of the Society [= Die Gesellschaft der Gesellschaft]. Suhrkamp Frankfurt/ Main.

Luhmann, N. (1995): Social Systems. Stanford University Press, Stanford.

Maturana, H. R./ Varela, Francisco J. (1992): The Tree of Knowledge. The Biological Roots of Understanding. Shambhala, Boston.

Piaget, J. (1953): The origin of intelligence in the child. Routledge; London.

Stracke, C. M. (2010a): "Quality development and standards in learning, education, and training: adaptation model and guidelines for implementations". In: Информатизация образования и науки [= Информике (Informika), ISSN

2073-7572]; Vol. 7 (3), 2010. Moscow (Russian Federation), 136-146 [online available on: http://www.qed-info.de/downloads].

Stracke, C. M. (2010b): Quality and Standards in Learning, Education, and Training: The Adaptation Model IDEA for the Introduction of Quality Development. In: Proceedings of the International Conference on the Past and Future of e-Learning Standards. Toyo, Tokyo. [also online available on: http://www.qed-info.de/downloads]

Stracke, C. M. (2009): Quality Development and Standards in e-Learning: Benefits and Guidelines for Implementations. In: Proceedings of the ASEM Lifelong Learning Conference: e-Learning and Workplace Learning. ASEM, Bangkok. [also online available on: http://www.qed-info.de/downloads]

Stracke, C. M. (2006a): Process-oriented Quality Management. In: Pawlowski J. & Ehlers, U. (Eds.) European Handbook on Quality and Standardisation in E-Learning. Springer, Berlin: 79-96.

Stracke, C. M. (2006b): Interoperability and Quality Development in e-Learning. Overview and Reference Model for e-Learning Standards. In: Proceedings of the Asia-Europe e-Learning Colloquy. e-ASEM, Seoul. [also online available on: http://www.qed-info.de/downloads]

Educators' Digital Literacies: The Role of Pedagogical Design in Innovation

Florence Dujardin

Sheffield Hallam University, Centre for Education and Inclusion Research,
City Campus, Sheffield S1 1WB, UK
a-f.dujardin@shu.ac.uk

Abstract: The role of educators is changing. In addition to mediating their discipline, educators need to mediate contemporary digital cultures to help students develop digital literacies. This paper explores how the pedagogical design for an online Master's module addressed these challenges by fore-grounding participation and knowledge creation. An auto-ethnographic action research approach was used to capture and reflect upon the decisions and roles adopted by the author during the introduction of collective blogging.

Keywords: auto-ethnography, blog, community, connectivism, design, digital literacies, knowledge creation, participation, pedagogy, professional education

1 Introduction

The debate about digital literacies in higher education focuses largely on undergraduates, and on whether they have the "capabilities which fit an individual for living, learning and working in a digital society" (Knight 2011) – capabilities which can be summarised as "digital tool knowledge + critical thinking + social awareness" (Newman 2009). But what about educators' own competences? Concerns about educators' ICT kills are not new but they are now focusing on their ability to embed digital literacies in the curriculum *while* maintaining quality in the student experience and learning outcomes (Beetham *et al.* 2009). New pedagogical designs are emerging in response to this dual challenge, inspired by connectivism, a "learning theory for a digital age" (Siemens 2005). Its "intense focus on the networked and shared (or sharing) experiences" (Tschofen and Mackness 2012) has implications for pedagogical design: educators need to plan how to network people, ideas, resources and systems since it is individual engagement in the various facets of networks that constitute learning.

At present, little guidance is available for educators to design activities using social software (Minocha 2009). The aims of this paper are to address this gap in the literature and to illustrate how innovation and quality can be articulated in a connectivist pedagogical design that takes into account students' digital literacies in the wider context of the knowledge society. The context is an online Master's programme in professional communication (MAPPC) aimed at professionals with many years' experience in organisational communications (e.g. public relations, marketing, technical support). Collective blogging was introduced on a year-long module in Reflective Practice. This paper provides an insight into the process of embedding digital literacies and the roles adopted as a result.

2 Literature Review

Three concepts guided pedagogical decisions. *Blogging* is becoming a common practice in higher education. It can take different forms depending on the meta-phor of learning used by educators; in the present study, blogging is framed as a reader-oriented practice (Smydra and Mitzelfeld 2012) involving participation and knowledge creation. *Academic Literacies* research is used as conceptual frame-work to place the discussion within wider debates about Web 2.0 in education.

Blogging

Blogging is a "paradigmatic" technology (Siles 2011, 792). The first blogs (or 'weblogs') appeared in the 1990s, making blogs the best established of all social technologies. They are now perceived as a core social technology for personal branding and in organisational digital strategies. Blogging has even been considered a key 21st century literacy (Penrod 2007), which makes it a valuable digital literacy for mature learners to develop. In the context of the knowledge society, these learners need to consider actively how digital literacies affect their employability, and to pre-empt possible labelling as "digital immigrants" (Prensky 2001a; b) by showing that, regardless of their age, they are capable of acquiring the literacies of "digital residents" (White and Le Cornu 2011).

Blogging has a particular value for educators supporting Reflective Practice modules, as studies suggest that it can enhance student reflection (Bouldin *et al.* 2006; Cotterill *et al.* 2010; Hall and Davison 2007; Palmer *et al.* 2008; Stiler and Philleo 2003). Shared collective blogs (as opposed to individual blogs) are well suited to support the social dimension of reflection identified by Kemmis (1985).

They make explicit to students similarities and differences in the topics they choose and in the approaches their peers take to reflect on those topics; blogs can also help students realise that "the true value of reflective writing is to be found in the responses it elicits from others" (Goodfellow and Lea 2007).

Using a collective blog to support reflection on practice has other benefits. First, it increases usability. Checking multiple individual blogs takes time, which may encourage 'blurking' (i.e. blog lurking) (Davies and Merchant 2007) rather than active participation; conversely, by interacting through one collective blog, students can spend time productively by engaging with their peers' outputs. Most importantly, using a collective blog enhances task authenticity for MAPPC students: there is evidence that large organisations use private collective blogs to enable their staff to share expertise and produce knowledge collaboratively (Huh et al. 2007; Jackson et al. 2007; Schuff et al. 2009).

Participating in knowledge creation

The metaphors that educators use to shape a pedagogical design can profoundly affect learning experiences and outcomes (Sfard 1998). Common metaphors are 'knowledge acquisition' and 'participation' in the learning community. In the fields of blogging and reflection, another key metaphor is the 'diary' which, like 'acquisition', emphasises privacy and monologism rather than social aspects of learning. It makes sharing and assessing reflection deeply problematic (Boud and Walker 1998; Creme 2005). Sfard points out the difficulty and inadvisability of ignoring powerful metaphors – such as that of the 'diary'. The key issue then becomes how to integrate it into a more fruitful metaphor.

The 'participation' metaphor is particularly useful in professional education because it emphasizes "situatedness, contextuality, cultural embeddedness, and social mediation" (Sfard 1998, 6). It positions learners as individuals interested in "the existing and functioning of a community of practitioners" (ibid), thus promoting a different kind of identity from that of a diarist. A key advantage of the 'participation' metaphor is its focus on "activities, i.e., on 'knowing', and not so much on outcomes or products" (Paavola and Hakkarainen 2005, 538). Sharing personal reflections with peers to improve professional practice allows a dialogic and social dimension in learning to develop, which is in keeping with connectivism. As a new form of literacy, blogging involves an "active sociality" (Lankshear and Knobel 2006) whereby learners post, comment, 'like', embed media, and subscribe to updates – practices that can signal 'digital resident' status. Paavola and Hakkarainen highlight the limitations of the 'participation' metaphor in "deliberately creating and advancing knowledge" (2005, 539), and put forward another metaphor of learning, that of 'knowledge creation'. Using the Vygotskyan emphasis on signs and tools to mediate human activity, Paavola and Hakkarainen show how this third metaphor can foster a trialogic approach to knowledge: students engage in internal reflective dialogues, interact with one another, and respond to the artefacts (such as blog posts and responses) created by their peers. This metaphor has an impact on the selection of software tools, "the most promising [being] the ones that guide participants themselves to engage in extensive working to produce knowledge through writing and visualization" (ibid, 549). The value of blogs becomes clear in this perspective.

Academic Literacies

The tenets of Academic Literacies research are that reading, writing, and ICT use involve more than skill acquisition or enculturation into academic disciplines; they are patterned by power relations and the prior understandings and expectations of students and educators alike (Lea and Street 1998). The focus of Academic Literacies research has focused extensively on students' meaning-making practices, but the field also recognises that it is "productive to explore the choices of lecturers, as recontextualisation agents, regarding which knowledge to privilege" (Coleman 2012, 335). An Academic Literacies lens is therefore used to problematise the issues that educators face when introducing Web 2.0 tools; Lea's pedagogical principles (2004) offer a useful tool to design learning tasks that are attentive to learner needs.

One of these principles acknowledges the "integral nature of relationship between literacies and technologies" (Lea 2004, 744). Coleman explores this idea further and notes that educators are "ideologically bound to broader sociological processes" (2012, 328) when they seek to mirror the digital literacy practices of the workplace in their courses, as is the case is the present study. Lea also makes it clear that educators have a responsibility in mediating technology. While Internet access may no longer be a major issue in Western societies, some students (in particular, mature students) may find it difficult to use Web 2.0 software because it redefines what it means to read and write in "a dominant political/ ideological order of high tech and global capitalism" (Tusting 2008, 319). Lea's call for creating spaces that help students explore different meanings and sense of identity (Lea 2004) still resonates in the digital age. Goodfellow and Lea go further and ask educators to nurture students' "critical confidence" in ICT (2007, 108) so they can challenge and/or contest the dominant order that Tusting identifies (2008).

3 Methodology

This study is part of a wider ethnographic action research (EAR) project into the introduction of social media on the MAPPC. A variant of action research, EAR originates from the field of Development Studies, and aims to support communities' use of ICTs in developing countries. EAR researchers "use ethnography to guide the research process and... action research to link the research back to the project's plans and activities" (Tacchi *et al.* 2003). EAR has been adapted to research educational contexts (Bath 2009) and social media use in developed countries (Hearn *et al.* 2009), and therefore seems well-suited to research technological innovation in professional education.

This paper presents the "baseline research" (Tacchi *et al.* 2003) for the collective blog project. Three EAR concepts can shed light on educators' design decisions.

Social mapping involves investigating the characteristics and needs of the target community and its relations to the wider social context. In the present study, professional characteristics and demographics influence pedagogical design. MAPPC students have with a wealth of professional experience to explore in the Reflective Practice module. However, as mature learners, they may be considered "digital immigrants" (Prensky 2001a; b). Though generational differences are probably overplayed (Bennett and Maton 2010; Madden 2010b; a), this creates new responsibilities for educators to address mature learners' possible issues with digital literacies.

The focus of an EAR project is to develop a *communicative ecology* which involves people, media, activities and relationships, linked through media repertoires, social uses of media, and social networks. To support the Reflective Practice module, I trialled three different software (discussed in the next section) in different stages of the action research, thus gradually widening the communicative ecology, strengthening the student network, and embedding literacies that mature learners need to contribute to the knowledge society.

The concept of *socio-cultural animation* is particular relevant to the present study. EAR researchers consider themselves to be "catalyst, mediator and facilitator" as they work with communities to mitigate the effects of the digital divide (Foth 2006, 642). Educators play similar roles when they intro-duce social media and help students understand its potential for learning (Minocha *et al.* 2011). They must also bear in mind the 'second-order digital divide' arising from age, gender and social capital (Hargittai 2010; Lichy 2012; van Deursen and van Dijk 2011).

This paper is auto-ethnographic in nature because "only someone actively involved in working with new technologies within an academic context during of their introduction and rapid development [can] have the opportunity to reflect on the task of design and record those influences from which a theory of design might emerge" (Duncan 2004, 9). Though auto-ethnography offers "highly personalized accounts that draw upon the experience of the author/ researcher", it does so "for the purposes of extending sociological understanding (Sparkes 2000, 21).

Data was collected from personal notes, a blog which is "useful for self-reflection" (Minocha 2009, 55), and a life-grid (Bane 1996; Murray et al. 2010). To address possible concerns about validity, I strove to meet Guba and Lincoln's criterion of "authenticity" for qualitative research (Guba and Lincoln 1994) by sharing the process of introducing collective blogging and by reflecting closely on decisions and roles. The study also identifies to wider themes, notably how "changing literacy practices are intimately associated with networks of changing social practices and technologies, from the local to global levels" (Tusting 2008, 317), so it is hoped that the paper achieves analytic generalisation value for educators wishing to widen their communicative ecology with social media.

4 Discussion

A wide range of issues were identified in the data. The literature was used to prioritise the following themes: the innovation process, socio-cultural animation considerations, and personal digital literacies.

Widening the communicative ecology – a process view

To embed blogging practices in the MAPPC, I explored different possibilities in three consecutive iterations of the Reflective Practice module, following the stages of innovation identified by Somekh (1998).

In a first *routine* stage (2008-9 module iteration), discussion forums were used within the virtual learning environment (VLE) since this medium has been shown to be successful in supporting students' reflection on practice (Rocco 2010). However, forums are the main means of student interaction on MAPPC modules, so using forums both for reflection and discussion proved somewhat confusing for students; the learning environment itself did not reinforce visually that a different type of approach to learning was required.

In the second **refinement** stage (first term of the 2009-10 module iteration), I activated individual blogs within the VLE. In addition to supporting the learning task, the aim was to help mature learners develop a sense of 'residence' in a 'paradigmatic' technology for the knowledge society. While individual blogs within the VLE worked reasonably well from the point of view of individual engagement, there were limitations in terms of collaborative knowledge making. This was mostly due to usability problems with the VLE and its limitations in supporting the complex set of rules, relations and codes normally found in blogs (Schmidt 2007). As McLoughlin and Lee note, VLEs often do not emulate Web 2.0 well (2007).

For the third **integration** stage (last two terms of 2009-10 and all three terms of 2010-11 iteration), I introduced the WordPress blogging platform – a significant move since the university does not support it. Taking on the role of learning technologist, I set up this blog as a password-protected space because MAPPC students may not wish to post their reflections on professional practice on the public Web. I also took the opportunity to switch from multiple personal blogs to a single collective blog, in order to: address usability problems; make students aware of the value of blogs as tools for information, identity, and relationship management (Schmidt 2007); and enhance task authenticity, by mirroring blog-based practices used in large organisations (as described in Dugan *et al.* 2010; Yardi *et al.* 2009). After initial reservations, students enthusiastically took to trialogic knowledge creation.

Planning socio-cultural animation

Beetham, McGill and Littlejohn (2009) provide a general framework to help educators to develop students' digital literacies in practice. It was adapted here to focus on issues relevant to knowledge-creation through collective blogging, and to include insights from Academic Literacies research into ICT use in higher education.

By recontextualising the corporate use of collaborative blogging, the module provides an **authentic context** for collaborative knowledge creation. Both the medium (blog) and the focus (workplace issues) create a potential for 'talk-back', which involves "readers in responding to written reflection in kind" (Goodfellow and Lea 2007, 102) thus developing trialogic ways of constructing professional and scholarly forms of knowledge. Furthermore, the practice of 'talkback' has relevance for some MAPPC students who engage with 'audience/producers' (Meyers 2012) as part of their workplace duties.

The learning tasks and resources provide **scaffolding** for students to develop new perspectives on blogging and reflection. They clarified what is expected of MAPPC students beyond reading texts; the idea of knowledge creation being a dialogic or even trialogic process (McLoughlin and Lee 2010) was unfamiliar to students as few had studied online and/or used blogs before. In addition, moderation included "explicit discussion of the draft nature of writing in this environment" (Goodfellow and Lea 2007, 104). Finally, the assessment grid identified the levels of reflection, scholarliness and participation that students were expected to achieve.

Lea (2004) emphasises the need to make **meaning-making** practices explicit to students. Blogging can accommodate 'transitional writing' (Creme 2008), that is, writing in which students can work with peers to refine their understanding of what it means to participate in knowledge-creation in a Master's course. In professional education, making meaning-making explicit also involves helping students draw on their workplace experience, to help them grasp differences between writing – and blogging – for academic and work purposes.

Conflicts may sometimes occur between different ICT-based practices. For example, Lea and Jones (2011) discussed the difficulties that undergraduates face when recontextualising their use of ICT to support learning. Following Ivanič et al. (2007), the design for the Reflective Practice module harnessed business-oriented practices familiar to MAPPC students: task design encouraged students to discuss explicitly knowledge-making in business and academic contexts, to help them develop a sense of ownership in the collective blog.

Like all mature learners, MAPPC students bring with them **prior concepts and understandings** of ICT practices (Lea and Jones 2011; Lankshear and Knobel 2006) and of educational practices (Lea 2004). To allay students' initial unease about writing blog posts rather than more familiar essays, I focused their efforts on reviewing workplace issues and emphasised the value of blogging for an audience of peers as a form of professional practice.

Tusting warns educators about "turn[ing] new literacies into a set of abstract skills and techniques" (2008, 325). By attending to all aspects discussed above, it was possible to contextualise digital literacies to address the needs of mature learners working in professional communications.

Implications for educators' own digital literacies

In the digital age, it is no longer enough for educators to act as "mediators of academic culture" (Dysthe 2002). They also need to mediate aspects of the digital culture that are relevant to their disciplines (here, Communication Studies) and to the needs of students as digital citizens. This called for identity work: rather than consider myself an "outsider" (Tusting 2008) or "digital immigrant" (Prensky, 2001a; Prensky, 2001b), I used White and Le Cornu's alternative framing (2011): they define 'digital residency' as an outcome of a developmental process – rather than a matter of generation – thus allowing me to reflect on my long-term experiences of software use (captured in a life-grid). Developing a digital resident identity was a requisite (Conole 2012; Schroeder *et al.* 2010) for the introduction of the blog. Without a personal experience of blogging, tweeting and social networking, it would have been difficult to address the technical issues of access and skills, and the higher order issues of digital knowledge-making and online identity.

Pedagogical approaches needed to be rethought to make innovation possible (Somekh 1998, Minocha 2009). Supporting individual learners remained important as ever; however, I also adopted community-focused approaches because "the way to prepare students for the new world is to facilitate playful, explorational communities of peers" (Tusting, 2008, 325) – hence the importance choosing 'participation' and 'knowledge-creation' as underpinning metaphors. Unexpectedly, a different style of e-moderation emerged: the initial 'guide at the side' stance gave way to that of a 'peer that steers' in response to the vitality of student engagement. As Somekh emphasises, "soft factors ... are essential to effective innovation" (1998, 12).

Harnessing the affordances of collective blogging, I used the three dimensions of pedagogy 2.0 – participation, personalisation, and productivity (McLoughlin and Lee 2008b) – to design the 2009-10 and 2010-11 module iterations. Like Bender (2002), I found that these approaches do not inherently support quality and criticality in knowledge-creation. Indeed, personalisation and the cult of the personal can be deeply deceptive, particularly when associated with employability in the context of the knowledge society, as they may distract educators from the key educational goals of individual agency and emancipation (Clegg and David 2006). As for participation and productivity, the professional background of MAPPC students made them able and willing to locate their efforts within the "rapid growth of digital popular-culture media" (Goodfellow 2011, 139). However, the pedagogical design only supported explicitly reflection on *personal* workplace practices, and did not encourage students to consider wider influences and explore how digital media has "allied itself to commercial and political interests that [are] themselves ideologically dominant" (ibid). There were therefore limitations in the design, in that it did not nurture an "expanded sociocultural concept of digital literacy" (Goodfellow 2011, 134).

5 Conclusion

This study is situated in a period of change for educators who need to consider their own digital identities as well as maintain the quality of learning experience and outcomes. As McLoughlin and Lee (McLoughlin and Lee 2008a) point out, social media can be used as a catalyst of changes in pedagogy. This paper presented an example of how this challenge was managed: in addition to mediating the discipline, I acted as 'catalyst' by embedding collective blogging in a module, as 'mediator' of contemporary digital cultures by using the key metaphors of participation and knowledge, and my role of 'facilitator' also underwent a subtle shift from 'guide' to 'peer'. Paraphrasing Newman (2009), the educator's digital literacies exhibited in this study can best be summarised as "digital tool knowledge + critical connectivist pedagogy + social awareness of the knowledge society". As it is a small-scale review of pedagogical design practice, the study has unavoidable limitations, so it is hoped other auto-ethnographic accounts will reveal the complexity of educators' decision-making regarding the introduction of Web 2.0 technology and of the role they play in helping students become active and critical contributors to the knowledge society.

References

Bane, D. (1996) Collecting retrospective data: Development of a reliable method and a pilot study of its use. *Social Science & Medicine,* 42 (2): 751-757.

Bath, C. (2009) When does the action start and finish? Making the case for an ethnographic action research in educational research. *Educational Action Research,* 17 (2): 213-224.

Beetham, H., McGill, L. & Littlejohn, A. (2009) *Thriving in the 21st century: Learning Literacies for the Digital Age (LLiDA project).* Bristol, JISC. http://www.jisc.ac.uk/media/documents/projects/llidareportjune2009.pdf

Bender, W. (2002) Twenty years of personalization: all about the 'Daily Me'. *Educause Review,* September/October 20-29.

Bennett, S. & Maton, K. (2010) Beyond the 'digital natives' debate: towards a more nuanced understanding of students' technology experiences. *Journal of Computer Assisted Learning,* 26 (5): 321–331.

Boud, D. J. & Walker, D. (1998) Promoting reflection in professional courses: the challenge of context. *Studies in Higher Education,* 23 (2): 191-206.

Bouldin, A. S., Holmes, E. R. & Fortenberry, M. L. (2006) "Blogging" about course concepts: using technology for reflective journaling in a communications class. *American Journal Pharmacy Education,* 70 (4): Article 84. Retrieved from: https://www.ncbi.nlm.nih.gov/pmc/articles/PMC1636988/pdf/ajpe84.pdf

Clegg, S. & David, M. (2006) Passion, pedagogies and the project of the personal in higher education. *21st Century Society,* 1 (2): 149-165.

Coleman, L. (2012) Incorporating the notion of recontextualisation in academic literacies research: the case of a South African vocational web design and development course. *Higher Education Research & Development,* 31 (3): 325-338.

Conole, G. (2012) Connectivity. *Journal of Learning Development in Higher Education,* 4. Retrieved from: http://www.aldinhe.ac.uk/ojs/index.php?journal=jldhe&page=article&op=view& path%5B%5D=159

Cotterill, S., Lowing, K., Cain, K., Lofthouse, R., Mackay, C., McShane, J., Stancliffe, D. & Wright, D. (2010) Blogs and e-portfolios: can they support reflection, evidencing and dialogue in teacher training? *Journal of Learning Development in Higher Education,* 1 1-21.

Creme, P. (2005) Should student learning journals be assessed? *Assessment and Evaluation in Higher Education,* 30 (3): 287-296.

Creme, P. (2008) A space for academic play: student learning journals as transitional writing. *Arts and Humanities in Higher Education,* 7 (1): 49-64.

Davies, J. & Merchant, G. (2007) Looking from the inside out: academic blogging as new literacy. In Lankshear, C. & Knobel, M. (Eds.) *A New Literacies Sampler.* New York, Peter Lang. Pp. 167-198.

Dugan, C., Geyer, W. & Millen, D. R. (2010) Lessons learned from Blog Muse: audience-based inspiration for bloggers. *CHI 2010.* Atlanta, GA.

Duncan, M. (2004) Autoethnography: critical appreciation of an emerging art. *International Journal of Qualitative Methods,* 3 (4): Article 3. Retrieved from: http://www.ualberta.ca/~iiqm/backissues/3_4/pdf/duncan.pdf

Dysthe, O. (2002) Professors as mediators of academic text cultures: An interview study with advisors and Master's degree students in three disciplines in a Norwegian university. *Written Communication,* 19 (4): 493-544.

Foth, M. (2006) Sociocultural animation. In Marshall, S., Taylor, W. & Yu, X. (Eds.) *Encyclopedia of Developing Regional Communities with Information and Communication Technology.* Hershey, PA, Idea Group Reference. Pp. 640-645.

Goodfellow, R. (2011) Literacy, literacies and the digital in higher education. *Teaching in Higher Education*, 16 (1): 131-144.

Goodfellow, R. & Lea, M. (2007) *Challenging E-Learning in the University: A Literacies Perspective.* Buckingham, Open University Press.

Guba, E. G. & Lincoln, Y. S. (1994) Competing paradigms in qualitative research. In Guba, E. G. & Lincoln, Y. S. (Eds.) *Handbook of Qualitative Research.* London, Sage. Pp. 105-117.

Hall, H. & Davison, B. (2007) Social software as support in hybrid learning environments: the value of the blog as a tool for reflective learning and peer support. *Library & Information Science Research,* 29 (2): 163-187.

Hargittai, F. (2010) Digital na(t)ives? Variation in Internet skills and uses among members of the "Net Generation". *Sociological Inquiry,* 80 (192-113).

Hearn, G. N., Tacchi, J. A., Foth, M. & Lennie, J. (2009) *Action Research and New Media: Concepts, Methods and Cases.* Cresskill, NJ, Hampton Press.

Huh, J., Jones, L., Erickson, T., Kellogg, W. A., Bellamy, R. K. E. & Thomas, J. C. (2007) BlogCentral: the role of internal blogs at work. *CHI EA '07* San Joe, CA.

Ivanič, R., Edwards, R., Satchwell, C. & Smith, J. (2007) Possibilities for pedagogy in further education: harnessing the abundance of literacy. *British Educational Research Journal,* 33 (5): 703-721.

Jackson, A., Yates, J. & Orlikowski, W. (2007) Corporate blogging: building community through persistent digital talk. *40th Hawaii International Conference on System Sciences.* Waikoloa, HI.

Kemmis, S. (1985) Action research and the politics of reflection. In Boud, D. J., Keogh, R. & Walker, D. (Eds.) *Reflection: Turning Experience into Learning.* London, Kogan Page. Pp. 139-164.

Knight, S. (2011) Digital literacy can boost employability and improve student experience (15 December 2011). *The Guardian.* London.

Lankshear, C. & Knobel, M. (2006) *New Literacies.* (2nd ed) Buckingham, Open University Press.

Lea, M. R. (2004) Academic Literacies: a pedagogy for course design. *Studies in Higher Education,* 29 (6): 739-756.

Lea, M. R. & Jones, S. (2011) Digital literacies in Higher Education: exploring textual and technological practice. *Studies in Higher Education,* 36 (4).

Lea, M. R. & Street, B. V. (1998) Student writing in Higher Education: an academic literacies approach. *Studies in Higher Education,* 23 (2): 157-172.

Lichy, J. (2012) Towards an international culture: Gen Y students and SNS? *Active Learning in Higher Education,* 13 (2): 101-116.

Madden, M. (2010a) Four or More: The New Demographic. 2010 (February). http://www.pewinternet.org/Presentations/2010/Jun/Four-or-More--The-New-Demographic.aspx

Madden, M. (2010b) *Older Adults and Social Media.* Washington, DC, Pew Research Center. http://pewinternet.org/Reports/2010/Older-Adults-and-Social-Media.aspx

McLoughlin, C. & Lee, M. J. W. (2007) Social software and participatory learning: pedagogical choices with technology affordances in the Web 2.0 era. *ascilite 2007.* Singapore.

McLoughlin, C. & Lee, M. J. W. (2008a) Mapping the digital terrain: new media and social software as catalysts for pedagogical change. *ascilite 2008.* Melbourne, Australia.

McLoughlin, C. & Lee, M. J. W. (2008b) The three P's of pedagogy for the networked society: personalization, participation, and productivity. *International Journal of Teaching and Learning in Higher Education,* 20 (1): 10-27.

McLoughlin, C. & Lee, M. J. W. (2010) Pedagogy 2.0: critical challenges and responses to Web 2.0 and social software in tertiary teaching. In Lee, M. J. W. & McLoughlin, C. (Eds.) *Web 2.0-based E-Learning: Applying Social Informatics for Tertiary Teaching.* Hershey, PA, IGI Global. Pp. 43-69.

Meyers, E. A. (2012) 'Blogs give regular people the chance to talk back': rethinking 'professional' media hierarchies in new media. *New Media & Society,* 14 (6): 1022-1038.

Minocha, S. (2009) *A Study of the Effective Use of Social Software by Further and Higher Education in the UK to Support Student Learning and Teaching.* Bristol, JISC. http://www.jisc.ac.uk/whatwedo/projects/socialsoftware08.aspx

Minocha, S., Schroeder, A. & Schneider, C. (2011) Role of the educator in social software initiatives in Further and Higher Education: a conceptualisation and research agenda. *British Journal of Educational Technology,* 42 (6): 889-903.

Murray, L., Stephenson, J. & Parnis, N. (2010) Exploring a 'Life Grid' approach in understanding the early HE experiences of students in one institution. 2011 (February). http://cloudworks.ac.uk/cloud/view/4192

Newman, T. (2009) Consequences of a digital Literacy literature review: from terminology to action. *'Digital Literacy: Shock of the Old 2009' Conference.* Oxford University.

Paavola, S. & Hakkarainen, K. (2005) The knowledge creation metaphor – an emergent epistemological approach to learning. *Science & Education,* 14 (6): 535-557.

Palmer, S., Holt, D. & Bray, S. (2008) The learning outcomes of an online reflective journal in engineering. *ascilite 2008.* Melbourne.

Penrod, D. (2007) *Using Blogs to Enhance Literacy: The Next Powerful Step in 21st-Century Learning.* Lanham, MD, Rowman & Littlefield Education.

Prensky, M. (2001a) Digital natives, digital immigrants - Part I. *On the Horizon,* 9 (5): 1-6.

Prensky, M. (2001b) Digital natives, digital immigrants - Part II: do they really think differently? *On the Horizon,* 9 (6): 1-9.

Rocco, S. (2010) Making reflection public: using interactive online discussion board to enhance student learning. *Reflective Practice,* 11 (3): 307-317.

Schmidt, J. (2007) Blogging practices: an analytical framework. *Journal of Computer-Mediated Communication,* 12 (4): 1409–1427.

Schroeder, A., Minocha, S. & Schneider, C. (2010) The strengths, weaknesses, opportunities and threats of using social software in higher and further education teaching and learning. *Journal of Computer Assisted Learning,* 26 (3): 159-174.

Schuff, D., DeLuca, J. A. & Hamilton, B. W. (2009) Business in the Blogosphere: Corporate Blogging. Philadelphia, PA, Fox School Institute for Business and Information Technology, Temple University.

Sfard, A. (1998) On two metaphors for learning and the dangers of choosing just one. *Educational researcher,* 27 (2): 4-13.

Siemens, G. (2005) Connectivism: a learning theory for the digital age. http://www.elearnspace.org/Articles/connectivism.htm

Siles, I. (2011) The rise of blogging: articulation as a dynamic of technological stabilization. *New Media & Society,* 14 (5): 781-797.

Smydra, R. & Mitzelfeld, P. (2012) Blogger: creating connections between writer, text, and reader in an English Honor's course on literary self-narrative. In Cheal, C., Coughlin, J. & Moore, S. (Eds.) *Transformation in Teaching: Social Media Strategies in Higher Education.* Santa Rosa, CA, Informing Science Press. Pp. 413-431.

Somekh, B. (1998) Supporting information and communication technology innovations in higher education. *Journal of information technology for teacher education,* 7 (1): 11-32.

Sparkes, A. C. (2000) Autoethnography and narratives of self: reflections on criteria in action. *Sociology of Sport Journal,* 17 (1): 21-43.

Stiler, G. M. & Philleo, T. (2003) Blogging and blogspots: an alternative format for encouraging reflective practice among preservice teachers. *Education & Training,* 123 (4): 789-797.

Tacchi, J., Slater, D. & Hearn, G. (2003) *Ethnographic Action Research: A User's Handbook Developed to Innovate and Research ICT Application for Poverty Eradication.* New Delhi, UNESCO.

Tschofen, C. & Mackness, J. (2012) Connectivism and dimensions of personal experience. *International Review of Research on Open and Distance Learning,* 13 (1). Retrieved from: http://www.irrodl.org/index.php/irrodl/article/view/1143/2086

Tusting, K. (2008) Ecologies of new literacies: implications for education. In Creese, A., Martin, P. & Hornberger, N. (Eds.) *Encyclopaedia of Language and Education* 2nd ed. ed. New York, NY, Springer Science+Business Media, LLC. Pp. 317-329.

van Deursen, A. & van Dijk, J. (2011) Internet skills and the digital divide. *New Media & Society,* 13 (6): 893-911.

White, D. S. & Le Cornu, A. (2011) Visitors and residents: a new typology for online engagement. *First Monday,* 9 (5). Retrieved from: http://firstmonday.org/htbin/cgiwrap/bin/ojs/index.php/fm/article/view/3171

Yardi, S., Golder, S. A. & Brzozowski, M. J. (2009) Blogging at work and the corporate attention economy. *27th international conference on Human factors in computing systems, ACM.*

Requirements for the Specialisation of Competence Metadata Schemas for the Description of Agricultural Skills and Professions

Charalampos Thanopoulos, Giannis Stoitsis, Jad Najjar, Yiannis Psochios

Agro-Know Technologies, Athens, Greece
[cthanopoulo; stoitsis; psochios]@agroknow.gr
Eummena, Leuven, Belgium
Computer Science Department, AL-Quds University, Jerusalem, Palestine
jnajjar@eummena.org

Abstract: A lot of metadata schemas have been developed, in order to support the general objectives of European initiatives, like European Qualification Framework, European Learner Mobility, aiming to improve the transparency and recognition of qualifications and competences. In this paper, the requirements for the specialisation of the Competence Metadata Schema for the identification and description of specialised agricultural competences are presented. The investigation of agricultural experts' opinions refers to the measurement of the importance of the Competence Metadata Schema in specific agricultural fields (hydroponics and irrigation). Based on this analysis the Competence Metadata Schema will be further evaluated, in order to meet the objectives of AGRICOM and Herbal.Mednet projects on the identification of the desired competences for agricultural professions.

Keywords: Competence Metadata Schema, metadata, competence, agriculture, job description, Vocational Education and Training (VET)

1 Introduction

Modern agriculture aims to succeed the better exploitation of land use, in order to increase the production, improving simultaneously the quality of agricultural products. Both aspects of quality and abundance of agricultural products are expressed via the intensive agriculture, like the protected agriculture in greenhouse, hydroponics and other forms of intensive agriculture or machinery agriculture. Continuous growth of agricultural techniques and practices requires a more pretentious labour market, including competent agronomists, consultants and practitioners, as well skilled enough farmers and workers.

Based on the intended outcome, the identification of agricultural competences can serve two different aspects. On one hand competences are defined in a way to describe the learning outcomes of learning courses (Najjar *et al.*, 2012b, eCOTOOL High-Level Competence Model Explanation, 2011) and on the other hand a list of essential and desired competences sets the outline of the job profile for specific working framework (Thanopoulos *et al.*, 2012), as farmers or workers with specific duties in the production chain of a farm (e.g. harvesting techniques, taking care a vegetables garden, pests and diseases control).

AGRICOM), Transfer of Water Competence Model to AGRIcultural COMpetences (http://www.agriculture-competences.eu), and Herbal.Mednet, Enhancing the Vocational Education and Training of Innovative Farming Trainers / Advisors in Area of Herbal, Medicinal and Aromatic Plants, are both co-funded projects by Lifelong Learning Program (LLP) and intend to support VET systems in Europe.

This paper presents the first version of the Competence Metadata Schema for the agricultural competences. Also, it explores the necessity of Competence Metadata Schema in agriculture and analyses the requirements for further specialisation of competences for the specific agricultural fields of hydroponics and irrigation.

2 Competence Metadata Schema for agricultural competences

Based on the initial design and development of the Competence Metadata Schema for agricultural competences, each competence is described with a number of metadata elements (Manouselis *et al.*, 2010, Palavitsinis and Manouselis, 2009 Palavitsinis and Manouselis, 2008, Diamantopoulos *et al.*, 2011), including title and description, categorisation, classification and relation to other components (e.g. competences and skills) (Grant *et al.*, 2011).

Competence Description Schema				No	Competence Description Schema			
Element	*Data Type	**Obligation	***Input Method		Element	*Data Type	**Obligation	***Input Method
Identifier			A	6.	Classification		M	
Catalog	CS	M	A	6.1	Purpose	V	M	M
Entry	CS	M	A	6.2	Type	V	M	M
Title			M	6.3	Category	V	O	M
Title	LS	M	M	6.4	Classification schema	-	M	M
Description		M	M					
ActionVerb	LS	O	M	6.4.1	Source	CS	M	A
Description	LS	M	M	6.4.2	Taxon	-	M	M
Level in Context			M	6.4.2.1	Id	CS	M	M
Level Schema	V	M	M	6.4.2.2	Entry	CS	M	M
Level	V	M	M	7.	Meta-Metadata		M	
Relation		O		7.1	Contributor	-	M	
Resource	-	M	M	7.1.1	Role	V	M	A
Identifier	-	M	M	7.1.2	Entity	CS	M	A
Catalog	CS	M	M	7.1.3	Date	DT	M	A
Entry	CS	M	M	7.2	Schema	CS	M	A
Source	V	M	M	7.3	Language	V	M	A
Level	V	M	M					
Operator	V	M	M					

Fig. 1. Competence Metadata Schema for identification and specialisation of agricultural competences (*Data Type: [CS]=CharacterString, [LS]=LangString, [V]=Vocabulary, [DT]=DateTime, **Obligation: [M]=Mandatory, [O]=Optional, *** Input Method: [A]=Automatic, [M]=Manual)

Competences were carefully selected, in order to provide farmers and people working in hydroponics and plant Irrigation with a variety of competences and skills that are needed, in order to meet the today's objectives of modern agriculture in terms of sustainability, maintenance and enhancement of intensive aquiculture.

An initial Competence Metadata Schema is developed for the identification of agricultural competences for specific field of water resources use in agriculture. It consists of the fields: (1) Title, (2) Description (Action Verb, Description), (3) Level in Context (Source, Level), (4) Relation (Competence Element, Source, Level, Operator) and (5) Classification (Purpose, Type, Category, Classification Schema) (Fig. 1).

Figure 1 depicts the initial metadata schema, designed under the directions of the AGRICOM experts for the development of the Competence Metadata Schema to cover the agricultural needs and the evaluation through pilots in hydroponics (Thanopoulos et al., 2011, Stracke, 2011).

3 Approaching the requirements of the implementation of the Competence Metadata Schema in agriculture

In order to measure and evaluate the importance of the specialisation of Competence Metadata Schema for the agricultural professions, an online survey was realised, in order to decide on the selected metadata elements (Manolis *et al.*, 2012). Participants of this survey are agricultural experts, mainly coming from the design of training curricula at University level or/and professional training level, as well career officers and consultants in agricultural topics.

Results intend to underline the usefulness of Competence Metadata Schema in the identification of desired competences and its implementation in specific agricultural fields. The Competence Metadata Schema will be tested firstly in specific fields of the use of water resources in agriculture (e.g. hydroponics, plant irrigation).

Initial requirements analysis is based on a small number (79) of responses from Greece, Germany, Italy and Netherlands, as well other European countries.

3.3 Rating the importance of agricultural competences

Based on this schema, a number of competences were identified for hydroponics and irrigation and divided in two sections, i) management and ii) water specific competences. Experts tried to rate the importance of the desired agricultural competences. This is the first step of the evaluation of the Competence Metadata Schema. In a second step, the Competence Metadata Schema will be tested in real cases of the description of agricultural professions related to the use of water resources in agriculture (like hydroponics and plant irrigation).

For the evaluation of competences, a 5-point scale is used, in which the level I is the first-lower level and level V is the highest level of importance, helping to classify the importance of each competence.

3.3.1 Importance of management competences in agriculture

In the majority, Management Competences are mentioned with the highest level of importance, underlining the success of the Competence Metadata Schema for the identification of competences (Fig. 2).

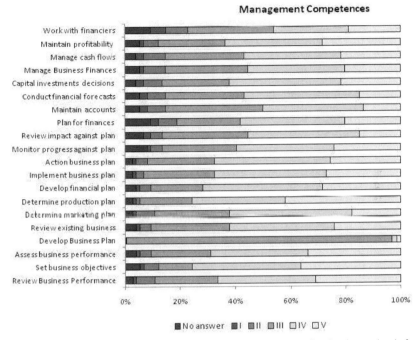

Fig. 2. Rating importance of agricultural management competences (level I = lowest level of importance, ..., level V = highest level of importance)

Specifically, for "Review Business Performance" competence, a noticeable percentage of 66.2% mentioned its importance, selecting levels IV (35.1%) and V (31.1%). While, 4.1% of the answers mentioned it as not so important (levels I and II), 23% gave a neutral answer (level III of importance) and 2.7% did not answer.

"Set Business Objectives" and "Determine Production Plan" competences are proved as two of the most crucial competence. 75.7% of experts revealed both competences as very important (levels IV and V) for the agricultural professionals. Low levels of were marked by 6.7% and 2.7%, respectively. Level III of importance was underlined by 12.2% and 18.9% of the respondents.

In addition, "Assess Business Performance", "Develop Business Plan", "Implement business plan" and "Action business plan" are proved as strong competences, with 68.9% and 67.6% respectively of the answers mentioning levels IV and V. Small percentages (5.4% and 6.7%, 4.1% and 5.4%), marked low levels I and II. 21-26 % gave a neutral answer and less than 4.1% did not answer.

Moreover, "Review existing business", "Determine marketing plan", "Capital investment decisions" and "Maintain profitability" are marked with equal levels of importance, according to experts with the percentage of 62.2% and 63.5% for the last one, choosing the levels IV and V of importance. Small percentages marked the levels I and II and the level III of the importance was underlined by 28.4%, 27%, 24.3% and 24.3% of the respondents respectively. Less than 5.4 % did not answer.

"Monitor progress against plan", "Review impact against plan", "Manage Business Finances", "Plan for finances", "Conduct financial forecasts" and "Manage cash flows" share almost equal level of importance with 59.4%, 55.4%, 58.1%, 56.7% 55.4% and 56.7% respectively of the answers mentioning the strong importance (levels IV and V) for the agricultural jobs. Small percentages marked levels I and II and the medium level III was underlined by 27%, 31.1%, 23%, 28.4%, 29.7% and 28.4% of the respondents, respectively. A percentage of 4.1 - 8.7 % did not answer.

Regarding "Develop financial plan", a noticeable percentage of 71.6% believe that it is a significant competence (levels IV and V). Only 5.4% of the respondents underlined the lower levels of importance (levels I and II). 18.9% mentioned level III of importance for the agricultural professionals and 4.1% did not answer.

For the competence "Maintain accounts management" half of the experts (50%) chose the levels IV and V of importance. A small portion of the answers marked the low levels of the importance 9.5%. The medium level III of the importance was underlined by the significant 35.1% of the respondents and 5.4% did not answer.

At last, "Work with Financiers" is proved as one of the most crucial components in the list of Management Competences. 45.9% of experts mentioned the highest levels of importance. A small portion marked the low levels of importance (13.5%) and a significant percentage of 31.1% of the respondents selected level III.

3.3.2 Importance of water specific competences in agriculture

Figure 3 depicts the results on evaluation of Competence Metadata Schema for the identification of Water Specific Competence, rating their level of importance for the successful performance of agricultural jobs.

For "Water storage" "Nutrients" and "Keeping up to date" competences, 67.6%, 68.9% and 68.9% of experts mentioned the levels IV and V. 6.7%, 4.1% and 2.7% respectively mentioned levels I and II. The percentages 21.6%24,3% and 24.3% gave a neutral answer (level III) and 4.1%, 2.7% and 4.1% did not answer.

Competence "Irrigation" is proved as the most crucial Water Specific Competence. 78.4% of experts revealed this competence as a very important one (level IV and V) for agricultural professionals. A small portion of the answers marked the low levels of the importance 6.7%. Medium level of importance (Level III) was underlined by 12.2% of the respondents, while 2.7% did not answer.

In addition, competences "Water quality", "Water availability" throughout the year / growing season and "Plant protection" are proved as strong competences as the irrigation with 73%, 77% and 75.7% respectively of the answers mentioning the high levels of importance (levels IV and V). Small percentages (5.4%, 5.4% and 4.1%) marked the first two levels (I and II). 14.9% and 13.5% and 16.2% respectively gave a neutral answer (level III of importance) and 6.7%, 4.1% and 4.1% did not answer.

Moreover, "Legal" and "Soils" competences are of the same importance according to the experts with the percentage of 62.2% and 64.9% respectively, choosing the levels IV and V of importance. Small percentages marked the first two levels (I and II) and the medium level III of the importance was underlined by 27% and 25.7%, of the respondents respectively. 4.1% and 2.7% did not answer.

"IT skills" is proved as one of the basic Water Specific Competence. The smallest percentage of experts, 60.8%, revealed it as the least important competence (levels IV and V). A small portion of the answers marked the low levels of the importance (10.8%) and a significant percentage of 25.7% of the respondents find more accurate the medium level of the importance and 2.7% did not answer.

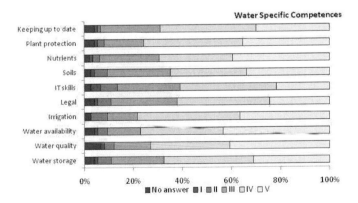

Fig. 3. Rating importance of agricultural water specific competences (level I = lowest level of importance, ..., level V = highest level of importance)

4 Conclusions and Future Work

Since the introduction of competences and schemas of competence models in several sectors (Stracke, 2011, Palavitsinis *et al.*, 2009), a lot of works have been realised in terms of the development of metadata schema for the recognition of competences. As an example, the ICOPER Reference Model supports the identification of Information and Communication Technologies (ICT) competences, which are relevant in the context of learning and teaching and described through metadata and identifier (Najjar *et al.*, 2012a).

In a similar way, the eCOTOOL Competence Model developed for the description of Europass Certificates Supplements, taking in consideration the description of agricultural competences (Stracke, 2011, eCOTOOL High-Level Competence Model Explanation, 2011). Additionally, the WACOM Competence Model describes competences for the water sector, through the identification of its components (knowledge, skills and other competences) (Stracke, 2011, Thanopoulos *et al.*, 2011).

In this paper, it is presented the initial work in the design and development of the Competence Metadata Schema for the agricultural sector, with a provision for pilot testing and further evaluation in hydroponics and irrigation fields of agriculture. For this reason, a fundamental step is the analysis of the requirements for the importance, implementation and evaluation of this schema for the specific fields of agricultural sector related to the use of water resources in agricultural practice.

As an initial step agricultural experts, who are involved in professional training, consultants and practitioners, were asked to evaluate the importance of the development of the Competence Metadata Schema. Even if they mentioned the high priority on the development and implementation of such kind of metadata tools for the specialisation of agricultural competences, the reasons that underline this necessity vary among their answers The majority of the participants expressed the opinion that better description of competences through the Competence Metadata Schema will positive support the understanding and acquisition of qualifications that required by the labour market, as well the improvement of the professional training in order to meet the objectives of the labour market in agriculture.

Concerning the evaluation of the agricultural competences in the fields of use of water resources in agriculture, as outcomes of the Competence Metadata

Schema, replies reveal the high importance (50-60%) or normal level of importance (20-30%) of these competences for the agricultural professionals.

In a second step the Competence Metadata Schema, will be finalised in terms of the data type and definition of the vocabularies terms, in order to evaluate real cases of agricultural professionals.

Acknowledgements

This work is funded with the support by the European Commission, and more specifically the projects "AGRICOM: Transfer of Water Competence Model to AGRIcultural COMpetences" (No DE/11/LLP-LdV/TOI/147 458) and Herbal.mednet (No 2012-1-FS1-LEO05-50453) of the Lifelong Learning Programme (LLP). This publication reflects the views only of the authors, and the Commission cannot be held responsible for any use which may be made of the information contained therein. Authors thank all the consortium partners for their contribution in the design and realization of the requirements analysis.

References

Najjar, J., Grant, S., Simon, B., Derntl, M., Klobučar, T., Crespo, R., Delgado, C., Nguyen-Ngoc, A., Pawlowski, J., Hoel, T., Oberhuemer, P. (2012a). D2.2 - Model for describing learning needs and learning opportunities taking context ontology modelling into account.

Grant, S., Sgouropoulou, C., Thanopoulos, C. (2011). A model for skills and competences and its application in the agricultural sector, In Proc of the 5th International Conference (MTSR '11), Izmir, Turkey.

Stracke, M.C. (2011). Competences and Skills in the Digital Age: Competence Development, Modelling, and Standards for Human Resources Development. Proceedings of the 5th International Conference (MTSR '11), Turkey, ISSN: 1865-0929, pp. 34-46.

Najjar, J., Thanopoulos, C., Manouselis, N. (2012b). Towards Outcome Based Online Learning: Applications and Standards, Proceedings of First International Conference on Information and Communication Technologies for Education and training (TICET 2012), May 7-10, Tunisia (In press).

Thanopoulos C., Protonotarios, V., Stoitsis, G. (2012). Online Web portal of competence-based training opportunities for Organic Agriculture, Agris on-line Papers in Economics and Informatics, Vol. IV (1): 67-86.

Thanopoulos, C., Manouselis, N., Kastrantas, K. and Psochios, Y. (2011). Design and Development of the ICT Tools for the Online Dissemination of the WACOM Competence Model (WCM). In Proc of the 4th European Conference: "Innovations in the Environmental Sector" Competence Models, E-Learning, Social Communities, Belgium, pp: 82-97.

eCOTOOL High-Level Competence Model Explanation (2011), http://www.competencetools.eu.

Manouselis, N., Najjar, J., Kastrantas, K., Salokhe, G., Stracke, M.C. and Duval, E. (2010). "Metadata Interoperability in Agricultural Learning Repositories: An Analysis", Computers and Electronics in Agriculture, Special Issue on Information and Communication Technologies in Biological and Earth Sciences, Elsevier, 70 (2), 302-320.

Palavitsinis, N. and Manouselis, N. (2008). "Agricultural Knowledge Organisation Systems: An Analysis of an Indicative Sample" in Sicilia M.-A. (Ed.), Handbook of Metadata, Semantics and Ontologies, World Scientific Publishing Co. (in press).

Manolis, H., Kastrantas, K. and Manouselis, N. 2012), "Revisiting an analysis of agricultural learning repository metadata: preliminary results", in Proc. of the 6th Metadata and Semantics Research Conference (MTSR'12), Cádiz, Spain. (in press).

Palavitsinis, N., Manouselis, N. (2009). "A Survey of Knowledge Organization Systems in Environmental Sciences", in I.N. Athanasiadis, P.A. Mitkas, A.E. Rizzoli & J. Marx-Gómez (eds.), Information Technologies in Environmental Engineering, Proceedings of the 4th International ICSC Symposium, Springer Berlin Heidelberg.

Palavitsinis, N., Manouselis, N., Sanchez, S. (2009). "Evaluation of a Metadata Application Profile for Learning Resources on Organic Agriculture", in Proc. of the 3rd International Conference on Metadata and Semantics Research (MTSR'09), Milan, Italy.

Diamantopoulos, N., Sgouropoulou, C., Kastrantas, K., and Manouselis, N. (2011) "Developing a Metadata Application Profile for Sharing Agricultural Scientific and Scholarly Research Resources", in Proc. of the 5th Metadata & Semantics Research Conference (MTSR'11), Izmir, Turkey.

A Content Analysis and Information Model for the European Qualifications Framework (EQF)

Kenji Hirata, Simone Laughton, Kazuhisa Seta, Christian M. Stracke

Expert Science Institute and i am & interworks inc., 2-26 Shirasagi Nakano, Tokyo, Japan
University of Toronto Mississauga Library, 3359 Mississauga Road N, Mississauga, ON, Canada
University of Duisburg-Essen, ICB, Essen, Germany
skillmgt@gmail.com, simone.laughton@utoronto.ca, seta@mi.s.osakafu-u.ac.jp, christian.stracke@icb.uni-due.de

Abstract: Combining competency with proficiency levels can be useful to support and define the attainment of educational objectives and certifications. Proficiency levels can be described in many different ways (e.g., numeric, alphanumeric, text descriptions, etc.), making it challenging to share this type of information. An information model can be used to support mutual understanding and to facilitate the exchange of information amongst different IT systems. The European Qualifications Framework (EQF) is intended to provide a common reference model that can relate various European national qualification systems. The eight EQF proficiency levels are widely used and consist mainly of textual information that is used to define or rank the understanding, knowledge, and ability of learners. A content analysis was conducted to better understand how this information is shared and combined, and then a proposed proficiency information model was applied to EQF.

Keywords: Competency, Proficiency Level, Information Model, Interoperability

1 Introduction for Proficiency Level Modelling

Informational modelling and standardization in Learning, Education and Training (LET) have been the focus of much attention and development efforts in the last decade. Modelling methods and information technology standards for competency or educational objectives have been developed concurrently. From the beginning of the 2000s, some industrial and academic associations have developed information technology specifications or frameworks for competency and learning objectives on a global level to address the interoperability requirements and environmental complexities of organizations. Some examples included work spearheaded by the following organizations, IMS Global Learning Consortium Inc. (IMS GLC Inc.), HR-XML consortium, IEEE Learning Technology Standard Committee (LTSC), and ISO/IEC JTC1 SC36 (ISO-SC36) (Hirata 2011), and a data specification for competency semantics was published by Society for HR Mark-up Language (HRMLs 2012). These specifications would be used in talent management systems for global companies.

These specifications do not clearly address the differentiation between competency itself and educational objectives. Educational objectives or learning outcomes are a specific form of competency information that is managed and used in the real world. There are a multitude of educational approaches that can be used for one skill or competency. For example, reading a textbook is an educational activity that can support the development of a learner's knowledge base to support the development of a competency. Role playing is another useful activity or approach that can be used to elicit learner demonstrations of competency, in specific contexts with defined conditions. Educational or learning objectives can be set for a competency. For example, for a mathematical calculation competency, the educational objectives in each grade in school are different in terms of the knowledge and understanding required and what the learner is required to do in terms of the complexity of the calculations and the application in different domains. The complexity of calculations or the range of domains could be determining factors in how the proficiency level is defined and understood. The combination of competency information and associated parts, such as level, are useful for expressing educational objectives and understanding competency constructs. However, they can be defined in many diverse ways making it challenging to share and transfer this type of information.

In addition to the complexities of competency construct definitions, proficiency or level concepts may be unclear or imprecise. Some national skills standards and the EQF (The European Qualifications Framework for Lifelong Learning, EC 2008) set proficiency levels for certain skills or competencies, but the translation of the levels may be difficult to apply or interoperate with IT systems residing in different countries, specific industries and individual companies. Proficiency level may be constructed by those with several and varied perspectives and diverse metrics. This can make it difficult to reach a shared understanding to support LET, assessment, and certification. A referable or standardized proficiency level semantics model is indispensable to support human development. It has the potential to foster mutual understanding and to allow for the sharing of proficiency level competency information and data for those who live in different counties, work in various industries and companies and require competency information and data for wide-ranging uses.

2 Purpose

Human assessment is used to assume the degree of learner competencies. The discovery of the potential of what one can do and the natural interest to learn about and from others is inherent to being human. Some questions that are asked include, "What can I do", "What can I do well?", "What can another person do?", and "What is the extent of their potential and talent?", "How well a person can do the things they do?". By asking and answering these questions, people get to know each other and themselves. They build relationships in school, workplace and ordinary life. The exploration of our natural abilities takes place throughout the entire span of our lives even in the absence of a common framework for expressing and defining proficiency level. Definitions and coding both of competency and proficiency level are key factors to manage and support human development, assessment, and talent management across the global. In this paper, through reviewing patterns of proficiency level structures and descriptions, we introduce a model for expressing and defining proficiency level. Then the model is applied to EQF in order to support the exchange and management of the proficiency level information among human and IT systems.

3 Information Model for Proficiency Level

Hirata, Laughton and Stracke (2010) proposed an ontology model for proficiency, and revised it to create a simpler structure that is easier to use (figure1: 2012). The proficiency level information model (PLI model) consists of several attributes and elements. Attributes are used to identify proficiency level information and can consist of several items, so these attributes are indispensable for data identification and verification. In Figure 1 below several examples of attributes are provided including, id, name, and description for a simple implementation. Other attributes can be added according to other approaches, such as the use of RDF schema to describe proficiency information. Although attributes are used to identify proficiency information, as noted below, elements and sub elements in PLI model are more important for expressing structure and content of a proficiency level.

As noted in Figure 1 below, the metrics element indicates schema of proficiency level characteristics. It can be used to specify differentiation in the competency proficiency level of learners, trainees, students, learning contents, and others. Metrics also is used to help with specifying and assessing what or how a competency proficiency level is measured (e.g., for grade, degree, level, class, stage, and so on). Four sub elements in metrics were set in the metrics element, "level number", "level sequence", "dimension number", and "dimension". Dimension element will be listed as "dimension number". If dimension number is "5", five data are required.

A metric element provides information of level or segmentation. For expressing level, two elements could be used, "level number" and "level sequence". Level number is the number or the pattern how many levels or the extent of the range of possible levels. For example, the data of level could be an integer for nominal level segmentation. For example if "low", "middle" and "high", are used a total number of level "3" expresses proficiency level concept. The level sequence is expressed from the smaller or lower of the level labels to the highest. For the example above, the lowest or minimum level as proficiency should be listed first, and the highest or maximum level as proficiency should be listed last {1="low"/ 2="middle"/ 3="high"}. The list sequence is important. As the data of level would be continuous range such as TOEIC test (English test), there is no obvious segmentation. In this case, level number is expressed as "continuance", and level sequence is expressed as "10-990". As additional information, sometimes TOEIC score can be expressed as nominal proficiency levels, such as level from E to A, in spite of "continuance". "Level E" takes range of 10 - 219, "level D" takes range of 220 – 469, "level C" takes range 470 - 729 and so on. So the element "metrics" can have several sub elements.

The metrics element also provides content information regarding proficiency. In this example, proficiency information was divided into levels, so at least one more viewpoint is needed for segmentation. Dimension is a way to identify that there are different aspects with specific levels that can be used to evaluate, and to assess proficiency level. The labels used to express the different aspects of something such as "dimension" could include many different factors, assessment elements or criteria. For expressing the content, the "dimension number" and "dimension" are set. It is easier to understand this example in the context of a use case of driving license in Japan. The driving test is conducted using several different aspects as dimensions, such as reviewing training archival record, paper testing, and practical driving skill examination. These evaluation methods are reflected by different dimensions. So a driving license in Japan is assessed by a combination of 3 dimensions at least. This means that the statement of the dimension number is "3". Dimensions are "general knowledge", "knowledge for driving", and "driving skill". However, it may not be easy to elicit and to define the metrics being used, because more detailed information related to the metrics that are being used may be hidden or implicit, and complex. So contents analyses are normally needed to figure out the dimensions or aspects of what is being assessed.

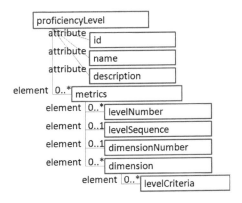

Figure 1 Proficiency Level Information Model

4 Contents Analysis for EQF Level

EQF acts as a translation device to make national qualifications more readable across Europe, promoting workers' and learners' mobility between countries and facilitating their lifelong learning. EQF is a common European reference framework that links countries' qualifications systems together, acting as a translation device to make qualifications more readable and understandable across different countries and systems in Europe. The eight reference levels are described in terms of learning outcomes. EQF recognizes that Europe's education and training systems are so diverse that a shift to learning outcomes is necessary to make comparison and cooperation between countries and institutions possible. EQF shows 8 levels for each three domain. These domains are knowledge, skill, and competence, and are related each other, but are defined separately. Using a more standardized structured way through the proficiency level information model to describe the domains could be a helpful approach to support the use of EQF.

Before the PLI model can be implemented with EQF, it would be advisable to analyze and clarify the content of EQF structure and level. As mentioned above, there are three domains, knowledge, skills and competence. Each of the three domains are connected but basically separated, and there was no integrated or summarized description for the 8 levels. The attributes and the first two elements in the PLI model can be easily fixed without additional analysis.

However, the last elements are not easy to define. So based on EQF documents, content analyses for EQF level table and descriptions can be conducted for each domain in order to spell out the dimension more clearly. The dimensions are abstract concepts and critical elements or views to distinguish each level. They can be open to interpretation, so by using the proficiency level information model, some of these ambiguities can be resolved establishing a basis for true interoperability. As noted below, a content analysis was completed regarding the 3 domains of knowledge, skills, and competence. The relevant factors are listed on the top of the tables below, and the concrete contents of the factors are chosen terms from sentences and listed on each table. The result of the knowledge domain is shown in table 1, the result of skill domain is shown in table 2, and the result of competence domain shows table 3. For example, level 6 in knowledge domain is defined by "specialty level: a field and highly specialized", "advancement: advanced", "range of content type: theories and principle", and "understanding: critical understanding". The differences of level 5 can be clear. Level 5 require only normal, but level 6 requires highly in specialty level. Level 5 requires only basic or normal level in advancement, but level 6 requires advanced level". Level 5 requires only memory for knowledge, but level 6 requires understanding. These are big differences between the two levels. The analysis is useful and can support mutual understanding.

Table 1   Contents Analysis of EQF Knowledge Domain

Factor	Specialty level	Advancement	Range of content type	Breadth of knowledge	Understanding
Level 1	General	Basic			
Level 2	A field		Basic factual		
Level 3	A field		Fact/ Principle/ Process/ General concept		
Level 4	A field		Factual/ Theoretical	Broad contexts	
Level 5	A field/ Specialized		Comprehensive/ Factual/ Theoretical	Boundaries	
Level 6	A field	Advanced	Theories/ principle		Critical understanding
Level 7	A field/ Highly specialized	Forefront		Interface between different field	Original thinking and research
Level 8		Most advanced		Interface between different field	

Table 2   Contents Analysis of EQF Skill Domain

Factor	Problem Type	How to solve	Skill width	Advance ment	Skill type	Responsibility in task
Level 1				Basic		carry out simple task
Level 2	Routine problems	Simple rules and tools		Basic	Cognitive/ practical	carry out tasks with info.
Level 3	Problems	Selecting and applying basic method/ tools/ materials/ information	A range		Cognitive/ practical	Accomplish tasks
Level 4	Specific problems	Generate solutions	A range		Cognitive/ practical	
Level 5	Creative solution	Develop	A compre hensive range			
Level 6	Complex/ Unpredictable problems in a specialized field			Advance d	Demonstrate mastery & innovation	
Level 7	Research/ Innovation	Develop new knowledge & procedure/ integrate knowledge			Specialized problem solving	
Level 8	Critical problems in research and innovation	Extend and redefine existing knowledge or professional practice/		Most advance d	Specialized/ Technique/ Synthesis & evaluation	

Table 3   Contents Analysis of EQF Competence Domain

Factor	Action Type	Independence/ responsibility	Management objects	Context	Flexibility
Level 1	Work	Under direct supervision		Structured	
Level 2	Work	Under supervision/ some autonomy			
Level 3	(1) Work) 2) Problem solve	1) for task completion			2) Adapt own behavior to circumstance
Level 4	(1) Work) 2).Supervise	1) Exercise self mgt. with guidelines 2) some of evaluation & improvement of activity	2) Routine work	Usually predicable	
Level 5	1) Manage & Supervise 2) Review & Develop		1) Work 2) Self & other performance	Unpredict able	
Level 6	1) Manage & Supervise 2) Develop professional		1) Professional activities or projects 2) Individuals & Groups	Unpredict able	
Level 7	1) Manage & Transform 2) Contribute & Review		Professional knowledge & practice/ Strategic performance of teams	Complex/ Unpredict able	1) New strategic approaches
Level 8	1) Demonstrate 2) Commute		1) Substantial authority, innovation, autonomy, and professional integrity 2) Develop new ideas or processes	forefront	

5   Proficiency Level Model Implementation to EQF Level

Following the results of the content analyses, each element of dimension number can be fixed as follows, knowledge domain is 5, skill domain is 6 and competence domain is 5. The 5 dimensions of knowledge domain are "speciality level", "advancement", "range of content type", "breadth of knowledge", and "understanding". The 6 dimensions of skill are "problem type", "how to solve", "skill width", "advancement", "skill type", and "responsibility in task". The 5 dimensions of competence are "action type", "independence", "management objects", "context", and "flexibility". The left side of table 2 shows an implementation of whole knowledge domain of EQF level into the PLI model as an example.

On the other hand, the PLI model can also adapt to not only whole concept of proficiency but also to each level. The right side of table 4 shows an implementation of EQF knowledge domain for the 5th level. There are 5 dimensions in EQF knowledge domain, but 3 dimensions are used to define the 5th level. So the dimension number is "3" in the figure. And three dimensions are listed for the dimensions, "speciality level", "range of content type", and "Breadth of knowledge". Additionally, each level was defined with more detail with content for each dimension. In the case of knowledge for the 5th level, this level should consist of or have condition of "a field" and "specialized". The range of content types includes "comprehensive", "factual" and "theoretical". Breadth of knowledge should expand to "boundaries" level.

6 Conclusion

Increasingly there are needs and requirements for the ability to exchange and better manage international content and system frameworks for learning and competency. The proficiency level also needs to be more clearly defined and include information system implementations based on common structures and guidelines to better support interoperability. EQF level has been well known a content framework of proficiency levels in European and other counties. EQF level have been used in various industries and counties, but it is challenging to come to a common understanding to support the exchange of data or qualifications (such as certifications) after being introduced in diverse contexts. To realize and encourage interoperability that will support human understanding and also foster better interoperability amongst information systems, an information model for proficiency level could be useful.

Based on the information model for proficiency level (PLI) model, which was proposed by Hirata, Laughton, and Stracke (2010), EQF levels were analysed and the PLI model was applied. Three content analyses were conducted for three domains of EQF, namely knowledge, skill and competence. The analyses indicated that each concept of proficiency consisted of 5 or 6 dimensions. The use of tables to portray a sampling of the results for the content analyses, the structure and construction of proficiency can be made more explicit to facilitate the application of the PLI model IT systems and data design used to support the management and exchange of competency information. In this initial study, the PLI model was applied to EQF to determine if it would promote interoperability. Initial findings are that it could be helpful. However, this research indicates that improvements are needed. The model needs to be revised to add that the parameter of condition of dimensions, for example "and", "or" or "priority". This could help to show the relationships amongst the dimensions more clearly and definitely. At this point more research is needed.

Table 4   EQF Knowledge Domain Model and 5th Level Model

attribute/element	EQF knowledge domain	EQF knowledge domain 5th level
Id	EQF_2008_k	EQF_2008_k_lv05
name	EQF_knowledge_2008	EQF_knowledge_2008_level05
description	EQF knowledge is structured by 8 levels by EU...	EQF knowledge 5th level is the 5 stage of 8, which is defined by EU.
metrics	EQF knowledge metrics	EQF knowledge metrics for level 5th
levelNumber	8	5
levelSequence	level {1, 2, 3, 4, 5, 6, 7, 8}	5/8
dimensionNumber	5	3
dimension	{specialty level} {advancement} {range of content type} {breadth of knowledge} {understanding}	{specialty level} {range of content type} {breadth of knowledge}
levelCriteria		specialty level [and] {in a field} {specialized}
		range of content type [and] {comprehensive} {factual} {theoretical}
		breadth of knowledge {boundaries}

References

EC. (2008). The European qualifications framework for lifelong learning (EQF). European commission.

Hirata, K. (2011). Developing a specification for competency semantics. In Competence modelling for human resources development and European policies. Stracke, C. Ed. Essen, Germany, GITO verlag.

Hirata, K., Laughton, S., and Stracke, C. (2010). Competency proficiency ontology. In Workshop proceedings of the 18th international conference on computers in education. p.292-299. Putrajaya.

Hirata, K., Laughton, S., and Strake, C. (2012). Working draft ISO/IEC 1 JTC 1/SC 36 N 2411, Information Model for Competency-Part 2: Proficiency Information Model.

HRMLs. (2012). Data specification for competency semantics. Hirata, K. Ed. The society for human resources mark-up language. Tokyo.

ISO/IEC TS 24763: Information technologies for learning, education and training - A conceptual reference model for competencies and related objects. ISO/IEC. 2011.

The ProInterNet Certification Process for e-Jobs Profiles and Training Programmes

Achilles Kameas, Ed Mahood, Michael Negri

Hellenic Open University, Greece
kameas@eap.gr
DEKRA Akademie GmbH, Germany
ed.mahood@dekra.com
FOM Hochschule, Germany
michael.negri@bcw-gruppe.de

Abstract: Recent reports have shown that, in the ICT sector, training programmes are mainly organized by or for large companies despite the fact that approximately 80% of all non-public employment is generated by companies with fewer than 20 employees (that is, very small and micro-enterprises). The aim of the ProInterNet (PIN) network is to set up a holistic approach of assessing and validating internet-related, employment-functional qualifications and profiles in SMEs. Part of this effort involves developing an approach toward labelisation, certification (validation) and normalisation of these qualifications by addressing the knowledge, skills, and competences requirements, on the one hand, and education and training development and provision, on the other. This includes a dynamic evaluation mechanism for internet-related functional-role profiles, training development and implementation guidelines corresponding to the agreed profiles, a prototype Label of Excellence (LoE) and a Seal of Market Compliance (SMC), with accompanying Certificate (as recognized quality standard).

Keywords: jobs observatory, job profiling, profile description, profile maintenance, profile certification, training certification, competence, eskills, eCF, EQF

1 Introduction

The Information and Communication Technology (ICT) sector is one of the economically most promising and significant business sectors in the European Union (EU). It makes an important contribution to the objectives of the Lisbon Agenda.

According to the most recent OECD outlook report (2010), the prospects for the ICT sector are improving in the wake of the financial crisis of 2008. The ICT sector accounts for 8% of business value added and countries with significant ICT manufacturing have comparative advantages in trade. Pressures on employment in the ICT sector within the OECD countries that began during the recession are beginning to ease and the numbers of available ICT vacancies are growing. As access to broadband internet is steadily increasing and the central role that networking plays in the commercial and non-profit sectors, the potential for employment growth in internet-related areas is increasing as well.

Though vacancies are becoming more plentiful, they are often difficult to fill as qualifications do not always match the requirements of the companies in this sector. In recent years, most projects aiming at the promotion of vocational and education (VET) standards in the ICT sector were initiated and driven by large companies. However, it should be recognized that approximately 80% of all non-public employment is generated by companies with fewer than 20 employees (that is, very small and micro-enterprises), and that the knowledge, skills and competences required by these smaller enterprises (SMEs) differ significantly from those required by larger organizations.

The ProInterNet (PIN) thematic network contributes to the main objectives of the Leonardo da Vinci programme as laid down in policy documents, starting with the Copenhagen process. It has created a network of key players in the area of ICT and Multimedia skills in SMEs aiming to improve the transparency, information and guidance systems with regard to competence and qualifications at European level for internet professions. The key stakeholders involve industry organisations that have in-depth experience of e-Jobs, Internet-related jobs and direct access to SMEs (technology suppliers and users); VET institutions with a focus on e-Jobs and Internet-related jobs; relevant public authorities and intermediary organisations.

Through its activities, PIN intends to contribute so as to improve the employability of job seekers, reduce the e-skills shortages on the EU labor market, improve the quality of Vocational Education & Training (VET) in the field of Internet related jobs and last but not least to make VET more transparent and comparable at European level. The network brings together complementary players such as VET, HE, certification organizations, jobs and enterprise associations for a proactive and continuous knowledge exchange in the area of Internet jobs.

The network's aim is to set up a holistic approach of assessing and validating internet-related, employment-functional qualifications and profiles in SMEs. Part of this effort involves developing an approach toward labelisation, certification (validation) and normalisation of these qualifications by addressing the knowledge, skills, and competences requirements, on the one hand, and education and training development and provision, on the other. The idea is to agree on an EU competence system for internet-related jobs. This includes, of course, a dynamic evaluation mechanism for internet-related functional-role profiles, training development and implementation guidelines corresponding to the agreed profiles, a prototype Label of Excellence (LoE) and a Seal of Market Compliance (SMC), with accompanying Certificate (as recognized quality standard).

2 e-Jobs Observatory

In order to foster the interaction between industry intermediary organisations and VET institutions, the e-Jobs Observatory (http://e-jobs-observatory.eu) was set up as part of PIN. It is intended as an information and guidance platform for the parties involved, bringing together international experts on the field of internet-related jobs. More concretely, the e-Jobs Observatory is a Web 2.0 platform that offers industry intermediary organisations the opportunity to express their needs in terms of training and qualification of employees and exchange thoughts with VET institutions, which, in return can adopt their trainings according to market requirements and attain the label of excellence and an official certification from the network (Figure 1). The direct benefits from participating in the e-Jobs Observatory include free access to all information and results of studies conducted by the Observatory and its related projects, and reinforcement of interaction between key participants. Every person or partner that participates in this interactive system has the ability to influence the ongoing development, multiplies its reach out and formulates a better picture of future trends and developments in the field. Moreover, one becomes part of a rapidly growing network of like-minded companies and associations interested in furthering the quality of professional qualifications in Europe.

3 Roles profiles

The functional (or job-description) profiles are the centrepiece of the e-Jobs Observatory approach. It is on the basis of these profiles, which are driven and verified by actual market needs, that training can and should be developed.

The identification of a given profile should be related in a clear, consistent way to a development within the industry itself or in an internet-related field. This should be made clear in the relevant part of the profile description.

Each internet-related function must be given a meaningful and wide-understood title (such as Webmaster, Online Community Manager, etc.). In addition, the profile description will be divided into two sections:

Figure 1. The e-Jobs Observatory home page

1.   Function Description

This will consist of a table as follows (all entries in italics are explanations for the items listed in the left-hand column):

Profile title	*<Title>*	
Summary statement	*<One-sentence description of the function.>*	
Mission	*<The reason the function is necessary.>*	
Responsibility	*<Brief overview of the primary responsibilities.>*	
Deliverables	Accountable	Contributor

Profile title	*<Title>*	
	<Deliverables for which the function is responsible.>	*<Deliverables to which the function provides inputs.>*
Main task/s	*<Listing of the main tasks to be performed by the function.>*	
Environment	*<Brief description the function's working environment.>*	
KPIs	*<Listing of key performance indicators (KPI) for the function.>*	

This table must be fully completed by the organisation that requires such a profile and wishes to have it included in the list of authorized profiles.

2.   Function Profile

This section consists of two subsections, each comprising a different table.

2.1 Profile summary

This table contains the Areas, Numbers, and Competences, which are based on the European eCompetence Framework (eCF) (2011) (Figure 2).

Profile		\<Title>		Technical					Behavioural												Business				
Area	No.	Competence	Importance	T01	T02	T03	T04	T05	B01	B02	B03	B04	B05	B06	B07	B08	B09	B10	B11	B12	M01	M02	M03	M04	M05
Plan	A.1	IS and Bus. Strat. Alignment																							
	A.2	Service Level Management																							
	A.3	Business plan Development																							
	A.4	Product/Project Planning																							
	A.5	Design Architecture																							
	A.6	Application Design																							
	A.7	Technology Watching																							
	A.8	Sustainable Development																							
Build	B.1	Design & Development																							
	B.2	Systems Integration																							
	B.3	Testing																							
	B.4	Solution Development																							
	B.5	Document Production																							
Run	C.1	User Support																							
	C.2	Change Support																							
	C.3	Service Delivery																							
	C.4	Problem Management																							
Enable	D.1	Info Sec. Strat. Development																							
	D.2	ICT Qual. Strat. Development																							
	D.3	Educ. & Training Provision																							
	D.4	Purchasing																							
	D.5	Sales Proposal Development																							
	D.6	Channel Management																							
	D.7	Sales Management																							
	D.8	Contract Management																							
	D.9	Personnel Development																							
	D.10	Info. & Knowledge Mgmt																							
Manage	E.1	Forecast Development																							
	E.2	Project & Portfolio Mgmt																							
	E.3	Risk Management																							
	E.4	Relationship Management																							
	E.5	Process Improvement																							
	E.6	ICT QM																							
	E.7	Business Change Mgmt																							
	E.8	Info. Sec. Management																							
	E.9	IT Governance																							

Column legends:

- T01: Has knowledge of netiquette, interactive virtual env., social networks, e...
- T02: Has knowledge of online usability requirements
- T03: Can promote and sell products or services online
- T04: Can create media elements
- T05: Can draft texts, clearly, concisely, correctly
- B01: Is creative, imaginative, artistic
- B02: is ethical
- B03: Is precise and aware of details
- B04: Is customer oriented
- B05: Is committed to corporate strategy and aware of corporate culture
- B06: Has good interpersonal skills
- B07: Has presentation/moderation skills
- B08: Can communicate (including in foreign languages if useful)
- B09: Can work in a team
- B10: Can seek, organize and synthesize
- B11: Can analyse (assess, evaluate, critique, test)
- B12: Can explain (defend, argue, justify)
- M01: Has Knowledge of project management principles
- M02: Has knowledge of budgeting/estimating issues and practices
- M03: Has knowledge of legal, environmental, labour, standards issues
- M04: Has marketing knowledge
- M05: Can lead a team

Figure 2. The role description table used by the e-Jobs Observatory

2.2 Detailed profile

For each eCF competence identified in the summary profile (above), an expanded version detailing the specifics of each competence and sub-competence must be produced, for example (whereby the entries in italics are explanations for the data required):

A.1 IS and Business Strategy Alignment

Dimension 2: Title and generic description	*<The title is as given; the description here should be modelled after the descriptions provided on the eCF website.>*	
Dimension 3: eCompetence proficiency levels	Level 1	*<These should be completed as*
	Level 2	*necessary for the profile, but modelled*
	Level 3	*after the descriptions provided on the*
	Level 4	*eCF website.>*
	Level 5	
Dimension 4: Knowledge and skills	*<There should be one entry for each of the master competences that have identified in the summary profile above.>*	

3.1 Profile definition, change and approval process

Any organisation holding the e-Jobs Observatory Label of Excellence (see below), or which is a member of the e-Jobs Observatory network, can propose changes to an existing profile or suggest the development of a new internet-related roles profile (Figure 3). Any profile that is to be included within the scope of these guidelines must be completed and submitted to the e-Jobs Observatory working group for approval.

3.2 Submitting a new profile for approval

The profile itself is to be developed in accordance with the requirements specified in the previous section. The working group will review the profile for completeness, accuracy, consistency, coherency, and relevance. If the submitted profile conforms to the formally established criteria above, the profile will be made available in a restricted area of the website for member review and comment. Members will be notified that their comments are requested. The profile will be available for review for a period of three (3) months. At the end of this period, the working group, will review the comments and incorporate any necessary changes into the profile.

Figure 3. The profile submission page of the e-Jobs Observatory

3.3 Submitting suggestions for changing an existing profile

Any organisation which has been awarded the e-Jobs Observatory Label of Excellence or any other member of the e-Jobs Observatory network may comment upon existing profiles and make suggestions for change. At such time that the e-Jobs Observatory working group assesses that a revision of a commented upon profile is appropriate, a task group will be established to make the necessary revisions and to ensure the profile meetings all requirements for completeness, accuracy, consistency, coherency, and relevance. The working group will create a revised profile which will be made available in a restricted area of the website for member review and comment. Members will be notified that their comments are requested. The profile will be available for review for a period of three (3) months. At the end of this period, the working group, will review the comments and incorporate any necessary changes into the profile.

The revised version of the profile will be released for a vote by the network membership. The voting period will last one (1) month. As the submitting organization is a member of the network, it will have full access to the status of the submitted proposal. Two results are possible:

1.   Approved: If a majority of the membership organizations vote positively on the proposed profile, it will be approved and included in the e-Jobs Observatory's list of approved profiles and published publicly on the website.

2.   Rejected: If rejected, however, the working group will provide a written assessment to the submitting organization outlining the changes and amendments that would need to be made before the profile could be accepted. The submitting organization can resubmit the profile after having made said changes, at which time the approval process would begin again.

4 The e-Jobs Observatory Label of Excellence

Labelisation is the first step along the certification path envisioned by the e-Jobs Observatory (Figure 4). It is an independent, stand-alone process that enables the applicant organisation to become involved in and associated with the network of stakeholders striving to improve ICT further training in Europe.

Figure 4. The Label of Excellence submission form

A dialogue with industry led the e-Jobs Observatory to establish a set of principles that provide a framework within which training and personnel development in the field of internet-related jobs can be promoted. Any organization should be able to subscribe to these basic principles, as they form the basis of the e-Jobs Observatory Label of Excellence (LoE), shown in Figure 5.

Figure 5. The e-Jobs Observatory Label of Excellence

These fundamental principles have been encapsulated in the e-Jobs Observatory Statement of Compliance, and are as follows:

1. The labour market in the internet-related sector is regularly and systematically analysed in order to identify valid and current market needs for crucial skills and competences.

2. Learning outcomes are more important than the learning path that a student takes to achieve them. Competence development in the broadest sense of the term is the top priority in training and learning. Training programmes should be expressed in terms of learning outcomes.

3. Learning outcomes should describe the knowledge, skills and competences the learner should have acquired or obtained by the end of a given unit of learning.

4. Training as a goal-directed activity aims at qualifying individuals in an organised, systematic and transparent way, hence the importance of identifying training requirements through relevant role profiles.

5. The so-called "soft skills" or key competences are recognized as an integral part of every training unit, module or programme.

6. Within the ICT sector, especially in regard to internet-related role profiles and training, the European eCompetence Framework (eCF) plays an important, central role in bridging the gap between market needs and training offerings.

7. The European Qualification Framework (EQF), as well as national and sectorial frameworks, provides a useful and helpful mechanism to increase the transparency of training programmes in regard to learning outcomes.

By subscribing to these principles and applying for the LoE, a training organization or institution asserts that they are willing to support these principles by attempting to incorporate them into their training offerings.

5 The e-Jobs Observatory Seal of Market Compliance and Certificate

Any organisation which has been awarded a e-Jobs Observatory Label of Excellence or any member of the network can submit a training programme, course, or unit for a given internet-related roles profile (Figure 6). In the following, the term "unit" is used to describe the training that has been submitted, irrespective of its complexity or duration.

Assessment and validation criteria

The following assessment criteria will be used in the approval and validation process of training units for internet-related jobs:

- Pre-Assessment of candidates: The institutions have to make sure that the candidates fulfil the basic requirements necessary to enter the program
- Detailed description of training contents
- Envisage and integrate changes of needs and requirements, ensuring up-to-date training.
- Expected training outcomes must be expressed in the terms of learning outcomes
- Methods must be clearly identified for training approach and tools, materials and media to be used
- Linkages between methods and outcomes must be clear, in order to ensure that targeted outcomes are achieved
- Integration of training on soft skills, which ensure the training of various soft skills by applying appropriate methods
- Assessment of training success

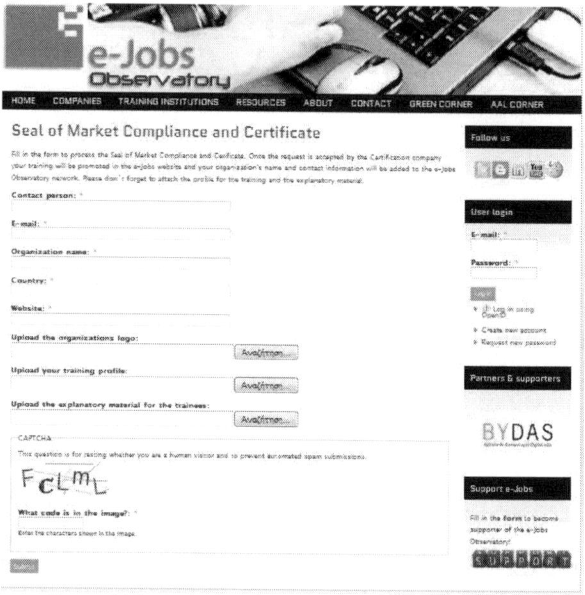

Figure 6. The Seal of Market Compliance submission form

5.1 Submitting a training unit for approval

The training is to be developed in accordance with the requirements specified above. Upon submittal, the e-Jobs Observatory working group will review the training unit for completeness, accuracy, consistency, coherency, and relevance and conformance to the formal documentation requirements. If the submittal does not meet these minimum requirements it will be returned with a written justification and suggestions for improvement to the submitting organization. If the submittal meets all preliminary requirements, it will be further analysed for content and completeness. The evaluation will be conducted by the authorized member of the e-Jobs Observatory working group, and will be in accordance with a set of criteria outlined in the Training Unit Approval Checklist. The resulting assessment will be communicated to the submitting organisation.

Three results to the process are possible:

1. Approved: The submitting organisation will be notified in writing and the training will be added to those being kept on the e-Jobs Observatory website. A "Seal of Market Compliance" and certificate will be issued.
2. Accepted, pending changes: The submitting organization will be notified in writing of the changes and amendments that need to be made before

the training can be approved. The submitting organisation can resubmit the training after having made said changes.

3. Not accepted: The submitting will be notified in writing outlining the reasons for the rejection. A resubmittal of the training in its current form is not permitted.

5.2 Approving a training unit

Figure 7. The e-Jobs Observatory Seal of Market Compliance

Training units which are evaluated and found to be in conformance with the requirements set out in these guidelines will be awarded the e-Jobs Observatory Seal of Market Compliance, which is depicted in Figure 7. This seal attests to the fact that the training unit in question has been submitted to and approved by the e-Jobs Observatory working group, thereby fulfilling the standards set forth herein. The seal is a guarantee of quality for this reason.

The organisation or institution submitting the training unit will also receive a Certificate of Market Compliance, which details the approval and sets the time limits for its applicability.

6 Certified Profiles and Training

One of the key project outcomes has been the identification and development of internet-related job profiles which serve as a baseline for the development of training modules that can be certified as described in section 4 above. A total of ten such profiles have been compiled, five resulting from the PIN project and an additional five which were produced within the context of the EQF-iServe (2012) project. These are:

1. Digital Animator /2D-3D Specialist
2. Internet Hotline Operator
3. Online Community Manager

4. Usability Specialist
5. Web Content / Multimedia Developer
6. Web Content Manager
7. Web Designer
8. Web Marketer
9. Web Seller
10. Webmaster

All of these profiles, of course, are available for download on the e-Jobs Observatory website (www.e-jobs-observatory.eu).

While these can be considered the "standard" profiles, sanctioned by the e-Jobs Observatory, market-driven training modules may be addressed to a full profile or, depending upon local market needs, to skills and competence subsets of these profiles. The guidelines for training development are in place, and the development of guidelines-compliant training units is in progress. Within the auspices of the project, at least one training provider per participating country has submitted or signalled intention to submit training modules for certification. The process is on-going, thus no validation data are available to date.

7 Conclusions

In today's fast-changing, technological environment, keeping up-to-date technically is a necessity. In an increasingly competitive global business environment, it is essential that workers keep not only their technical skills current, but also ensure that they are suited for the changing demands of work itself. As ProInterNet Synthesis Report (PIN, 2010) has shown, the so-called "soft-skills" (or key competences, that is, behavioural and managerial skills and competences) are very much in demand by industry, in addition to expected technical knowledge and skills. This set of skills has been confirmed by roundtable meetings with industry representatives that were conducted in all partner countries as well. These will need to be considered, of course, in any approach that claims to improve the quality of training available.

More information about the e-Jobs as well as templates for applying for new profiles, labelisation or certification can be obtained from the e-Jobs Observatory website. All submittals shall be in electronic form via the e-Jobs Observatory platform. Upon submittal, the e-Jobs Observatory working group will review the training unit for completeness, accuracy, consistency, coherency, and relevance and conformance to the formal documentation requirements.

Acknowledgement

This document was prepared as part of the ProInterNet (PIN) Thematic Network Project, Agreement no. 2009-2204/001-001, under the auspices of the Leonardo da Vinci Programme. The authors wish to thank all the colleagues working in the project.

References

EQF (2008) *The European Qualifications Framework for Lifelong Learning*, Luxembourg, Office for Official Publications of the European Communities.

EQF-iServe (2012) Apply approach and methods developed within EQF-Code to internet-related services professions, Lifelong Learning Project Number 2010-1-FR1-LEO05-14477, Project website: http://groupspaces.com/eqfiserve/

OECD (2007) *Qualifications Systems: Bridges to Lifelong Learning*, Paris, OECD.

OECD (2010) *Information Technology Outlook 2010 Highlights*, Paris, OECD.

ProInterNet (PIN) (2010) *Synthesis Report*, Technical Report delivered as part of Work Package 1, ProInterNet Project [online], available at http://e-jobs-observatory.eu/sites/e-jobs-observatory.eu/files/Synthesis%20Report%-20Final.pdf

Learning Quality in Vocational Education and Training and the Case of TUT: A 3P Model for Leading Integrative Change

Hua-Hui Tseng

Tainan University of Technology, Music Department, No. 128 Po-Ai 1st Road, Kao-Hsiung, Taiwan
t50005@mail.tut.edu.tw

Abstract: The purpose of this paper is to use the International Personnel Management Association's (IPMA, 2002) people, process, and products (3P) model to analyze and explore the process of learning and giving students tools in education that would lead them to become successful and responsible learners. Consideration will be given to areas and practices of the 3P model in a school system that creates a department-wide commitment to use flexible curricula to engage students. In this paper, an attempt is made to provide a general overview of the 3P model for leading integrative change and show how the seven components of the 3P model can be used as an index to measure the progress of change. The case of the Tainan University of Technology (TUT), Taiwan, is used to gain insight into some of the implications and excitement about teaching issues. The findings demonstrate that a true assessment of success is a sustainable future that is realized by raising the quality of education, research, and development that support the vision of collegial governance and academic freedom.

Keywords: change processes, quality, value

1 3P Model for Leading Integrative Change

Burnes (1996) noted organizational change refers to understanding alterations within organizations at the broadest level, among individuals and groups at the collective level, across the entire organization (Kezar, 2001, p. 12). It is critical that change begin with a modification of behavior and attitudes. Within the last decade, organizations have been operating in an environment of increased competitiveness and change. Successful organizations are those that can change effectively, either through creating new markets or meeting new goals for existing products. Most higher education administrators, however, think in terms of good ideas or noting trends in institutionalization or diffusion rather than true change (Kezar, 2001, p. 13). At the same time, many practices and structures take on the features of legitimacy without becoming institutionalized.

Technology and a shrinking world have quickly pushed Taiwan into the global arena. As leaders of educational institutions encounter an array of new questions and challenges, the leaders of TUT sometimes wonder what their efforts to prepare and adapt to change will bring. In order to create something of value, it is necessary to have the proper materials, knowledge, and skills and use materials creatively and with imagination to implement unique designs for the creation of an object. Theories of diffusion constitute the approach Tainan University of Technology (TUT) is taking with respect to its educational change processes.

In this study, the integration challenges the TUT faculty, staffs, and students are facing will be described and an overview given of the TUT's vocational education and human resource development and solutions to stimulate excellence in integrative mechanisms and initiatives. Thereafter, the process implemented at the TUT for influencing change in new workplaces and among providers of workforce preparation will be described. Finally, the components (people, products, and processes) that comprise the TUT's vocational education and human resource development will be outlined.

2   Designing an Innovative Model for Implementing Top-Down Change in an Organization

The International Personnel Management Association's (IPMA, 2002) method, the people, process, and products (3P) model, consists of expanding concentric circles. Each circle represents a stage in the process of an organization moving from the status quo to enthusiasm and willingness to commit to change. **Higher education** institutions serve as key **change agents** in transforming **education** and society (Goswami, Gupta, & Pathak, 2010). In the first circle or stage, which is called *building support,* the core group of people who will spread the message are assembled. In the second stage, *individual commitment* is built through personal growth, learning, and personal results. It is in the third and final stage, *organizational results,* where the collective mindset is changed and new organizational processes and systems put in place to produce lasting change for the organization.

3 Innovative Programs

Building Support: A Wider Sustainability

Change processes are unique and depend on the organizational life cycle of a college or university (Kezar, 2001, p. 92); nonetheless, the IPMA (2002) found the following:

> Change starts with a few key people who are not only willing to commit their time and resources but who also believe in the change being introduced. We call these individuals "passionate champions." Our approach has been to use current managers to help us develop and implement solutions, expanding the number of people involved each time. (p. 1)

With the TUT principal's approval, faculty invited the Teaching Excellence Committee of the Music Department to steer and oversee the change effort. The group sponsored a department-wide survey of the TUT's 335-strong workforce. The results of the survey not only helped faculty define the problem areas, but also provided a way for individual faculty members to participate. Early on in the process, the Committee asked 15 of current senior chairs to identify the traits of a successful chair. The results of this exercise formed the basis for a list of leadership competencies. Then, the Committee asked managers of the human resource department to set priorities for change. The managers chose three areas on which to focus, namely, cross-curriculum sub-objectives, model lessons, and enrichment. The Committee convened a panel to work with the Teaching Excellence Committee for a week to define the project, determine its focus, and develop solutions to address concerns in each of the three priority areas. The panel suggested using a 3P model for leading integrative change. The panel has since become the known as the Integrative Committee and its members guide the effort. Members of the Integrative Committee are perhaps the integrative curriculum's most passionate champions.

From the core group, the Integrative Committee moved outward and spread the message throughout the school. The Integrative Committee began weekly briefings for the principal's Chief of Staff and the Commissioner of the Department of Administrative and Financial Services. An overview of the 3P model for leading integration was provided to the principal's team. In addition, members of the team were asked for their support, which was forthcoming. Senior management teams of all the academic departments, the TUT's human resources managers, and the alumni of the TUT association, consisting of a professional development program for senior managers, were briefed. In

February 2010, 67 school administrations attended a half-day forum, hosted by the principal, who introduced the 3P model for leading integrative change and answered questions. Members of the Multiple Learning Integrated Curriculum (MLIC) hosted two open briefings for administrators, providing an overview of the MLIC and answering questions. A website and newsletter were created to provide ongoing, current information about the 3P change model.

Individual Commitment: Broad-Based Knowledge Sharing

Vocational schooling requires the continuous renewal of its content and structures in order to respond to changing employment structures and occupational skills. The integration of teaching and learning is a meaningful, fruitful exercise when practiced in the context of vocational training. This area of discipline lends itself readily to the integrative process. New curricular constructs ('learning fields' and 'learning spaces') promote integrative learning that link the perspective of integrative curriculum development with current policy agendas. From curriculum development, including qualification goals, use of existing training models, and integration to other components of the curricula, the Integrative Committee had drawn attention to the possibility of developing different complementary working perspectives within a joint research-supported curriculum redesign initiative.

Organizational Results: Effective Learning Environment

The goal of the 3P model, which measures how well a system is implemented with all the key components of the integrative education model, is focused on the process of learning or giving students tools with which they can become successful and responsible learners. Jacobs (1989) and Shoemakers' (1989) researches involved the implementation of curriculum integration and supported the 3P model. System changes, including implementing an on-going evaluation plan, are envisioned.

The Creating Integrative Change Template (CICT) helped with applying the relevant parts of the 3P model to Music Department at the TUT to build new instructional approaches to reach every student. The seven components included in the CICT template have been critical to building integrative change in a 3P school system and created a department-wide commitment to using flexible curricula to engage all students. Because every school and department is unique, it is likely that a subset of these components may be effective or essential; however, in applying the template in other contexts, new components may emerge. Form 1A, with examples from the 3P model, offers a more comprehensive set of implementation strategies within the seven main components of the model.

Form 1A: Creating Integrative Change Examples from the 3P Model

Technology Infrastructure
- Wiring for Internet and Intranet
- Computers, software, and network
- Technology coordinator staff
- Commitment to digital curricula
- Widely available software and digital resources
- School-wide and departmental servers
- Classroom connections to Internet and Intranet
- Departmental Web site; Class Web site
- Within-building tech support

Teacher Training
- Multiple, ongoing training strands, required
- Classroom teachers opportunity to mentor others
- Teachers have option to be trained for new part-time roles
- Teachers as part-time technology coordinators
- Multiple summer institutes
- Continuous collaborative support
- Open atmosphere to share problems and solutions

Collaborative Curriculum Planning
- Vocational education, educational technology, and regular education staff plan together
- Group analyzes curriculum barriers/solutions
- Focus is on curricular flexibility, not student disabilities

Creative Funding
- Reallocation of vocational education and technology funds to create a pool
- Joint grant applications with non-profitable organizations
- Small grant from national and municipal foundation
- Department-wide commitment to increase willingness to be flexible
- Commitment shared across disciplines

Administrative Support
- Advocates present to administrators and school board
- Some administrators/principals spearhead work
- Administrators support grant writing
- Administrators support flexible fund allocation
- Commitment to PDL at superintendent level

Redefined Roles
- Vocational education teachers collaborate with technology staff
- Vocational education teachers collaborate with Academic education teachers
- Vocational education specialists focus on mainstream curricula
- Classroom teachers increase flexibility of curricula

• Look ahead to potential barriers • Pre-build solutions to increase learning for all • Commitment shared across disciplines	• Teachers participate in digitizing and creating units **Parent/Community Involvement** • Parent participation in digitizing and resource collection • PTO informed and committed to PDL initiatives • Parental involvement via Web in classrooms and students' work • Seek buy-in from community to pool resources

Form 1B, the blank template, offers structured support for selecting those parts of the 3P model that might apply in departments at the TUT and adds new components as well as specific implementation strategies.

Form 1B: Creating Integrative Change Blank Template

3P/New Model Component	Implementation Examples
1. Technology infrastructure	Using multimedia for teachers at the undergraduate level and graduate schools (PEOPLE)
2. Administrative support	Developing and evaluating a department-based framework for managing quality and standards at the undergraduate level (PROCESS)
3. Teacher training	Planned and deliberate strategies and processes for academic management at the undergraduate level and graduate schools (PRODUCTS)
4. Redefined roles	Codified interdisciplinary teaching in a mandated planning process at the undergraduate level (PRODUCTS)
5. Collaborative curriculum planning	Developing and producing knowledge objects for classroom setting at graduate schools (PRODUCTS)

6. Parent/community involvement	Realizing the free self-determination of a personality with its subordination to external objective normative structures for a person at the undergraduate level (PEOPLE)
7. Creative funding	Organizing workplaces and industries in an evidence-based plan for renewal at school level (PROCESS)

4 Workforce Development & Alignment

The present: The role of the Teaching Excellence Center in promoting impeccable diversified vocational education and maintaining competitiveness. The 21st century will be an era in which the development of a knowledge-based economy is essential. Whether knowledge-based innovations and research can be further advanced hinges on events in higher education. Higher education is already a primary arena for competition among many countries with regard to knowledge creation and human resource development. Not only does higher education play a decisive role in national development, but also, higher education is a vital source from which enhancements in national competitiveness spring. Moreover, the fast-changing social landscape, political liberalization and democratization, rapid economic growth, industrial restructuring, and increasingly pluralistic social values over the last few years have brought new challenges for higher education in terms of its traditional functions and stewardship role.

The competitiveness of a country's higher education is an important indicator of its competitiveness as a nation. For competition to thrive, students must receive accurate information about products and processes. One part of the **TEC**'s basic mission is to promote teaching and learning effectiveness. The **TEC** serves to bridge the gap between research and teaching by establishing models and criteria of effective teaching.

The future: Key external factors in the TEC's environment. Due to the rapid change of many sectors of education, it is critical the TEC's enforcement process be a dynamic one. The Center must constantly review itself as a "value platform" to help guide the TUT's development. The following identifies those changes in education most likely to affect the TEC's ability to achieve its two goals. The TEC's two goals are:

> 1. Publicly recognize faculty members for their dedication, creativity, honed insights, and skills.

2. Contribute to the realization of a high-quality learning environment for TUT students.

With respect to achieving Goal 1, the Spotlight on Teachers is a collection of profiles that offer insight into what individual faculty members think about teaching and how to best facilitate student learning. With the help from faculty and staff, a collective portrait of how TUT faculties, through a wide variety of philosophies and approaches, pursue teaching excellence on campus can be built.

With respect to achieving Goal 2, in January 2006, the Faculty Federation was established to honor outstanding teachers amongst the TUT faculties with the Teacher of the Year award. In these profiles, the Teacher of the Year reflects on what being a teacher means to him or her and how, over his or her career, he or she has come to facilitate the learning of his or her students so effectively.

5 Conclusion

Leaders must create business strategies that add to their organizations' future viability and the well-being of people and communities (Anderson & Anderson, 2001, p. 203). In order to face the challenges that accompany changes, Taiwan's Ministry of Education (2006) is actively working to establish an educational foundation to support the concept of a "knowledge-based economy" (p. 1). In 2005, an overall assessment of university administration was conducted; a plan was launched to reward universities for teaching excellence with the expectation that universities will be encouraged to emphasize teaching and enhance the quality of university education through performance-based incentives" (Ministry of Education, Taiwan, 2006, p. 49).

The "explosion" of knowledge, the increase of state mandates related to a myriad of issues, fragmented teaching schedules, concerns about curriculum relevancy, and a lack of connections and relationships among disciplines have all been cited as reasons for a move towards an integrated curriculum (Jacobs, 1989). Implementation of the 3P model has significant implications for creating excitement about teaching and has helped the TUT look forward. It is helping students to take control of their own learning. The seven components of 3P model can be used as an index to measure the progress of change. However, a true assessment of success is a sustainable future realized by raising the quality of education, research, and development that support the vision of collegial governance and academic freedom.

References

Anderson, D., & Anderson, L. A. (2001). *Beyond change management.* San Francisco, CA: Wiley.

Burnes, B. (1996). *Managing change: A strategic approach to organizational dynamics.* London: Pitman.

Fogarty, R. (1991). *The mindful school: How to integrate the curricula.* Palatine, IL: Skylight.

Goswami, V., Gupta, S., & Pathak, P. (2010, October). Quality enhancement in Indian higher education. *Journal of Social Welfare & Management, 2*(4), 155-160.

International Personnel Management Association. (2002). *A model for change: Maine's application.* Retrieved from http://www.nwrel.org/scpd/sirs/8/c016.html mainegov-images.informe.org/bhr/mms/IMPA-second.pdf

Jacobs, H. H. (1989). *Interdisciplinary curriculum: Design and implementation.* Alexandria, VA: Association for Supervision and Curriculum Development.

Kezar, A. J. (2001). *Understanding and facilitating organizational change in the 21st century: Recent research and conceptualizations.* New York: John Wiley & Sons.

Ministry of Education. Taiwan (2006). Introduction to higher education in Taiwan. Retrieved from http://www.edu.tw/EDU_WEB/EDU_MGT/KMS/EDU0000002/25.htm?FILEID=14 3578&UNITID=4&CAPTION=Introduction

NAFSA's 52nd Annual Conference. (2000). *An update on education In Taiwan.* Retrieved from http://www.tw.org/TaiwanUpdate.html

President's Council on Sustainable Development. (1994). *Education for sustainability: An agenda for action.* Retrieved from http://www.gcrio.org/edu/pcsd/index.htm

Shoemaker, B. (1989). Integrative education: A curriculum for the twenty-first century. *Oregon School Study Council, 33*(2), 1-57.

Innovative Development of the Russian Education System based on Standardization and Certification of e-Learning

Boris Pozdneev, Yury Kosulnikov, Maxim Sutyagin

Moscow State Technological University "STANKIN", Information System Department, 1, Vadkovsky pereulok, 12794, Moscow, Russia
bmp@stankin.ru
iourik@stankin.ru
Gazprom Corporate Institute, IT Department, 16-2, Nametkina str., 117997 Moscow, Russia
M.Sutiagin@institute.gazprom.ru

Abstract: One of the main directions of innovative development of Russian education system is a large-scale use of e-learning in educational institutions at all levels (primary, secondary, and higher school and postgraduate professional education, skills development in industries). The adoption of the Russian Federal Law "On the e-learning" resulted In a significant increase in the number of educational institutions that use e-learning in educational activities. However, the specific e-learning requires a systematic quality assurance processes, training, information and educational environment, teaching staff and electronic resources. Problems of quality and quality assurance e-learning are considered in the aspect of conformity (voluntary certification) e-learning components to meet the requirements of international and national standards harmonized with international standards.

Keywords: innovation, e-learning, learning, education, training, quality, quality management, quality assurance, standardization, certification, ISO/IEC JTC1/SC 36, TC 461.

1 Introduction

At present, information and communication technologies contribute to the development of national and international educational systems, transformation of traditional technologies and teaching methods, create new forms of e-learning and the formation of cross-border and transnational educational structures of the new generation.

The main task of the Russian educational policy - providing modern quality education based on the preservation of its fundamental and current and future compliance needs of the individual, society and state. To solve this problem it is necessary to modernize the Russian system of education. The purpose of modernization of education is to create a mechanism for sustainable development of the education system. To achieve this goal it is necessary to address the following priorities, interrelated tasks:

- provision of state guarantees of equal access and opportunities for meaningful education;
- achieving a new modern quality preschool, general and vocational education;
- formation of the educational system of legal, organizational and economic mechanisms to attract and use of extrabudgetary resources;
- improving the social status and professionalism of educators, strengthening their government and public support;
- development of education as an open state-of the social system based on the distribution of responsibility between the subjects of educational policy and the role of all participants in the educational process - student, teacher, parent, educational institution.

The Russian system of education brings more than 1,000 universities, 10,000 vocational schools, 40,000 schools, which are distributed over a vast territory. The need to provide equal opportunities to obtain education for all citizens of Russia necessitates the use of e-learning in the educational process.

These features will be reflected in the new law "On education", a project that is now being actively debated in society. Some of the most important provisions that will be included in the new law have already acquired legal force. Adopted in 2012, the federal law "On e-learning", legalized the use of e-learning in all forms of education. The next step in this direction will be the adoption of the Federal Law "On the Industry e-learning (e-Learning)". The subject of legal regulation are relations associated with the creation and operation of e-learning industry in the Russian Federation. The law shall fix the legal status of e-learning industry and determine the duties of the State to take necessary measures to support the establishment and operation of e-learning industry.

Creating a competitive e-learning systems in the field of engineering education should be based on a set of requirements (see Fig. 1-3) contained in the federal state educational standards (FSES), international and national standards, professional standards and standards organizations (higher vocational, corporate, industrial education).

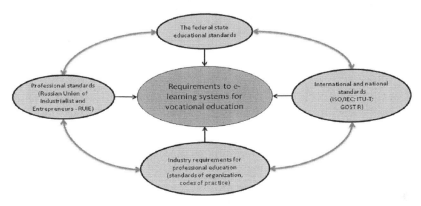

Fig.1 Structure of requirements to e-learning systems

Fig.2 The harmonization of normative documents on standardization in the field of IT LET at national and international levels

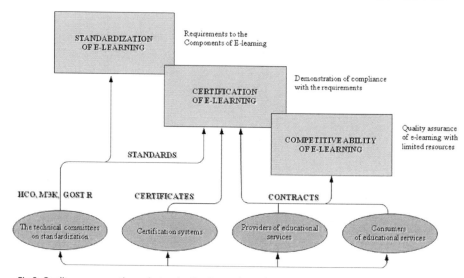

Fig.3 Quality assurance through standardization and certification of personnel, processes, products and services in the field of e-learning

2   National and International Standardization

Russian and international experience shows that the effective application of standards is the basis for improving the quality and competitiveness of information and educational media, electronic educational resources and educational services

International and national standards help to gain such a confidence in the world. One of the major goals of standardization is to provide a comprehensive trust. Systems, products and services are functioning as expected by the customer, because they correspond to the basic requirements set out in international standards.

Standards provide quality products and services, environmental safety, reliability, interoperability, efficiency and effectiveness. Allow manufacturers to be sure that their products have the opportunity to enter international markets, since it can be used everywhere.

Interoperability creates scalability and ensures users that they will receive the same services wherever they are. Thus, the standards equally provide benefits to consumers, manufacturers and service providers. It should be noted that in developing countries, the use of international standards accelerates the spread of new products and services and thus stimulate economic development.

Quality assurance and management of e-learning are possible when considering e-learning systems in terms of their compliance with international and national standards that contain requirements for e-learning technology, information and educational media and electronic educational resources.

According to the fundamental principles of international standard ISO 9000 quality of e-learning should be understood as the degree of compliance with the requirements set of inherent characteristics. Accordingly, a set of requirements must be defined in professional standards, federal state educational standards, as well as national and international standards for quality management, information technology, open systems interconnection, information sharing, data protection, etc. (Fig. 4).

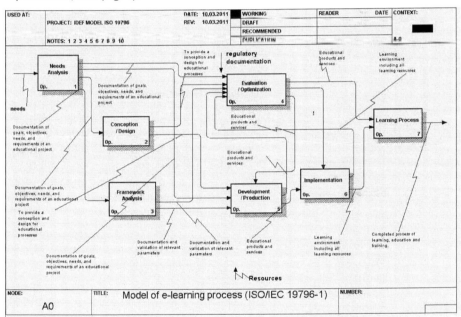

Fig. 4 Model of e-learning process. ISO/IEC 19796-1 (DIN PAS 1032-1)

In 2004, Russia had established a national technical committee on standardization of "Information and Communication Technologies in Education" (TC 461), which brings together six subcommittees (see Fig. 5 and [2]). More than 100 highly qualified experts from the educational and research institutions, the leading domestic IT companies and other organizations are working in subcommittees of TC 461. Since 2006, the Russian national delegations actively participate in the work of ISO / IEC JTC1/SC36.

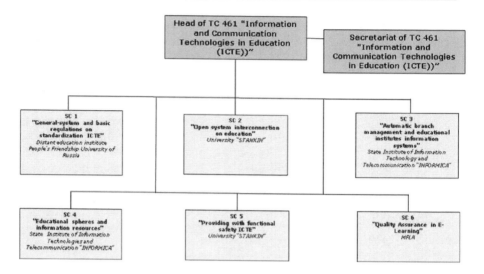

Fig. 5 Structure of Technical Committee 461 ICTE

The result of seven year work of TC 461 is development of more than 20 national standards that form the basis of a set of standards on IT LET. TC 461 plans in the years 2013-2015 the development of at least 20 national standards, which will be 100% harmonized with international standards.

The list of already developed national standards is presented in Appendix 1. All standards of this list can be grouped into six main areas that together represent profile of e-learning standards. These areas are:

1. General Terms and Definitions.
2. Quality Management.
3. Management Information Systems for Educational Institutions.
4. Learning Management Systems.
5. E-Learning Resources.
6. Training Facilities.

Developing of national standards aimed at ensuring harmonization with international standards and at the same time takes into account country-specific development of education, information society, technical regulation in Russia. In connection with the formation of the Customs Union and the Common Economic Space of the three countries (Russia, Republic of Belarus, Kazakhstan) standards developed by the TC 461 acquire the status of interstate standards (GOST).

Thanks to the development of Russian legislation (the new Law on E-learning, and the new Education Law) the national profile of standards for IT can be the basis for the application of e-Learning in Corporate educational structures (association of universities, industry training system et al.).

The basis of a national profile are standards for terminology and quality management:

GOST R 52652-2006 Information and communication technologies in education. General provisions.

ISO / IEC 2382-36 Information technology. Vocabulary. Part 36. Learning, education and training.

GOST R 53625 (ISO / IEC 19796-1:2005) Information technology. Learning, education and training. Quality management, quality assurance and metrics. Part 1. General approach.

GOST R 53723 Information technology. Guidance on the application of GOST R 53625 -2009.

Thanks to GOST R 52653, adopted in 2006, identified 35 of the terms and definitions in ICTE.

Key terms of the standard have been harmonized with the basic international standards including ISO / IEC 2382-36, which at that time was in the development stage.

Subsequently, a national standard ISO / IEC 2382-36, which is a direct application of the international standard ISO / IEC 2382-36, which provided a complete harmonization of terminology. With the introduction of these two standards it was possible to streamline the terminology in the preparation of publications and the development of normative and organizational documents in the field of information science and education.

National Standard GOST R 53625 was developed based on the modification of ISO / IEC 19796-1. This modification has been associated with the reduction and systematization of the data portion of an international standard. Parallel to this, an original national standard GOST R 53723 was developed, which provides recommendations to establish a common approach to quality, based on the integration of standard process models presented in ISO 9001 Quality management systems - Requirements and ISO / IEC 19796 Learning, education and training - Quality management, assurance and metrics. This allowed developers to focus at quality management systems of educational institutions to expand the traditional process models taking into consideration the features of the educational activities using e-Learning.

In addition, a wide range of developers of information management tools for the e-Learning has been properly oriented to the functional interaction of the e-Learning components in the process approach (ISO 9000 and ISO 9001). Information management tools are electronic resources, educational environment, digital libraries, information management systems for educational institutions. This made it possible to unify information management tools for the e-Learning and to assess their quality during the subsequent certification.

3   Certification of E-learning

The Russian legislation contains several ways to assess the quality of products and services. One option is voluntary certification. Several Bodies (systems) for Certification carry out in Russia voluntary certification of products and services of ICT (Fig. 6 - 7). They work closely with each other on the base of mutual agreements.

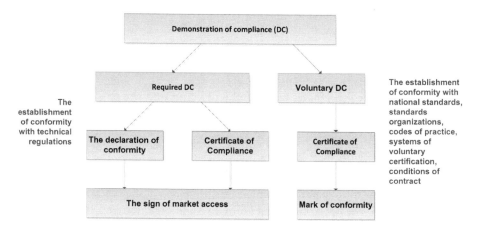

Fig. 6 Schemes of conformity assessment of products under the Federal Law "On technical regulation" of 27.12.2002

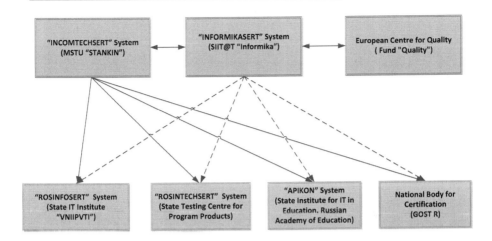

Fig.7 The relationship of certification systems in education and science and their relationship with national and European authorities

In 2004 MSTU "STANKIN" registered in the Federal Agency on Technical Regulating and Metrology the system for voluntary certification of ICT in education (system "INKOMTEHSERT"). MSTU "STANKIN" is defined as the governing body of the "INKOMTEHSERT". The Governing Body of the System "INKOMTEHSERT" plays the role of industry body for standardization, certification and registration of information resources in the education system. As part of the developed system are a number of certification bodies and regional testing laboratories in Moscow, Tambov, Petrozavodsk, Voronezh, Ufa, Tomsk, Samara, Perm, Kemerovo, Saratov, Krasnoyarsk. Main functions of "INKOMTEHSERT" system are described in [3].

Along with the current system "INKOMTEHSERT" and "ROSINFOSERT" in education and science were established three certification systems related to conformity assessment of ICT: A system of voluntary certification of hardware and software and information systems educational purposes (system "APIKON"), a voluntary system certification of information technology for the formation of state information resources (system "ROSINTEHSERT") and the system of voluntary certification "INFORMIKASERT". The main characteristics of existing certification systems in education are presented in the table 1.

Tab. 1 Voluntary Certification Systems for ICT in Education and Science

Name	Registration Certificate	Mark of Conformity	Governing Body	Structure
Voluntary Certification Systems for ICT in Education ("INCOMTEHSE RT" System)	26.11.2004 № POCC RU.B135.04И K00		State Educational Institution for Higher Vocational Learning Moscow State Technological University " STANKIN" (MSTU "STANKIN")) http://www.stankin.ru/	Governing Body – 1 Certification Body – 1 Testing Laborato-ries - 14
The system of voluntary certification of hardware and software and information systems of educational purposes (System "APIKON")	06.12.2004 № POCC RU.Д149.04А O00		State Science and Research Institution "Institute for Information Systems in Education» of Russian Academy of Education (SS&RI IISE RAE) http://www.iiorao.ru/	Governing Body – 1 Certification Body – 1 Testing Laborato-ries - 3
The system of voluntary certification (in Educaiton and Science) «INFORMIKASE RT»	17.12.2009 № POCC RU.B612.04И Ц00		Federal State Institution "State Science and Research Institute of ICT" (FSI SS&RI ICT "INFORMIKA") http://www.informika.ru/	Governing Body – 1

4   Conclusion

Russia's WTO accession and integration into the global educational environment necessitates extensive use of e-learning in educational institutions at all levels (schools, universities, training and skills development).

As a result of active work of TC 461 in ISO/IEC JTC1/SC36 a set of basic national standards (GOST R), harmonised with international standards (ISO/IEC) in e-learning and taking into account the national specifics of Russian education.

For confirmation of compliance e-learning components of the essential requirements of national and international standards in Russia created two systems of voluntary certification (INKOMTEHSERT and INFORMIKASERT), accredited certification bodies (CB) and the testing laboratories (IL) at leading universities and research organizations. These interacting organizations provide the necessary testing and certification of:

- quality assurance systems for educational institutions;
- information educational media;
- electronic educational resources;
- telecommunications services; and
- staff (heads of educational institutions, teachers, technicians).

References

B. Pozdneev, Yu. Kosulnikov, M. Sutyagin "The prospects of training and retraining of engineering personnel on the basis of e-Learning Technologies".

Periodical "Higher Education in Russia", 2009, # 7, pp. 9-12.

http://www.stankin.ru/

http://infocert.stankin.ru/

Appendix 1

Appendix 1. List of already developed national standards

1. GOST R 52652-2006 IT LET in education. General Provisions.
2. GOST R 52653-2006 IT LET in education. Terms and Definitions.
3. GOST R 52655-2006 IT LET in education. The integrated automated control system of the high professional educational system. General requirements.
4. GOST R 52656-2006 IT LET in education. Federal level educational internet-portals. Ceneral requirements.
5. GOST R 52657-2006 IT LET in education. Federal level educational internet-portals. Information resources system of heading.
6. GOST R ISO/IEC 8825-4-2009 Information technology.ASH.1 encoding rules. Part 4. XML encoding rules (XER).

7. GOST R 53625 -2009 Information technology (ISO/IEC 19796-1:2005) Information technology. Learning, education and training. Quality management, assurance and metrics. Part 1. General approach.
8. GOST R 53723 -2009 Information technology. Application guide for GOST R 53625 -2009 (ISO/IEC 19796-1:2005).
9. GOST R 53620 -2009 Information and communication technologies in education. Electronic learning resource. General regulations
10. GOST R 53626 -2009 Information and communication technologies in education. Training equipment. General statements.
11. GOST R 53909 -2010 Information and communication technologies in education. Training equipment. Terms and definitions.
12. GOST R 54818 -2011 Information and communication technologies in education. Information and communication technological systems for educational buildings. General statements.
13. GOST R 54818 -2011 Information and communication technologies in education. Information and communication technological systems for educational buildings. Terms and definitions.
14. GOST R 54816 -2011 Information and communication technologies in education. Training equipment. General statements.
15. GOST R ISO/IEC 19778-1 Information technology. Learning, education and training. Collaborative technology. Collaborative workplace. Part 1. Collaborative workplace data model.
16. GOST R 54837 (ISO/IEC 19796-3:2009) Information technology. Learning, education and training. Quality management, assurance and metrics Part 3: Reference methods and metrics.
17. GOST R ISO/IEC 19778-2 Information technology. Learning, education and training. Collaborative technology. Collaborative workplace.
18. Part 2: Collaborative environment data model.
19. GOST R ISO/IEC 19778-2 Information technology. Learning, education and training. Collaborative technology. Collaborative workplace. Part 3: Collaborative group data model.
20. GOST R ISO/IEC 2382-36-2011 Information technology. Vocabulary. Part 36: Learning, education and training.
21. GOST R ISO/IEC 24703-2011 Information technology. Participant Identifiers.
22. GOST R ISO/IEC 15836 Information and Documentation. The Dublin Core metadata element set.

Blended Multicampus Education for Lifelong Learners

Katie Goeman, Stijn van Laer

Hogeschool-Universiteit Brussel, Faculty of Economics and Management,
Educational Research and Development, Brussels, Belgium
Katie.Goeman@hubrussel.be
Katholieke Universiteit Leuven, Media & Learning Unit, Heverlee, Belgium
stijn.vanlaer@dml.kuleuven.be

Abstract: The main objective of the 2-year MULLLTI project is to implement highly flexible academic and professional higher education for lifelong learners. Since 2011, different partners within the Association of the University of Leuven have been collaborating in order to develop blended multicampus courses aimed at working students. Lecturers from several regions in Belgium, appointed at a series of universities and colleges for higher education, work in pairs to create eighteen courses in various subject fields. Ideally, the experiences should lead to a consistent theoretical framework, as well as a series of guidelines for good practice. In this paper we report on the rationale and the specific approach of the project, including the continuous quality improvement framework that has been put into place. In this way we hope to offer relevant insights for practitioners and researchers interested in multicampus education, blended and/or lifelong learning.

Keywords: multicampus education, lifelong learning, blended teaching, MULLLTI

1 Objectives of the MULLLTI Project

How can we provide more and better opportunities to lifelong learners? In this paper the reader will find a description of a 2-year project whereby several higher education institutions cooperate closely in order to scrutinize the benefits and boundaries of blended multicampus education i.e. blended course provision on multiple campuses, for mature (working) students.

The main objective of the Multicampus Education for Lifelong Learning Project (MULLLTI) is to (re)design eighteen courses for mature working students in Social Work, Management and Teacher Education. For that purpose lecturers employed at five different campuses within the Association K.U. Leuven work in pairs and apply the instructional design principles of blended learning. Each pair jointly decides on how to combine off- and online media and teaching methods, and which multicampus format to apply in order to reach congruent learning objectives. As a consequence, a huge number of interesting case studies have arisen that give insight into the opportunities and limitations of multicampus education for lifelong learning. In addition, the project partners hope to get a better understanding of which blended learning variants provide the best match in terms of learning objectives, content or type of learners.

In order to achieve this main objective several sub goals were put forward:

1) the identification of essential dimensions and tools for successful blended learning - according to literature and experts, and agreed on by the project partners;

2) the development of a multi-actor framework for blended multicampus teaching, including procedures, conditions and implications for learners, lecturers and the organization;

3) the design, delivery and evaluation of eighteen courses in a multicampus setup;

4) the elaboration of an in-service training module, focusing on the building blocks of blended learning, the (re)design, development and delivery of multicampus courses, as well as their monitoring and (e-)support.

2 Instructional Design for Blended Learning in a Multicampus Context

The MULLLTI project group has defined blended learning as "the systematic, integrated combination of online and offline teaching and learning activities". In line with Annetta et al. (2010, 153) "it encompasses both classroom sessions and technology resources (e.g., Web sites, course management systems, or learning management systems)".

The specific profile of working students plus the multicampus context impel lecturers to (re)think didactics and the deployment of media so as to create open and flexible learning spaces and carry out student-centred activities, face-to-face as well as at a distance. The lecturers within the MULLLTI project can rely on support of instructional designers and education experts when in doubt about choosing didactics that have the best fit with the learning goals and the characteristics of lifelong learners, as well as the organisation with its distinct support system and multicampus reality. The same considerations apply to finding the ideal mix and match of (electronic) study materials, whether self-developed, open or commercial. In this respect it is very convenient that within the Association of the University of Leuven there is one common digital learning environment. This is complemented by open source, user friendly and broadly-accepted software.

Figure 1 visualizes the framework that is applied when project partners confer on the instructional design for blended learning. The design process starts with whole tasks, i.e. a description of one's task with a particular profile in a specific position. To make these tangible, lecturers specify competences and learning goals, which are legally embedded in education programmes. In order to be able to achieve the learning goals, students need to carry out certain learning activities. These activities are elicited using specific didactics and by means of learning tasks, tailored to the learners and the context. Next one chooses one or more media, and decides how to blend the physical with the virtual on the basis of the functionality of media in the instructional process. As a consequence some aspects of the physical learning environment will be more suitable for particular learning tasks, while other learning tasks evoke better results by means of online media. For each environment three kinds of media are set forth, each focusing on information, communication or evaluation. In addition, preliminary stages are defined and possibly external actors steer, support or influence to a certain extent the off- and online teaching and learning activities. It is the complex interplay of input, interaction and the way(s) in which the building blocks supplement or complement each other that will define the effectiveness and efficiency of the blended learning environment.

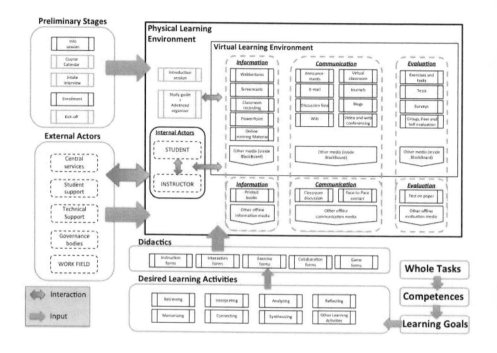

Figure 1. Instructional Design for Blended Learning

3 Continuous Quality Improvement Framework

In line with the objectives and specific approach of the MULLLTI project, a quality framework was drawn up. It is aligned with the idea of Continuous Quality Improvement (CQI) of the SLOAN Consortium i.e. to help "people to set goals, identify resources and strategies, and measure progress towards the institution's ideal vision of its distinctive purpose" (Moore 2005, 3). It rests on five pillars: learning effectiveness, cost effectiveness and institutional commitment, access, faculty satisfaction and student satisfaction.

The project group has embedded instruments and procedures in order to monitor in a systematic way a series of essential components. Table 1 gives an overview. By means of practice-based research, according to Furlong and Oancea (2008, 9) "an area situated between academia-led theoretical pursuits and research-informed practice, and consisting of a multitude of models of research explicitly conducted in, with, and/or for practice", we attempt to answer three questions: 1) Who participates, under which conditions? 2) What works (or not)? And 3) Are they satisfied with their learning/teaching experiences?

The framework for continuous quality improvement of blended multicampus education includes, on the one hand, indicators to keep track of levels of access, performance, participation and drop-out of lifelong learners, as well as students' and faculty members' levels of satisfaction. On the other hand different kinds of data are collected about the course design and use of tools for blended learning by students and educators, as well as about the aspect of *co-production* (Panetsos et al., 2009). Logically multiple research techniques for data collection and analysis should be integrated into the complete scheme of quality assurance.

Criterium	Indicators	Method	Target groups
Access and Characteristics	• enrolment numbers • motivation and expectations • socio-demographics • distance/travel time to campus • job conditions • study background • technology ownership, knowledge and attitudes • learning strategies	Questionnaire Secondary data	Students Organisation
Performance and Participation	• formal evaluation/exams: participation and success rate • course evaluation/ assessment of teaching	Secondary data	Students Instructors Organisation
Study Progress and Drop-out	• study efficiency: short-term, cumulative • rate of formal drop-out (a) • rate of informal drop-out (b) • reasons for (a) and (b)	Secondary data Interview Questionnaire	Students Organisation

Course Design and Tool Use	• differentiation • media characteristics: synchronism and user friendliness • balance distance/contact	Secondary data Log data	Students Instructors Organisation
Satisfaction	• aptitude of course and/or programme	Interview Focus group Questionnaire	Students Instructors
Co-production	• coherence • power of decision • transparency	Interview Secondary data	Students Instructors Organisation

During each semester parallel studies are carried, each study following a typical plan-do-study-act work flow with a continuous feedback loop. The research findings have immediate consequences for the institutions' approaches to blended multicampus education. Based on them the project partners hope to have answers to questions such as: what kind of centrally organized support is needed in the domains of didactics, technology and administration (or other)? What arrangements related to quality assurance and shared courses and curricula can help to build a sustainable approach to blended multicampus education? Results of each academic year are passed on to those involved in organizing and managing the education programmes and other different stakeholders, including students and instructors, management, supporting and/or administrative services, including study path counseling.

4 Reflections

This paper has described MULLLTI project. During a period of two years a team of lecturers, instructional designers, researchers and education experts are exploring the opportunities and boundaries of blended multicampus education. The main idea is to find ways of teaching working students by means of the *optimal blend* in a multicampus context. Parallel with course creation, an instructional design framework and a series of quality assurance indicators have been set up. Soon the first results will be analyzed, and critical feedback generated. In this way the MULLLTI team is trying to improve blended multicampus education aimed at mature (working) students, so that they perform successfully and instructors and learners feel satisfied.

This paper is a report on work-in-progress. After one year of intensive co-operation some critical comments can be made concerning the attrition of??? burden placed on some lecturers and the time-consuming process of (re)designing courses. In spite of this, a group of lecturers have jointly created for the first time blended courses which will be taken by students on several campuses during the next semester.

References

Annetta, L.; Folta, E.; Klesath, M. (2010). V-Learning: Distance Education in the 21st Century Through 3D Virtual Learning Environments. Dordrecht: Springer.

Furlong, J.; Oancea, A. (2005). Assessing Quality in Applied and Practice-based Educational Research. A Framework for Discussion. Oxford: Oxford University, Department of Educational Studies.

Moore, C. (2005). The Sloan Consortium Quality Framework and the Five Pillars. Sloan-C.

Sugrue, B.; Clark, R. (2000). Media Selection for Training. In: Tobias, S; Fletcher, D. (eds.): Training & Retraining: A Handbook for Business, Industry, Government and the Military. New York: Macmillan, pp. 208-234.

Panetsos, S.; Zogopoulos, A.; Tigas, O.; Gubaidullina, A. (2009). Quality Development in Education. In: Lytras, M.; Ordóñez de Pablos, P.; Damiani, E.; Avison, D.; Naeve, A.; Horner, D. (eds.): Communications in Computer and Information Science. Best Practices for the Knowledge Society. Knowledge, Learning, Development and Technology for All, Part 1. Berlin: Springer, pp. 146-153.

ROLE Learning Ontology: An Approach to Structure Recommendations for Self-Regulated Learning in Personalized Learning Environments

Marcel Berthold, Ingo Dahn, Andreas Kiefel, Pablo Lachmann, Alexander Nussbaumer, Dietrich Albert

[1]Knowledge Management Institute, Graz University of Technology, Graz, Austria
{marcel.berthold,alexander.nussbaumer,dietrich.albert}@tugraz.at
[2]Knowledge Media Institute, University of Koblenz-Landau, Germany
{ingo.dahn,andreas.kiefel,pablo.lachmann}@uni-koblenz.de
[3]Department of Psychology, University of Graz, Graz, Austria
{dietrich.albert}@uni-graz.at

Abstract: In the field of technology-enhanced learning and self-regulated learning many different approaches were presented to support learners. In this paper we introduce a Learning Ontology for responsive open learning environments. The ontology builds on a connection of learning phases of a Psycho-Pedagogical Integration Model to learning strategies, techniques and activities. In addition, it is shown how these SRL entities are linked to functionalities and therefore bridge psycho-pedagogical information and learning tools (widgets). At the end of the paper two practical applications are presented, manifested in the description of the Mashup Recommender and Activity Recommender.

Keywords: ontology, recommender, self-regulated learning, personalized learning environments.

Introduction

Small applications with limited functionally, so called, apps, widgets or gadgets, have become very popular in the recent years. Especially in the context of web-based learning these widgets foster a large number of different learning scenarios. Such widgets can be integrated into already existing learning environments such as Moodle or can be compiled to a personalized learning environment (PLE) at according platforms (e.g. iGoogle, ROLE-Sandbox). The latter feature enables learners to create, adapt and personalize their own learning environment easily. However, the number of web-applications is already in the hundreds of thousands and still growing. As a result learners become overloaded by selecting widgets and creating their own learning environment (Ulrich, Shen & Gillet, 2010).

Though, there are many activities to create small applications and mashup technologies, there is still a lack of support to create pedagogically sound PLEs.

The European research project Responsive Open Learning Environments[7] (ROLE) aims to achieve progress beyond the state of the art in providing personal support of creating user-centric responsive and open learning environments. Learners should be empowered to create and use their own PLE consisting of different types of learning resources in a psycho-pedagogical sound way.

Therefore, this paper introduces a learning ontology that creates a foundation to recommend useful learning widgets and learning activities tailored to the learners' needs and competences. The ontology is based on a Psycho-Pedagogical Integration Model (Fruhmann, Nusshaumer, and Albert, 2010) and the research on literature about self-regulated learning (SRL), learning strategies, techniques and activities.

This approach extends existing approaches regarding ontologies of learning activities. For example, in (Amorim et al., 2006) a semantic scheme is presented how IMS Learning Design (IMS LD) can be expressed and in (Zhu, 2009) an approach is presented to sequence learning activities based on ontology and activity graph. In contrast to these and similar approaches, this paper focuses on self-regulated learning and involves meta-cognitive activities. In a future step an investigation can be made, how to align this approach with existing learning ontologies.

This paper is organized in the following way: In section two the pedagogical background is outlined. Section three describes the ontology and in sections four practical approaches are presented. In section five the realization of the proposed ontology and their application are discussed and future work plans proposed.

2 Pedagogical background

This section provides the psycho-pedagogical background for the ROLE Learning Ontology. The actual idea of PLEs is that learners compile their learning environment freely. The ROLE approach suggests following psycho-pedagogical

---

[7] www.role-project.eu

guidelines for learning with widget (for details see Berthold et al., 2012). These guidelines, which were produced following the framework based on the Psycho-Pedagogical Integration Model (PPIM). The PPIM comprises four phases (Fruhmann et al., 2010): (1) learner profile information is defined or revised, (2) learner finds and selects learning resources, (3) learner works on selected resources, and (4) learner reflects and reacts on learning strategies, achievements and usefulness. The PPIM follows the cyclic self-regulated learning model proposed by Zimmerman (2002) and was slightly extended and modified. In addition to these phases, a taxonomy of learning strategies, learning techniques and learning activities has been defined in order to operationalize the four phases of the PPIM.

To distinguish between learning strategies, techniques and learning activities it is important to create an ontology that provides the basis for appropriate recommendations. Relevant terms are defined as (see also: ROLE Glossary[8])

Learning strategy: It is a sequence of learning activities (concrete activities and decision activities, see below). In terms of a learning aid it can be described as a sequence of learning strategies, learning techniques, and concrete activities that are useful for task processing. An example is an elaboration strategy, which comprise learning techniques and activities that foster deeper understanding of the learning content (Friedrich & Mandl, 2006).

Schiefele and Pekrun (1993) suggest two major groups of learning strategies: cognitive and meta-cognitive strategies. This is a high level categorisation including almost all other strategies (elaboration, organisation, monitoring, reflection strategies etc.). Metacognitive strategies refer to learning and controlling the learning process itself, whereas cognitive strategies refer to learning new content or processing learning tasks.

Learning technique: It is a special case of a learning strategy consisting only of concrete activities (see below). Thus it describes a sequence of concrete activities that is assumed to be useful for the processing a task at hand. They can be compared to learning instructions that can be applied according to demand. Learning techniques are linear procedures which can be applied in predictable and controllable learning contexts where no methodical inclusion of prior knowledge for successful execution is needed. An example of a learning technique is brainstorming (Osborn, 1963). A group of learner collects usually

---

[8] https://ilias.uni-koblenz.de/ilias.php?ref_id=948&letter=L&cmd=listTerms&cmdClass=ilglossarypresentationgui&cmdNode=kd&baseClass=ilGlossaryPresentationGUI

collaboratively bullet points to a given topic and each member can contribute her ideas without being censored.

Learning activity: It describes an action that is appropriate to be performed for completing a learning task. Either it is a *concrete* activity, a learning step that helps in the learning process, or a decision activity, where learners have to think about and have to decide on how to proceed further. A learning activity is a constituent of a learning strategy or learning technique. Decision activities refer to learning strategies that can be selected in this decision activity. E.g. a cognitive organization strategy like a general strategy for creating presentations may comprise other more in-depth strategies that focus particularly on the content of the presentation.

These definitions enable us to connect the PPIM phases to learning strategies, techniques and activities. Taking the example from the definitions: An elaboration strategy is considered to deepen the understanding of the learning content and therefore refers rather to a cognitive learning strategy. The third phase of the PPIM is considered as a cognitive phase, because here the learner actual learns the content, whereas the other phases are rather seen as metacognitive phases. In this regard only learning techniques or activities considered as connected to cognitive strategies should be recommended for the third learning phase. In this sense a cognitive learning strategy contains cognitive learning techniques (brainstorming).

3 The ROLE Learning Ontology

The ROLE Learning Ontology (LO) models the concepts, described in the previous Section, in a machine readable way. In particular, it connects learning phases, learning strategies, learning activities and the functionalities needed for these activities.

The ROLE LO consists of two parts – the small concept ontology, defining the classes and properties used – and the large set of instances of these classes with their properties. It is possible to re-use the concept ontology without necessarily adopting all the instances defined for it. The following figure depicts the classes of the ROLE LO (see Figure 1).

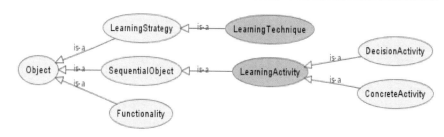

Figure 8 The classes of the ROLE Learning Ontology

The top class Object provides basic properties inherited by all other classes being subclasses of the Object class, like having a name, a description and an icon URL to associate an iconic representation of the object.

According to the definition given above, learning strategies are sequences of activities. The ontology models this by letting each *LearningStrategy* instance point to all its activities using a *strategyHasActivity* property. LearningActivity instances are defined as *SequentialObjects*, i.e. they can be ordered by a transitive relation *doesRequireBefore* indicating that one activity should be completed before another activity can start. It is worth observing that, by defining this relation, a strict order on the activities of a strategy may be enforced, but that this must not necessarily be the case. It is quite possible that there are dependencies between some of the activities of a learning strategy, but no dependencies between others. In this case, the activity instances may be sequenced in any way respecting the *doesRequireBefore* property. This provides, on one hand, the self-regulated learner with the freedom to re-arrange the activities of a strategy, while it, on the other hand, provides learning planners with enough information to issue a warning, should such a re-arrangement violate some dependencies modeled in the LO.

The class of learning activities is the union of the classes of **concrete** *activities* and of **decision** *activities*, which are mutually disjoint. The distinguishing feature between those classes of activities is, that *decision activities* may point to learning (sub)*strategies* among which the self-regulated learner may chose, while *concrete activities* don't offer this, they may only point to the *functionalities* which are needed to perform them.

The class of all *learning techniques* is defined in the ontology as being the same as the class of all *strategies* which have only *concrete activities*. Just as *concrete activities*, *learning techniques* can have assigned functionalities needed to perform them. This is to care for the case, when there are specialized tools available to implement particular techniques. For example some tools provide all functionalities to organize information for an *outlining* technique. When such tools are not available, it can be nevertheless possible to combine widgets with more restricted functionalities, e.g. word processors, for the particular activities being part of the outlining technique.

On the other, proper strategies, i.e. strategies containing decision activities cannot have functionalities assigned as the set of required functionalities will depend on the choices made by the learner during the decision activities, which cannot be predicted at design time.

By its design, the ROLE LO can support a variety of learning strategies. The PPIM strategy, mentioned above, is realized as an instance of class *LearningStrategy* with four *decision activities* corresponding to the four phases of the PPIM model. For each phase a particular *strategy* can be chosen, underpinned with *activities* for realizing particular *techniques*, for example for the time management activity needed in the planning phase of the PPIM.

The LO is connected with other ROLE components in several ways:

- Strategies provide the basic information for the ROLE Activity Recommender (AR)
- Pedagogic models, edited manually for use with the AR, can be translated into instances of the class LearningStrategy in the ontology
- The instances of the class Functionality are used by the ROLE Widget Store to describe available widgets (Nussbaumer et al., accepted).
- Through the functionality property, the ROLE Mashup Recommender can recommend mashups of widgets from the ROLE Widget store (Nussbaumer et al., accepted), which can be used to realize particular learning activities, which had been recommended by the ROLE AR
- The class of functionalities is shared with the ROLE Tool Ontology, thus providing a link between the concepts from the LO, used by pedagogic experts, and those from the Tool Ontology, used by software developers.
- Classes of the ontology point to their definitions in the ROLE Glossary, where further explanations and examples can be found.

Thus the ROLE LO serves as a hub connecting various other activities. In order to ease its use and maintenance, further efforts are required. There exists already an easy-to-use editor for the pedagogic models used by the ROLE AR. As the underlying information models are identical, it is now a straightforward task to transform those pedagogic models (in XML), into instances of the ontology's LearningStrategy class.

This ontology is formally expressed in RDF/OWL and publically available on SourceForge   (https://role-project.svn.sourceforge.net/svnroot/role-project/trunk/ model/learning_ontology/).

4 Practical Approaches

4.1 Mashup Recommender

The Mashup Recommender widget (MR; see figure 2) can be seen as a filtering system that provides more or less widgets that can be added to the PLE depending on the used template. The MR contains predefined templates e.g. a SRL template. This template could include the four phases of the PPIM and if the user selects such a phase according widgets that support this phase are presented. For example if the learner selects the planning phase calendar widgets and To-Do-Widgets could be suggested by the MR. For this purpose the MR calls SRL entities from the ontology. In this case the ontology service is questioned for the respective functionalities of the SRL entities (learning strategies, techniques and activities) and the widget store returns the associated widgets. Such templates can be created using a special authoring tool (Nussbaumer et al., accepted).

The MR can be used to provide guidance on different levels and for different stakeholders. A high level of guidance is the preparation of complete predefined PLEs based on a specific template by a teacher or tutor. Later the tutor can share this PLE with her students who can use it or modify it. A lower level of guidance can be provided if the teacher just shares the template with the students, so that they have to create their own PLE. For example, a teacher could select the SRL entities goal setting, resource searching, note taking, and reflecting for a template. Teachers or learners using this template could easily search these SRL entities for widgets and include them in a PLE. In this way the PLE consists of widgets for each SRL entity. Learning strategies are on a higher abstraction level, which results in a greater number of widgets that can be recommended. Learning techniques are on a lower abstraction level, which leads to a smaller number of related widgets that can be recommended. While in the first case the learner gets more widgets recommended and thus less guidance, in the second case the level of guidance is higher because of the smaller number of recommended widgets. For a detailed description of the MR and its technical background see Nussbaumer et al. (2012).

4.2 Activity Recommender

In following the Activity Recommender (AR) created for fostering self-regulated learning in personal learning environments will be introduced.

The AR (see Figure2) is a portable web-enabled application that follows the learning activity recommendation approach. It guides the learner through the learning process by providing the declarative, procedural and conditional knowledge about learning strategies and techniques for a particular task through displaying respective learning steps or activities related to the PPIM phases and additional information helping to carry out the learning activities. AR provides guidance for learners with different competence levels. Learners with higher SRL competency are able to skip recommendations in case the recommended information is already known or too detailed for them. Otherwise, the learner is guided with a step-by-step approach helping to cope with a problem. Unlike direct instructions the learners have a free choice on recommended learning activities they want to perform.

Once learner has decided to use a recommended learning strategy, the AR widget sends respective learning activities to the e.g. "To-Learn list" widget (see Figure2) that enables learners to compile an individual learning plan by accepting received recommended activities or by adding own learning activities, e.g. remind to take a break after a long learning session.

To select appropriate learning tools to support performing learning activities, the AR is able to send out messages with information about certain activity. These messages can be received and interpreted by other widgets, e.g. MR (see Figure 2 or see section 4.1) which subsequently offers matching tools.

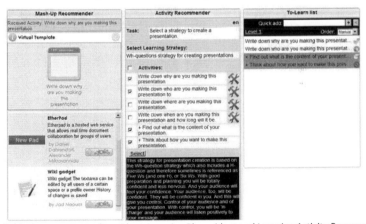

Figure 2. Mashup recommender widget, Learning Plan widget and Learning Activity Recommender widget running in the ROLE environment.

In contrast to collaborative and content-based filtering approaches handling with large community-generated data-sets, the Arwidget is working with data predefined and structured according to the PPIM model by the educational experts. The experts prepare the recommendations by defining pedagogical models, which contain learning strategies, techniques and matching activities for learning tasks, using an authoring tool. The underlying information model is identical to that of the ROLE LO. The prepared data is finally stored in a XML file that serves as the basis for generating pedagogical recommendations by the AR.

5 Outlook and future work

This paper presented the proposed ontology which is based on a Psycho-Pedagogical Integration Model (PPIM) and the connection of the phases of this PPIM to learning strategies, learning techniques and learning activities. The link of learning techniques and learning activities to functionalities bridges psycho-pedagogical information and widgets. This allows recommender tools to support the learner through their self-regulated learning process by offing guidance on different levels.

Further work will focus on aligning the ontology with existing approaches used in elearning standards. An investigation will be made if those data schemes are suitable to express the learning activities and their relations as presented in this paper.

Acknowledgements: The work reported has been partially supported by the ROLE project, as part of the Seventh Framework Programme of the European Commission, grant agreement no. 231396.

References

Amorim, R. R., Lama, M., Sánchez, E., Riera, A., & Vila, X. A. (2006). A Learning Design Ontology based on the IMS Specification. Educational Technology & Society, 9(1), 38-57.

Berthold, M., Lachmann, P., Nussbaumer, A., Pachtchenko, S., Kiefel, A., & Albert, D. (2012). Identifying Requirements for a Psycho-Pedagogical Mash-up Design for Personalising the Learning Environment. Advances in User Modeling perspectives - selected papers from UMAP 2011 workshops, LNCS, Heidelberg: Springer, pp.161-175.

Friedrich, H.F. and Mandl, H. (2006). Lernstrategien: zur Strukturierung des Forschungsfeldes. In: H.F. Friedrich & H. Mandl (ed.), Handbuch Lernstrategien. Hogrefe: Göttingen, pp. 1-23.

Nussbaumer, A., Berthold, M., Dahrendorf, D., Schmitz, H-C., Kravcik, M. & Albert, D. (2012). A Mashup Recommender for Creating Personal Learning

Environments. 11th International Conference on Web-based Learning 2012 (ICWL 2012), 02.-04.09.2012, Sinaia, Romania.

Nussbaumer, A., Scheffel, M., Niemann, K., Kravcik, M. & Albert, D. (accepted). Detecting and Reflecting Learning Activities in Personal Learning Environments. Workshop Paper (to be presented) at ARTEL Workshop at European Conference on Technology-Enhanced Learning 2012 (EC-TEL2012), 18.09.2012, Saarbrücken, Germany.

Osburn, A.F. (1963). Applied imagination. New York: Scribner.

Schiefele, U., & Pekrun, R. (1993). Psychologische Modelle des fremdgesteuerten und selbstgesteuerten Lernens. In E. F. Weinert (Ed.), *Enzyklopädie der Psychologie* . Göttingen: Hogrefe, pp. 249-279.

Zhu, F., Yao, N (2009). Ontology-Based Learning Activity Sequencing in Personalized Education System. In: Proceedings of the Internatinal Conference on Information Technology and Computer Science (ITCS 2009), pp.285-288, 25-26 July 2009.. Doi: 10.1109/ITCS.2009.64

Zimmerman, B. (2002). Becoming a Self-Regulated Learner: An Overview. *Theory Into Practice* 41, pp. 64-70.

How LLP Projects use Internet and Social Media for Communication Purposes: A Desktop Research

Ju-Youn Song, Katerina Zourou

University of Luxembourg, Campus Walferdange, LCMI/ DICA, Route de Diekirch, L-7201
Luxembourg
jun.song@uni.lu
Web2learn, Kritis 10, 54625 Thessaloniki, Greece
katerinazourou@gmail.com

Abstract: The effective use of Internet social media tools, and their embeddedness in the communication strategies are becoming fundamental to the success of the Lifelong Learning Programme (LLP) projects in this digital era. This desktop research is aimed at identifying how projects integrate social media to valorise project dissemination and communication activities and what kinds of social media applications are actually used in LLP projects. This research, based on the first analysis emerging from the selection of 150 LLP projects, has provided a first step towards establishment of a state-of-the art regarding practices developed in LLP projects and associated needs for further development of skills and competences.

Keywords: LLP project management, social media, social web, training in emerging technologies, LLP projects

Rationale

The Web2LLP project ("Improving Internet strategies and maximizing the social media presence of Lifelong Learning Programme (LLP) projects", http://www.web2llp.eu/) is a two-year project running from January 2012 to December 2013. The partnership consists of six project members: University of Luxembourg, Web2Learn, ATiT, Coventry University Entreprises, Pixel and PAU Education. The original idea for the project stemmed from the need that we felt, as project managers and members involved in LLP projects for several years, for skills and competences that were missing - in both technical and communication terms - regarding the effective use of Internet social media tools, and their embeddedness in the communication strategies that are fundamental to the success of an LLP project.

We realized, through informal exchanges with colleagues at EACEA Info days and other project meetings, that although the social web is a reality that cannot be disregarded, its communication potential for LLP projects has not so far been exploited, due to a) a lack of information and appropriation opportunities regarding ways of effectively using these tools as part of a communication strategy, and b) lack of visibility of good practice regarding what is reasonable and achievable in an LLP context. Moreover, although communication is a fundamental piece of every LLP project proposal (one of the required work packages and also a feature under which the project is evaluated both in the intermediary and final reports), there are no guidelines on how to set up a coherent Internet strategy featuring social media tools appropriate to the project. Our project was designed to respond to these needs and it has been selected for funding in 2012 in the highly selective (7% success rate) KA4 action.

1 Selecting the sample of 150 LLP projects

The desktop research is a core element of the needs analysis that is completed by:

a) An online questionnaire[9] addressed to LLP project teams, aimed at gathering information about the types of skills really needed for the communication and dissemination activities of their project. At the time of preparation of this article, 100 responses to the survey have been received and the data analysis is expected for September 2012.

b) Interviews with selected LLP project managers highlighting project good practices, to be featured in a video showcase on our website, available in December 2012.

The desktop survey, based on the grid available online[10], initially looked at how LLP projects integrate social media to valorise project dissemination and communication activities and what kind of social media applications are actually used in LLP projects.

For the desktop analysis we consulted EACEA project compendia and the ADAM database[11]. All sub-programmes were chosen except the Jean Monnet one, due to the lack of at least one digital communication platform such as a

---

[9] Form available at http://goo.gl/Va5lh

[10] http://goo.gl/PIHwS

[11] http://eacea.ec.europa.eu/llp/results_projects/project_compendia_en.php and http://www.adam-europe.eu/adam/homepageView.htm

website. Out of 289 LLP projects selected for funding in 2010, our desktop research focused on a sample of 150. The methodology adopted (table 1) was designed to cover equally:

- all LLP sub-programmes (or Actions) and
- all project types, i.e. multilateral projects (MP) and networks (NW).

We sampled across LLP sub-actions with the aim of providing a comprehensive overview of the current status of social media in use, regardless of the different objectives of each sub-programme.

The 150 projects were selected at random from the 2010 funded projects only. The reason for focusing on 2010 beneficiaries was the ability to survey complete or almost complete projects whose Internet and social media tools were set up and project activities were in full swing at the time of the research (Spring 2012). The sample, by LLP sub-programme and type of project, is shown below.

Table 1. Overview of the 150 projects selection

(*MP = Multilateral project, NW = network ** KA1 SCR = Studies & Comparative Research).

LLP action	MP funded	MPs*: Web2LLP selection	NW funded (**KA1 for SCR)	NW*: Web2LLP selection	Total by action	Web2LLP selection by action
Comenius	33	17	7	4	40	21
Erasmus	50	26	8	4	59	30
Grundtvig	50	26	3	2	53	28
Leonardo da Vinci	38	20	5	3	44	23
KA1 Policy cooperation and innovation in Lifelong Learning	28	14	6	3	34	17
KA2 Languages	24	12	1	1	25	13
KA3 Information and communication technologies (ICT)	24	12	2	1	20	13
KA4 Dissemination and Exploitation of Results	10	5	0	0	10	5
Total of 2010 selection	257	132	32	18	289	150

The overview of the 150 LLP projects by sub-programme is shown below.

LLP projects selection

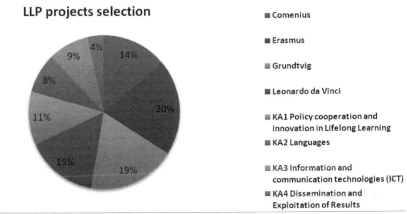

- Comenius
- Erasmus
- Grundtvig
- Leonardo da Vinci
- KA1 Policy cooperation and innovation in Lifelong Learning
- KA2 Languages
- KA3 Information and communication technologies (ICT)
- KA4 Dissemination and Exploitation of Results

Figure 9. Overview of the selected 150 LLP projects by action

2 Types of social media application

In general terms, we conceived social media categories as widely, easily and actually used, in the sense of user driven social applications. Therefore, the typology included categories that, on the one hand, were present in LLP projects so far and, on the other hand, were apt to be taken up by the target group, thus comprising a hypothetical element for data analysis. In this sense, we considered three features of user driven social applications that are applicable to our context:

- Applicability (actually): Could the application actually be used for disseminating or valorising LLP projects?
- Functionality (widely): Does/Did it work? Any good example from LLP projects?
- Usability (easily): Is/Was it easy to use? Do we need specific skills to use it?

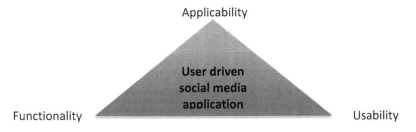

Figure 10. Three pillars of user-driven social media applications, inspired by Schreefel (2012)[12] and adapted by Song to LLP projects

The next step was the categorization of tools relevant to LLP projects. Among typologies of social media tools, the one elaborated by Conole & Alevizou (2010)[13] best fits this particular context and has been used as the basis for building our typology:

1. social networking sites; (i.e. Facebook, LinkedIn, Ning)
2. blogs
3. microblogging tools; (i.e. Twitter)
4. presentation repositories (i.e. Slideshare)
5. video sharing tools; (i.e. YouTube, Vimeo)
6. social bookmarking applications; (i.e. Diigo, del.ici.ous)
7. web 2.0 picture repositories (i.e. Picasa, Flickr)
8. RSS feed (allowing users to receive messages on their RSS aggregator, i.e. Google reader)

We added one more application that we considered useful to LLP projects:

9. shared web 2.0 public libraries (i.e. ObjectSpot, Mendeley).

Finally, we added two more features enhancing social media presence that we considered useful in our context:

10. easy sharing and bookmarking services (e.g. the "Add this" button) allowing users to share a static page through web 2.0 tools and
11. a feed embedded in the website enabling content flow from social media applications (i.e. from Twitter, Flickr, Picasa).

3 Data analysis

The data analysis comprises data on each of the types of Internet and social media tools presented above.

---

[12] Schreefel. E. (2012), "101 Web 2.0 Tools for Teachers You Should Know About" Blog post published on March 6, 2012 http://www.goedonline.com/101-web-tools-for-teachers#.T2Sn8H7kTBQ.twitter

[13] Conole, G. & Alevizou, P. (2010). A literature review of the use of Web 2.0 tools in Higher Education. Report commissioned by the Higher Education Academy. http://www.heacademy.ac.uk/assets/EvidenceNet/Conole_Alevizou_2010.pdf

3.1 The project website

139 out of 150 projects, around 93% of the sample, had a project website. 7% of the sample did not have an Internet presence at all, raising some doubts about project communication practices.

3.2 Social media applications

3.2.1 Social networking sites (SNS) and microblogging tools

47 projects (31% of the sample) have an SNS, which is clearly the most widely used social media application in the 150 LLP project desktop analysis.

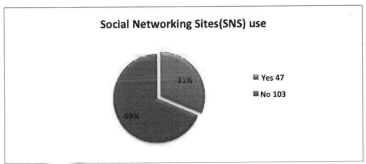

Figure 11. SNS use

Moreover, 6 out of the 47 LLP projects (11% of projects with a single SNS, and 4% of the entire sample) used more than one social networking site. The most popular SNS is Facebook (43 projects), followed by LinkedIn (8 projects) and Ning (2 projects).

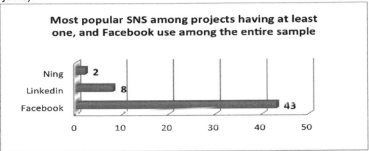

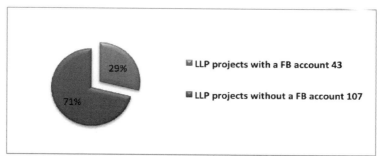

Figure 12. Most popular SNS among projects having at least one (among 47 projects that use one or more SNS), and Facebook use among the entire sample

Regarding microblogging tools, Twitter, the most popular in our sample, scores 15%, making Twitter one of the most widely used applications after Facebook (43 projects, 29%), making Twitter a popular tool for dissemination of project related resources as well as general communication.

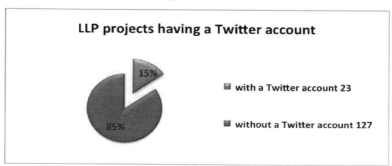

Figure 13. LLP projects having a Twitter account

Although less popular, 7% of LLP projects keep a blog. Out of the 11 blogs identified, we narrowed down our analysis to determine whether these blogs had been used as the main digital platform of the project instead of a (mainstream) website, due to the fact that in our sample (see 3.1) there was no website for some projects. The hypothesis was not confirmed- blogs coexist with the projects' websites and projects not having a website do not have a blog either.

3.2.2 Media sharing tools and syndication

When it comes to media sharing, the LLP projects analyzed opt for YouTube and Vimeo for video sharing, Flickr and Picasa for image sharing. The proportion of media sharing tools embedded in a website is only 8%. The purpose of using media sharing applications is to share project resources, such as video tutorials, expert interviews and project events, and (video or image) materials created in a workshop, making them publicly available.

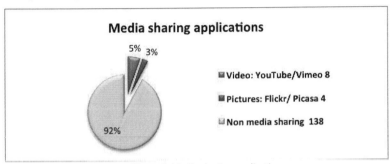

Figure 6. Media sharing applications

Only 18 out of 150 projects (12%) offer an RSS service allowing users to receive content updates without visiting the project website each time.

3.2.3 Social bookmarking applications, shared web 2.0 public library and presentation repositories

Only one project uses a social bookmarking application (0.6%), while none of the 150 projects uses Presentation repositories (0%) or a web 2.0 public library (0%).

3.2.4 Widgets enabling rapid sharing of content through social networks

Widgets enabling rapid sharing of content through social networks, via the AddThis button or similar devices were used by 24 projects, almost 16% of our sample. A feed, embedded in the website from a social media application such as Twitter, Flickr or Picasa, is used by 8 projects, around 5%.

4 Investigating actual training needs of LLP project teams

This desktop research is only a first step towards establishment of a state-of-the art regarding practices developed in LLP projects and associated needs for further development of skills and competences. It is completed by a survey that we have sent to LLP project members regarding a) tools they find appropriate for communication and valorization of their project activities and b) their specific training needs. The survey, made available online14, attracted 100 responses between May and July 2012, and the feedback gathered will be instrumental in the development of training materials we plan for early 2013.

Some preliminary findings (answers to the online form) include:

- Diversified training needs, ranging from the novice user (requests for training on setting up a Twitter account or a Facebook page) to the experienced user ("I'd be more interested in learn more about the technologies underlying future social media implementation (for instance html5 and css3").

- The need to focus on the appropriateness of tools in a given LLP project, beyond their mere use, thus moving from a technology-centred approach to a socio-technical approach based on clearly identified needs ("Managing the mix, [I need to have a] strategic approach to that"// "Harmonisation and optimisation of the combination of all of the above mentioned elements, tailored to the individual project (every project is different, therefore e.g. a video or reference repository might not be necessary in one, but essential in another").

- Opportunities for engagement with the public: ("I would be very interested in how to thoroughly involve and animate an online community (I find REAL and FUNCTIONAL online discussions impossible to initiate/maintain").

- Viability of Internet and social media presence after the project life circle ("I would like to address sustainability issues of the use of social networking within LLP projects: how are the social networks maintained during and especially after the project?")

5   A final comment regarding innovation and quality

Given that the conference theme is innovation and quality, the results of our desktop research leave little room for doubt on the interest for LLP project teams of tooling up their project communication practices with a website containing social networking applications and enablers (easy sharing buttons and feeds, categories 10 & 11). This element can be regarded as innovative compared to more traditional communication tools. Nevertheless, quantitative data show that practices are still in their infancy, as is demonstrated by the low percentage of

---

14 http://goo.gl/WWQ1Y

SNS that are emblematic of web 2.0 supported interaction with target groups (i.e. Facebook, Twitter and LinkedIn) and by the extremely low level of media sharing applications used.

The overall limited exploitation of social media applications also highlights the apparent discrepancy between the communication means of LLP projects and the web 2.0 communication tools that can be considered nowadays as mainstream interaction means. This indicates a possible mismatch between communication tools set up by projects and the general context of interaction with digital technologies. We are far from the possibility of detecting innovative practice in this area. This preliminary finding is likely to be exemplified by the series of interviews with project managers due to be completed in December 2012, and by the full analysis of the project managers' needs analysis survey, see section 4.

This desktop research is far from being exhaustive, and results cannot be generalized. It also has several limitations, including for example the randomly selected sample, the choice of only one year of EACEA funded projects, and the lack of any investigation of stances and mindsets regarding the digital communication choices of the randomly selected projects.

Innovation and quality in LLP projects do not happen in a top-down approach, independent of target groups' activities, motives and intentions. On the contrary, they stem from interaction with the target groups. Social media are a requisite for engagement with these groups in a mutually beneficial manner. However, the objectives and choices of tools, and the careful planning of human and technical resources, are dimensions that must be carefully designed, as dimensions of the training framework and digital materials that we are developing in this direction.

Acknowledgements

We would like to thank all the Web2LLP team members for their engagement in the project: Charles Max (University of Luxembourg), Nikki Cortoos, Silvia Miola, Alberto Nantiat and Sally Reynolds (ATiT), Alexandros Kalamantis and Maria Perifanou (Web2learn), Eleni Anoyrkati and Sunil Maher (Coventry University Entreprises), Elisabetta delle Donne and Federico Fragasso (Pixel Firenze), Agnès Aguilo, Montse Delgado, Valentina Olariu and Sabine Schumann (PAU Education).

Special thanks to Nikki Cortoos for feedback on an earlier version of our desktop research grid.

iPads as Mobile Laboratories in Science Teaching e-Learning Scenarios using iPads and Sensors

Manfred Lohr

BG/BRG Schwechat, IT Coordinator, www.bgschwechat.ac.at
Ehrenbrunngasse 6, 2320 Schwechat, Austria
manfred.lohr@gmail.com

Abstract: This work describes the didactic concept and the implementation of e-learning sequences in teaching physics using the iPad. The intention of this project was to investigate the capabilities of iPads in science teaching with a focus in the use of measuring sensors connected to iPads. The project was carried out at the BG / BRG Schwechat with 4th and 5th grade classes (pupils aged 14 to 16) in the subjects physics and physics' lab in the school year 2011/12. Teachers used 30 iPads, which are available to all students designated as a mobile e-learning unit for learning sequences in class. The motivation for using the iPad was the very good quality of scientific content provided in the so-called apps, which are available on the iPad and the opportunities that arise through the use of internal and external sensors for making measurements on the iPad. Analysing surveys of the involved pupils carried out on the learning platform moodle and assessments of teachers and stakeholders showed that the goal of increasing interest in this type of e-learning in science classes has been achieved.

Keywords: e-learning; science education; mobile learning; secondary school; case study; emerging technologies; mobile leearning.

1 Introduction

"We need to nurture a generation of creative learners capable of dealing with the immense challenges of this century" according to David Puttnam, Futurelab Chairman.

The project's aim was to develop an innovative learning environment for teaching physics, which enables mobile learning both in class and in other environments.

E-learning sequences were designed by teachers based on the concepts of inquire based teaching, project based teaching, as blended learning sequences or teaching focussed in competences. The learning material was provided on the content management system moodle and implemented by the use of 30 school-owned iPads.

The impact of the iPad on e-learning can be felt in a number of ways. The size and slenderness of the iPad makes it easy to interact with, the touchscreen offers intuitive interactivity with no need for peripherals like a mouse or keyboard and therefore saves space on a desk of pupils during the use of blended learning sequences.

One of the remarkable advantages of the work with iPads is the in haptic cognition – students act by "touch and try" – which offers another dimension of learning. Touching and moving of objects and direct interaction with the content enable special learning experiences. There is no need of distracting explanations regarding the operating system, which stays using an iPad in the background, in the center is learning content. iPads offer a mobile learning environment to physics education where students access to a wealth of information and data. The content which is part of Apps can then be interpreted independently or in groups.

A key feature of this project is the usage of iPads as measuring instruments, iPads are able to hear, see know where they are and how they are moved. The data that are recorded by various built-in sensors or sensors connected to the iPad by Bluetooth, data acquisition and read out is made in real time.

In this paper I present learning scenarios that have been implemented at BG /BRG Schwechat, a school in higher secondary education with about 1000 pupils aged from 10 to 18 taught by about 100 teachers. Since 2006 the BG / BRG Schwechat has been working in the so-called eLSA (e-learning im Schulalltag) network of Austrian schools. eLSA and e-learning have been a driving force for continuous school development at BG / BRG Schwechat.

In the academic year 2009/10 the school was awarded by the Federal Ministry for Education, Arts and Culture as one of 11 eLSA advanced schools in Austria for innovative teaching concepts in the field of e-learning. In this context, pedagogical approaches have been developed to promote learning with mobile devices. As part of this concept blended learning sequences were implemented in some subjects with the help of 30 school-owned iPads.

This paper is organized as follows: in Section 2 the educational concept of using the iPad in physics lessons is described, chapter 3 deals with the learning activities in the context of physics teaching in 4th and 5th classes with the help of iPads. In Chapter 4, I present opinions of students, teachers and stakeholders, which were collected as a part of an evaluation of the project, Chapter 5 offers a short comparison of iPads in education in Austrian schools and Chapter 6 gives a short conclusion.

Fig. 1. Group work with iPads

2   The Pedagogical Approach of the Use of iPads

One of the goals of a modern physics class is to promote young people's interest in science and technology, not least in order to achieve a numerically higher rate of people interested in scientific studies. By the classical experimental designs in the physics lab, where students ultimately only see moving pointers in analogue measuring instruments, this goal cannot be reached in the age of digital media.

The use of modern tablet PC not only for visualising physical relations but also as a measuring device motivates students to a large extent, to deal with scientific issues. The availability of scientific content on mobile devices such as iPod, iPhone, etc. which are also used by students privately, increases this effect and motivates students to occupy themselves with scientific topics outside the school environment.

The application of iPads in the framework of the described project is concentrated in four points:

1. Use of applications (so called Apps) that serve the visualization and exploration of scientific contexts.
2. Use of the iPad's built in sensors (acceleration sensors, GPS sensor, magnetic field sensor and sound sensor) in order to carry out and record measurements.

3. Use of external sensors connected to the iPad via Bluetooth in order to measure and record data, for instance air pressure, temperature, humidity, infrared and UV radiation.
4. Working with "augmented reality" apps which enable e.g. capturing a ball's speed in a video or determining celestial objects depending on the location and the angle of view.

These tools are used in the framework of various pedagogical concepts: The use of the content offered by Apps enables teachers to design learning scenarios which offer students to explore scientific processes following the concept of inquiry based learning.

Project based learning sequences supports the students' communicative learning. The use of iPads greatly encourages partner and group work. When working with iPads students are much more willing to participate In communicative learning activities than they are in the computer room where students often disappear behind their computer screens reluctant communication with classmates.

Teaching focused in competences enables students to organise their knowledge, to gain experiences and to draw conclusions. The iPads' built in and external sensors transform a normal classroom to an experimental laboratory for all students. The learners are able to collect their own data and interpret their experiments.

3   Learning Activities

The content management system moodle plays a key role in the implementation of learning scenarios. Moodle (modular object oriented dynamic learning environment) is a free learning platform, which offers some very helpful tools for educational purposes, e.g. assignment submission, discussion forums, a grading system and customizable online quizzes and wikis.

In the framework of the given project the working instructions which students are asked to follow are prepared by the teacher on the learning platform. In moodle courses students have the ability to upload their proposed solutions by the use of the assignment tool, teachers use the feedback feature to give hints for improvements of suggested solutions. A final assessment of the work of the pupils can be conducted in moodle by test questions. All these activities can be performed directly on the iPad, there is no need to consult a computer room.

At the beginning of each session students and teachers have to log into the moodle learning platform, which can be achieved with the help of the mTouch iPad application that allows access to all features of the learning platform. The students will be provided by their teachers not only with work instructions, but there are also educational activities such as forum, wiki, polls, and multiple choice tests available on the learning platform. By checking and evaluating each of the students' accomplished activities, they receive feedback on their submitted work.

As part of this project, tasks on subjects such as meteorology, astronomy and mechanics have been worked out interactively on the iPad using scientific applications. The possibility to explore interactively the boundary between day and night on Earth and other planets facilitated students the understanding of the physical laws.

By using the applet "Living earth" they found out the reasons for the sequence of the four seasons and by virtually flying through the solar system with the help of the "solar system" applet they considered if there are seasons on other planets. During their investigations they found out about some facts that surprised them (e.g. that there are regions on the earth, where the sun never

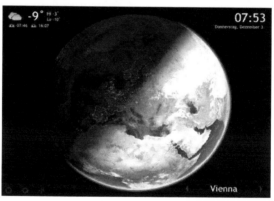

Fig. 2. Exploring the length of day and night

rises in December).

After solving and interpreting the tasks using applications, the next step was to start their own measurements with the help of sensors. Those measurements are based either on data from the sensors integrated in the iPad or on recorded data from external sensors that are coupled to the iPad with Bluetooth.

In the school building the students explored the relationship between air pressure and altitude, compared the infrared radiation emitted by various objects and analysed the sound pressure and frequency of different sounds. In order to encourage the development of social skills, again the work was done in groups. The students reported on the results of their measurements in a discussion forum in moodle.

Fig. 3. iPad connected with an air-pressure sensor

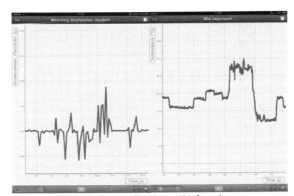

Fig. 4. Data from the acceleration and infrared sensor

Astronomical applications that access the built-in GPS and magnetic sensors of the iPad enable a very impressive exploration of the sky. Celestial objects are displayed depending on time of the day, location and the direction of view, so that the orientation in the sky is much easier. The variation of date and location allows an analysis of celestial events of the past or future. As additional tool the iPad offers the possibility to control the movement of a telescope – you have only to choose an astronomical object on the iPad and the GoTo command moves the telescope to the selected object.

When teaching mechanics the camera integrated in the iPad allows the recording

Fig. 5. Analysis of movements by videotaping

and analysis of motion. This improves the pupils' understanding of the

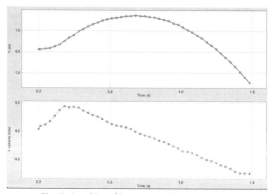

Fig. 6. Graphics of location and speed vs time

relationships between time, velocity and acceleration in different types of motion. Students record the moving object by video and track the object frame by frame. The App captures location and speed and analyses the object's acceleration. Students are able to conduct their own experiments and the related graphs will be created interactively on the iPad.

4 Evaluation and Assessment

An evaluation of the project "iPads in physics education" was carried out at three levels:

First, with the help of the participating students, secondly, teachers of the BG / BRG Schwechat and eLSA advanced partner schools from all over Austria were given the opportunity to express their views on e-learning with iPads in the course of a workshop, and third, as part of the EduDays2012 at the Danube University in Krems the audience of the lecture "iPads in physics instruction" gave their feedback.

Students were able to give their feedback on the project anonymously by using the moodle feedback tool.

The feedback questions focused on the ease of use of the iPad, on the learning outcomes with iPads and on the additional interest that evokes this kind of learning for science topics.

85% of those questioned said that the iPads, its applications and the sensors connected with Bluetooth were easy to use. Another important result of the survey was that working in teams would cause no problems and each task would be fulfilled in cooperation with the group members. 68% of students questioned felt that by learning with iPads greatly improved their understanding in scientific concepts. For all students, it was very motivating to work with iPads in educational context.

As part of the workshop "eLearning with iPads" teachers of different subjects at the BG / BRG Schwechat had the opportunity to get in touch with the didactic approaches to learning with iPad in order to develop their own ideas for their lessons. At the beginning of the workshop teachers got an introduction to the usage of iPads and how to design learning sequences with these devices. Teachers already acquainted with the use of a touch screen smartphone were quickly able to access all the features of the iPad and they needed no more briefing by the trainer after some minutes. The design of learning sequences integrating the learning platform moodle however required more detailed instructions, especially in the field of moodle feedback and assessment tools.

Every teacher participating in the seminar saw great potential in the use of iPads in the classroom and developed ideas for learning scenarios in their subjects. The mobility of the devices for blended learning sequences for which we do not want to go with the class in the computer room was highlighted.

Some teachers criticized that it is impossible to load data to the iPad via USB, others pointed out the lack of compatibility with Flash and Java files.

As an important addition to e-learning with tablet PCs, many teachers would welcome interactive textbooks available on the iPad.

The audience at the Danube University Krems had already gained some experience with iPads in the classroom. New to them, however, was the concept of science teaching with iPads, as described above. The use of external sensors and related applications received very positive feedback, as well as augmented reality simulations in mechanics and astronomy.

The author of this work was invited to "Apple's Leadership Series," in the course of the "British Educational Training and Technology Show" which was held in London in early January 2012. In exchange with other schools that use the iPad in the classroom too, there were valuable experiences gained.

5 References

In Austria, the iPad is used for teaching purposes both in primary and middle schools as well as in high schools.

At the moment there is the elementary school Breitenlee VS 22 in Vienna, the middle school Jennersdorf in Burgenland, the Business Academy in Eisenstadt in Burgenland and the BG / BRG Schwechat in Lower Austria, where the author of this paper is employed. Fundamental differences can be seen in the organizational structure of the iPad usage in the schools mentioned before and the BG/BRG Schwechat. The Schools in the Burgenland and Vienna focus on a one-to-one usage, which means that in an "iPad class" each student uses his personal iPad. At the BG / BRG Schwechat there are 30 iPads available to all students and teachers of all subjects designated as a mobile e-learning unit for learning sequences in class.

The use of the iPad at the elementary school VS 22 is subject of a research project with the following two objectives: the promotion of creativity and an improvement of the communication between students, parents and teachers with a class blog as a communication hub, which is accessible via internet.

At the HS Jennersdorf all students of one class (21 students) were equipped with an iPadin the course of the project "iPad in education". Over a period of 4 years, the educational opportunities and the potential of tablet computers are being tested in all subjects of secondary education in the classroom and will be evaluated afterwards.

At the HAK Eisenstadt a project similar to the one at the HS Jennersdorf is running where they examine the use of tablets in a school with a focus on economy.

The aim of these iPad- classes is to investigate e-learning content on their pedagogical and didactic value and set content standards. As part of the one-year project that is supported, scientifically monitored and evaluated by the College of Education Burgenland, the optimal conditions for the use of electronic learning content on various electronic devices - from laptops to tablet PCs – will be explored.

Some of the schools within the Austrian eLSA network are currently in preparation of plans for the use of tablets in the classroom. Through the cooperation of these schools, the opportunity of comparing the advantages and disadvantages of the different tablet providers will arise. There will be a focus on both the differences in hardware and on the quality of the software.

http://www.hs-jennersdorf.at/gelebte-schulpraxis/ipad-klasse/
http://members.aon.at/bzuliani/Der_Einsatz_des_iPads_in_der_Volksschule_-
_Forschung/home.html
http://elsa20.schule.at/topmenu/english-site/

6 Conclusion – Perspective

The use of iPads enriches in my opinion the opportunities of e-learning. Based on the feedback of students and teachers collected in the framework of the described project, it is legit to say that the iPad is a valuable tool for education. The use of iPads combined with e-learning scenarios enables learning activities that cannot be done on a PC in a computer lab. As one result of the use of iPads in science classes teachers perceived a significant increase in students' motivation to engage in scientific issues.

A future intention of the author is to implement mobile learning with the use of iPads in the framework of the Open Discovery Space project. Open Discovery Space (ODS) is funded by the European Commission and is the result of collaboration between 51 organisations from 23 countries. The aim is to create a socially-powered, multilingual open learning infrastructure to boost the adaptation of e–learning resources in Europe.

The wide range of already existing content for mobile learning in repositories like mobile COSMOS (http://portal.discoverthecosmos.eu/node/14461) and mobile   CERN (http://portal.discoverthecosmos.eu/2010_04_moCern_website/index_en.html) gives great opportunities to develop further "visionary" aspects of e–learning.

Improving Pronunciation of Secondary School Teachers through Computer Assisted Learning: An Experience

M. Naeem Mohsin

Associate Professor, G.C University Faisalabad, Pakistan
mnmohsin71@gmail.com

Abstract: This paper concerned with an experience of using computer assisted learning for improving pronunciation of secondary school teachers with a focus on English language and linguistics oriented training. The 50 subjects were given one month training. Before conducting training, a group discussion was managed, and a Pretest of pronunciation (individual sounds, word stress and intonation) was administered. The pretest results showed that subjects were unable to pronounce individual sounds, stress words correctly, and intonate properly, but after training through computer assisted learning the results of the post test showed significant improvement in pronunciation of teachers' individual sounds; long and short vowel sounds, diphthongs, word stress and intonation in connected speech.

Key Words: Learning, training, pronunciation, teachers

1 Introduction

English language learners face many problems due to different reasons, while learning English from primary to tertiary levels and pronunciation problem is one the biggest which remains with the students throughout their academic career and haunts them when they are in practical life. But if this is the constant problem of teachers Although teacher try their utmost to teach English pronunciation through printed pronunciation material which is either available in the course outlines or self-made by the teacher educator. But there are less teacher educators available whose own pronunciation is above board and the perspective teachers are surely left on the mercy of circumstances.

Pakistan, despite being a third world country, is the biggest user of Internet and Universities have tried to equip their campuses with Internet facilities by establishing Internet Labs, Smart rooms etc., which provide sufficient opportunities to teacher as well as perspective teachers to use computer aided/assisted programmes for multifarious purposes. This study is one the endeavours conducted on secondary school teachers, who were to undertake four weeks training. They were given training, by keeping in view the below stated study question, through CALL for improving English pronunciation and were exposed to pre and post test before going to classroom. Different Internet sources, CDs, DVDs, etc., were utilized to provide sufficient drills and practice for improving pronunciation to the subjects after the pre-test.

During the recent times there has been a growing demand to use technology for educational purposes as well as to learn English with special focus on pronunciation. Various types of computer hardware have been introduced and a survey of the literature shows an emerging interest among language teachers and researchers in the benefits of computer-assisted pronunciation instruction (Albertson 1982, Molholt 1988, Molholt, Lane, Tanner, & Fischer 1988, Pennington 1988, Chun 1989, Perdreau and Hessney 1990, Johnson and Rekart 1991).

On the other hand many educators are hesitant to embrace a technology that still seeks acceptance by the language teaching community as a whole (Kenning & Kenning, 1990). But in this context many reasons have been assigned to this reluctance by keeping in view the restricted availability of computer assisted instructions. Among them are the lack of a unified theoretical framework for designing and evaluating CALL systems (Chapelle, 1997; Hubbard, 1988; Ng & Olivier, 1987).

Experimental studies conducted in last years have focused on the effects of various types of pronunciation instruction on learners' overall levels of intelligibility and comprehensibility. Intelligibility is "the extent to which a listener actually understands an utterance" (Derwing & Munro, 2005, p. 385) and is often evaluated through transcription or listening comprehension tasks performed by a listener. Comprehensibility is "a listener's perception of how difficult it is to understand an utterance" (Derwing & Munro, 2005, p. 385).

Developments in technology have allowed automatic speech processing to be incorporated into pronunciation teaching (Hua, 2006). A number of researchers (e.g. Molholt, 1988; 1990; Harless, Zier & Duncan, 1999; Eskenazi, 1999a, 1999b; Neri, Strik & Boves 2002; Butler-Pascoe & Wiburg, 2003; Kim, 2006) have investigated the advantages of computer assisted pronunciation training (CAPT) software for enhancing English learners' pronunciation. On the other hand Internet has done marvels and has also appeared a pedagogical strategy. Today, the Internet is regarded as a pedagogical device to develop language teaching and the learning process (Lee, 2000).

Computer Assisted Pronunciation Training (CAPT) systems, as an example, are designed to provide learners with private, stress-free practice with individualized and instantaneous feedback on pronunciation. The introduction of CAPT applications has initiated a debate on the relationship between pedagogy and technology, and the role of the language teacher in the classroom (Neri et al. 2002).

2 Methodology and procedure

The study is participatory cum empirical effort and the subjects (50 secondary school teachers) were exposed to a pre-test (appendices A, B & C) and their proficiency was observed by using a checklist and then the results of the pre and post-test were compared to check their improvement in the mentioned areas, i.e., individual sounds (20), word stress (32 two syllabic) and intonation (1 sentence with at least 7 possible ways to pronounce) after the semester.

3 Findings and conclusions

It was found that a majority of subjects were able to pronounce individual sounds so far as consonants were concerned and were capable of pronouncing most of the vowel sounds of English except long and short vowel sounds like / i: / , /ɑ:/ , / ɔ: / , or /u:/. Similarly a majority of subjects were not able to pronounce diphthongs and mixed up one with the other without gliding the tongue while pronouncing them.

It is possible that lack of practice in pronouncing English vowels sounds, separate words and intonation has hardened their vocal cords as well as less practice of speaking English language in daily life, academic and social, might have doubled the problem but the results of post test reflect that their vocal cords have still the capacity to adapt new habits which has been given to them through drill through CALL. We also see that intonation understanding was hardly found in the beginning as most of the subjects read the sentence in a monotone but regular use of CALL with the help and guidance of teacher educator they were capable of stressing words to get the required meaning in the sentence.

Further, we find that teachers developed liking for CALL programmes and consistently utilized computer facilities as well as the available CALL programmes in the Lab and on Internet. But it is very important to consider that without the help of teacher educator, who himself/herself, pronounces English words with appropriate pronunciation the task for overcoming such difficulties will remain the same because it is the teacher educator who is to steer the boat of the pronunciation of perspective teachers in right direction in the beginning as Dhaif (1989) claims computers can never replace the 'live' teacher, especially in language teaching where the emphasis is on mutual communication between people. We find that there is big improvement in the understanding and performance of the subjects as the results of the post test manifest.

The subjects improved their word stress by pronouncing the individual sounds correctly with consciousness of intonation pattern to pronounce word in the sentence with stress to make the meanings clear. It was also found out that subjects were in the position to make distinction between long and short vowel sounds, learnt the word stress in accordance with the requirement, i.e., either verb or a noun or adjective, etc. Similarly in the connected speech the subjects demonstrated positive improvement as they came to know what sort of meaning they have to communicate with the stress on one particular word.

Hence, the study seems to answer that the perspective teachers, who are taught English pronunciation through CALL by the teacher educators, can better their articulation so far as individual sounds, word stress and basic intonation are concerned in light of the results of both pre and post tests because after a semester's training through CALL they were capable of improving their individual sound articulation, word stress, especially two syllabic words, and intonation in the connected speech and demonstrated in a better way.

4 Recommendations

Technological advancements should be considered as blessing in disguise for the learning of refined pronunciation. Language teachers, teaching English at tertiary level to perspective teachers, should equip themselves with computer skills to use Internet in a befitting manner. Universities should promote language teaching through computers so that every teacher may consider it mandatory for the improvement of his/her as well as students' pronunciation. Universities/Colleges (having teacher education programmes) must allocate funds for better and Internet equipped computer labs so that after training from the teacher educators, perspective teachers may become independent learners so for as good pronunciation/articulation is concerned. Government/policy designers should take CALL as a call of the day required for posterity.

References

Albertson, Kathleen. (1982). Teaching pronunciation with visual feedback. *NALLD Journal*, 17.18-33.

Butler-Pascoe, Mary Ellen & Wiburg, Karin M. 2003. Technology and teaching English language learners. MA: Pearson Education, Inc.

Celce-Murcia, M., & Goodwin. (1991). 'Teaching Pronunciation' in Celce-Murcia, M. (ed.) *Teaching English as a Second or Foreign Language*. Boston: Heinle & Heinle Publishers, pp. 136-153.

Chapelle, C. (1997). CALL in the year 2000: Still in search of research paradigms? *Language Learning & Technology*, *1*(1), pp. 19-43.

Chun, Dorothy M. (1989). Teaching tone and intonation with microcomputers. *CALICO Journal* 7.21-46.

de Bot, Kees& Kate Mailfert. (1982). The teaching of intonation: Fundamental research and classroom applications. *TESOL Quarterly*, 16.71-107.

de Bot, Kees. (1983). Visual feedback of intonation 1: Effectiveness and induced practice behavior. *Language and Speech*, 26,4.331-350.

Dhaif, H. A.(1989).Can computers teach languages? *English teaching forum*. 27(3), pp. 17-19

Dunkel, P. (Ed.). (1991). *Computer-assisted language learning and testing: Research issues and practice.* Philadelphia: Penn State University Press.

Eskenazi, Maxine. (1999a). "Using automatic speech processing for foreign language pronunciation tutor: Some issues and a prototype". Language Learning and Technology 2:62-76.

Eskenazi, Maxine. (1999b). "Using a computer in foreign language pronunciation training: What advantages?" CALICO Journal 16:447-469.

Harless, William. G., Zier, Marcia. A. & Duncan, Robert. C. (1999). "Virtual dialogues with native speakers: The evaluation of an interactive multimedia method". CALICO Journal 16:313-337.

Holland, Melissa, Kaplan, Jonathan & Sabol, Mark. 1999. Preliminary tests of language learning in a speech-interactive graphics microworld. CALICO Journa, 16:339-359.

Hişmanoğlu, Murat. 2010. "Online Pronunciation Resources: Hobbies or Fobbies of EFL Teachers?" IJONTE, 1(2), pp. 40-53.

Holland, M. (1995). The case for intelligent CALL. In M. Holland, J. D. Kaplan, & M. R. Sams (Eds.), *Intelligent language tutors: Theory shaping technology*. Mahwah, NJ: Lawrence Erlbaum Associates.

How to improve pronunciation? Retrieved May 16, 2011 from http://www2.elc.polyu.edu.hk/CILL/pathways/improve_pron.htm

Hubbard, P. (1988). An integrated framework for CALL courseware evaluation. *CALICO Journal*, Dec., 51-72.

Hua, Tsai. 2006. "Bridging pedagogy and technology: User evaluation of pronunciation oriented CALL software". AJET 22:375-397.

Kaplan, Jonathan, Sabol, Mark, Wisher, Robert & Seidel, Robert. 1998. "The military language tutor (MILT) program: An advanced authoring system". Computer Assisted Language Learning 11:265-287.

Kenning, M. M., & Kenning, M. J. (1990). *Computers and language learning: Current theory and practice*. London: Ellis Horwood.

Kim, In-Seok. (2006). "Automatic speech recognition: Reliability and pedagogical implications for teaching pronunciation". Educational Technology & Society 9:322-334.

Johnson, Karen E., & Deborah Rekart. (1991). Computer-assisted English pronunciation training for international teaching assistants. *TESOL Matters*, 1, 5, p. 17.

Johnson, Karen E., Patricia Dunkel, & Deborah Rekart. (1991). Computer-assisted English pronunciation training. Presentation at the Third National Conference on the Training and Employment of Graduate Teaching Assistants.

LaRocca, Stephen., Morgan, John. & Bellinger, Sherri. (1999). "On the path to 2X learning: Exploring the possibilities of advanced speech recognition". CALICO Journal 16:295-310.

Lee, Lina. (2000). "Using Internet to enhance foreign language teaching and learning". Retrieved May 13, 2011, from http://www.unh.edu/spanish/lina/internet1.html.

Neri, Ambra., Cucchiarini, Catia., Strik, Helmer. 2006. "Selecting segmental errors in L2 Dutch for optimal pronunciation training". IRAL 44:357-404.

Neri, Ambra, Cucchiarini Catia, Strik Helmer and Boves Lou (2002). The Pedagogy-Technology Interface in Computer Assisted Pronunciation Training, in: "CALL Journal" 15/5, 441-467.

Ng, K. L. E., & Olivier, W. (1987). Computer-assisted language learning: An investigation on some design and implementation issues. *System*, *15*(1), 1-17.

Pennington, M. (1988). Using the Visi-Pitch to illustrate and validate findings in second language research. Presentation at the 1988 TESOL Convention.

Perdreau, Connie, & Carrie L. Hessney. (1990). Pronunciation improvement through visual feedback. Presentation at the 1990 TESOL Convention.

Pronunciation: Changing Meaning through Word Stress. Retrieved 16 December, 2010 from http://esl.about.com/cs/pronunciation/a/a_wordstress.htm

Purcell, E., & R. Suter. (1980). "Predictors of pronunciation accuracy: A reexamination." *Language Learning*, 30, 2: 271-87.

Richmond, Edmun B. (1976). A visual display device for teaching pronunciation of speech sounds. *Educational Technology*, 16.43-45.

Schwartz, Arthur H., J. Markoff, J. & N. Jain. (1991). Intensive instruction for accent modification. Presentation at the Third National Conference on the Training and Employment of Graduate Teaching Assistants.

Suter, R. (1976). 'Predicators of Pronunciation accuracy in second language learning' *Language Learning,* 26: 233-53.

Vardanian, Rose Marie. (1964). Teaching English intonation through oscilloscope displays. Language Learning, 14.109-117.

Warschauer, M. (1996). Computer-assisted language learning: An introduction. In S. Fotos (Ed.), *Multimedia language teaching* (pp. 3-20). Logos International: Tokyo.

Weltens, Bert, & Kees de Bot. (1984a). Visual feedback of intonation II: Feedback delay and quality of feedback. *Language and Speech*, 27. 79-88.

Weltens, Bert, & Kees de Bot. (1984b). Visual feedback of intonation II: Feedback delay and quality of feedback. *Language and Speech*, 27. 79-88.

Appendix A

Pre & Post Test No. 1 (Individual sounds)
Consonants: **Vowels:**   **Diphthongs**

f	d	iː	eɪ
v	k	ɪ	aɪ
θ	g	e	ɔɪ
ð	tʃ	æ	əʊ
s	dʒ	ʌ	aʊ
z	m	ɑː	ɪə
ʃ	n	ɒ	eə
ʒ	ŋ	ɔː	ʊə

h	l	ɜ:	
p	r	ə	
b	j	ʊ	
t	w	u:	

Appendix B

Pre & Post Test No. 2 (word stress)

Sr. No	Ordinary Script	Phonetic Script	Sr. No	Ordinary Script	Phonetic Script
1	Abstract	æbstrækt (n)	17	Convert	konvɜ:t(n)
2	Abstract	əbstrækt (v)	18	Convert	kənvɜ:t(v)
3	Accent	æksent (n)	19	Excess	ekses(n)
4	Accent	əksent (v)	20	Excess	ikses(v)
5	Access	ækses(n)	21	Excuse	iksju:s(n)
6	Access	əkses(v)	22	Excuse	iksju:z(v)
7	Concept	konsept(n)	23	Present	prezənt(n)
8	Concept	kənsept(v)	24	Present	prizənt(v)
9	Conduct	kondʌkt(n)	25	Produce	prodju:s(n)
10	Conduct	kəndʌkt(v)	26	Produce	prədju:s(v)
11	Conflict	Konflikt(n)	27	Project	prodʒekt(n)
12	Conflict	kənflikt(v)	28	Project	prədʒekt(v)
13	Contest	kontest(n)	29	Subject	sʌbdʒikt(n)
14	Contest	kəntest(v)	30	Subject	səbdʒekt(v)
15	Contrast	kontra:st(n)	31	Reject	ri:dʒekt(n)
16	Contrast	ka:ntra:st(v)	32	Reject	ridʒekt(v)

Appendix C

Pre & Post Test No. 3 (Intonation)

Sr. No	Sentence	Intended meaning
1	I said she might consider a new haircut.	Not just a haircut.
2	I **said** she might consider a new haircut.	It's a possibility.
3	I said **she** might consider a new haircut.	It was my idea.
4	I said she **might** consider a new haircut.	Not something else.

5	I said she might **consider** a new haircut.	Don't you understand me?
6	I said she might consider a **new** haircut.	Not another person.
7	I said she might consider a new **haircut**.	She should think about it. It's a good idea.
		Answers to the questions
		I said she might consider a new haircut. *It was my idea.*
		I **said** she might consider a new haircut. *Don't you understand me?*
		I said **she** might consider a new haircut. *Not another person.*
		I said she **might** consider a new haircut. *It's a possibility.*
		I said she might **consider** a new haircut. *She should think about it. It's a good idea.*
		I said she might consider a **new** haircut. *Not just a haircut.*
		I said she might consider a new **haircut**. *Not something else.*

Courtesy: http://esl.about.com/cs/pronunciation/a/a_wordstress.htm

Appendix D

Pre test results

Able to pronounce consonants sounds	Able to pronounce vowel sounds other than long & shorts vowel sounds	Able to pronounce all long & short vowel sounds	Able to pronounce all diphthongs sounds	Able to stress two syllabic words	Able to stress words in sentence
38	38	4	3	5	5

Post-test results

Able to pronounce consonants sounds	Able to pronounce vowel sounds other than long & shorts vowel sounds	Able to pronounce all long & short vowel sounds	Able to pronounce all diphthongs sounds	Able to stress two syllabic words	Able to stress words in sentence
43	41	41	38	42	41

The Innovative Features of the Automated Digital Literacy Testing System

Renata Danielienė, Eugenijus Telešius

Information Technologies Institute,
K. Petrausko 26, LT-44156 Kaunas, Lithuania
renata.danieliene@gmail.com
et@ecdl.lt

Abstract: The article analyzes the situation of the Lithuanian automated digital literacy skills' testing system. In this article, different test delivery methods are being introduced. It also explains that these testing delivery methods are used in specific situations. In addition, various versions and modified innovations of digital literacy testing system are being presented. These testing systems were developed by a public institution of Information Technologies Institute. A new learning process is being described which was introduced for the e-GUARDIAN project.

Keywords: digital literacy, Internet-based testing, automated testing system.

1 Introduction

Today, we see the influence of computers all around us. Consequently, it is very important to choose specific tools for digital literacy training, constantly track innovations, analyze them and properly apply them. Lately, there has been very much attention given to the development and improvement of the automated testing systems. Testing can be inventive in a number of different ways. The test content, testing process and results scoring are the most known aspects where the contemporary features can be applied. During the past ten years of the testing system development various innovative solutions for digital literacy testing system were used by the public institution of Information Technologies Institute (ITI) in Lithuania.

2 ITI Activities

The public institution of Information Technologies Institute (ITI) was established in 1997. ITI can be described as an organization which creates temporary working groups for projects to design information systems in a professional manner. ITI has experience in corporative information systems design and computerization of administrative work (Lotus Domino infrastructures). From year 2000 ITI started activities in ECDL (European Computer Driving License) programme implementation in Lithuania and now is the official ECDL Foundation Sub-licensee for Lithuania [1]. Currently the development and dissemination of ECDL-related products and activities are the major targets for ITI. ITI team has developed the automated multilingual ECDL Test System which was approved by the ECDL Foundation. Currently, ITI is involved in the development of localized test bases and automated test administration and evaluation systems for ECDL, e-Citizen, ECDL CAD and e-Guardian programmes in Lithuanian, Latvian, Russian, and English languages.

3 Participation in projects

Recently, under the Leonardo da Vinci programme, Information Technologies Institute together with other institutions had participated in some projects that were related to digital literacy testing.

During the Leonardo Transfer of Innovation CECA project, ECDL Computer Aided Design (CAD), tests were developed in Lithuanian language and implemented into the Lithuanian Test System. The general objective of the Leonardo Development of Innovation euCAD project was to develop an innovative technique through which adults, at their work place or at home, could be supported in acquiring knowledge and certifying their skills on 2-D and 3-D CAD for industrial applications. In the euCAD project, the main target for ITI was the development of an innovative framework of vocational training system. The Lithuanian representative managed to develop and create the euCAD Test Engine where people could evaluate their knowledge in CAD application areas.

The main goal of Leonardo Transfer of Innovation project "Development and certification of skills for European educators focused on safe ICT and cyber threat prevention" e-GUARDIAN (LLP–LDV–TOI–2010–LT–0071) was to create an e-safety training and certification programme, which could help the European teachers to gain more knowledge about the Internet threats and how to overcome these threats.

Project participants combined and adapted their initial products with additional leading methodological materials into a complete e-GUARDIAN training and certification programme. The e-GUARDIAN programme has been submitted to the certification of the European teachers' knowledge on safer Internet. This programme has been adapted to pedagogues of educational institutions, who seek safely to use their computers and the Internet, to teach their students, and to protect them from the Internet threats.

Project outcome: Syllabus, Methodology guide, Training programme, E-course, Student's guide, Barometer tests (http://dev.ecdl.lt/project/eguardtest/), and Certification tests.

e-GUARDIAN Barometer test is used to identify an initial knowledge of the test-taker. When the test is finished, recommendations and individual learning plan are presented. The test-taker can individually learn by using this distance learning module.

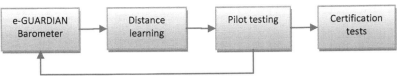

Fig. 1. e-GUARDIAN learning and certification process

When the training is finished, he has to perform pilot testing. If results are not satisfying, then he has to go back to e-GUARDIAN Barometer and repeat the process again (see Fig. 1.).

4 The automated testing system

Nowadays, computer-based testing is used for testing knowledge in various areas. Originally, simple computer-based tests of fixed length were used. Later on, as there arose the need for security of questions and the need of a more effective assessment of the test-takers' knowledge and individual generation of questions, computer-based testing was improved in order to solve the emerging problems . As a consequence, several questionnaire design methods were developed. Even in some educational institutions most exams are being replaced by tests. Therefore, such testing should be done qualitatively. Qualitative testing is extremely important in specialized testing systems, such as testing people's digital literacy knowledge' [3].

Currently, in Lithuania, ECDL tests can be taken using an automated testing system, which is installed on ITI server www.ecdl.lt. The testing system has been designed in accordance to the traditional IS design methods hence it works consistently. This testing system is authorized by ECDL Foundation and is competitive with other commercial products. Lithuanian ECDL testing system is multilingual: tests can be taken in Lithuanian, Russian and Latvian languages.

In the Lithuanian ECDL testing system, test questions are delivered consecutively. The test is formed from 36 questions. Skipped questions in the test can not be answered later on. When the test is finished, the status of passing/failing the test is shown. There is no skill level assigned to users depending on earlier tests results. The ECDL test questions can have four different answer types [4]:

- Multiple choice with four answers, where only one answer is correct. However, creating these questions can take a longer period of time and this is because creating incorrect answers can be difficult. The probability of students guessing it is relatively low.
- Multiple choice with an image and four answers, where only one answer is correct and other answers are incorrect. In this case, image visually shows the essence of question and thus it is easier for the test-taker to comprehend the question.
- True/false questions. In this case, the test-taker gets the statement and must decide if this statement is right or wrong. This type of question is easy to create, but the test-taker has relatively high probability of guessing (50%).
- Hotspot questions. In this case, the test-taker must click on a picture in order to answer a question. Usually the picture has several correct and incorrect answers. This type of question is designed for assessment of practical skills.

4.1 Test generation methods

Currently, in the Lithuanian ECDL testing system, tests are generated in two different ways. As soon as questions are randomly selected then these questions are grouped in sets by Syllabus items (thematic). During the test, questions are selected from these sets. Such test generation method is used for e-Guardian, CAD, and e-Citizen tests.

Lithuanian testing system also uses another, a more improved way to generate test questions. Moreover, questions are created in accordance with the existing ECDL Syllabus version. During the test, questions are chosen randomly from each item of the ECDL Syllabus. In this way, question sets for each student will be different. Such test generation method is used only for ECDL tests.

4.2 The new test delivery method for ECDL testing system

After a few years of research, a solution to digital literacy testing was introduced. This resolution enables to use it according to people's occupations and their area of activities, thus reducing frequency of question exposure and compact test composition. Compact test composition is considered as a complex term: (1) test shortening according to the test completion condition; (2) test items delivery according to occupational parameters. So far, there has not been developed a specific way for selection of questions for testing people of different occupations with different area skills. Usually, test questions are selected in a fixed order, random order or adaptively assessing reliability. Also, they are selected by the test length, the size of the questions bank, the number of test-takers, etc. The level of knowledge in the proposed test design method can be assessed by the help of variables that have not yet been used in testing, i.e. occupation, education, age, experience of work with the computer, etc. For the research of these variables (quantitative and qualitative) intelligent methods were applied [3].

Currently, in a real commercial use, tests of ECDL testing system are based on computer fixed test (CFT) delivery method. The main advantage of CFT is that it is based on a pencil-and-paper test model. The testing system based on the CFT can be quickly and easily implemented [2].

However, students' examination must be performed by evaluating more characteristics [5]. This cannot be accomplished very accurately by using traditional students' testing. After analysing computer-based testing and standard testing systems [3,4,5] we have chosen an adaptive testing theory for ECDL testing system. This will help to assess students' knowledge more accurately and will increase testing efficiency.

During the test, questions are chosen randomly from each item of the ECDL Syllabus item bank. Questions are also created in accordance with the existing ECDL Syllabus version. Since there are more Syllabus' items than questions in the test (36 questions), it is necessary to make a decision of how and which questions must be chosen for the test. For that reason, ECDL Foundation has manually designed some sub sets of knowledge area items. Each test-taker gets randomly questions from these sub-areas. The test generation process is shown in figure 2.

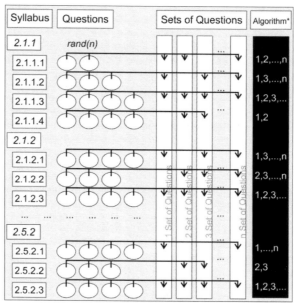

Fig.2. ECDL test generation process

This innovative test construction's algorithm was implemented on our test engine and the experiment with over more than 100 test-takers was made. During the suggested question formation, the test was formulated individually for each test-taker according to how he answered previous questions. Since the test was flexible, the length of the test was variable. In this way, testing time was economized and the number of question exposures was minimized. Therefore it decreases the possibility of cheating and question leaks. The experiment results showed that the shortening of the test (up to a certain number) does not influence the assessment.

4.3 In-Application test engine

Currently, Lithuanian testing system (ATES) is under the maintenance, and we are looking for the innovative solutions to improve testing system. Our team has been creating an In-application demo test. In-Application testing is the latest and the most advanced technique of digital skills evaluation. Traditional multiple choice and hotspot testing does not always accurately evaluate user's computer skills. In certain cases, the creation of multiple choice questions is complicated because the correct answer must always be given out among choices. The simulation based testing is a better solution than the multiple choice and the hotspot testing, however, it does not always allow real life scenarios testing. In-

Application testing allows to evaluate user skills in real life scenarios, it also gives a possibility to check the best practice questions.

ATES administration system that was approved by the ECDL Foundation level, is able to store all skill cards, tests and testing data, statistics in one place. It also allows a quick and easy way of information management, testing management, statistic review and other day-to-day tasks.

ATES administration system comes with ECDL Foundation Approved testing system which is based on hotspot and multiple choice questions.

In-Apps Test Engine is implemented as an additional module to ATES Administration System. It uses the same web based interface for skill card management, result review and question editing. Web based interface allows management practically from anywhere.

Features of ATES In-Apps Test Engine:

- Automatic web update features offer an easier management of installations. At the beginning of every session, In-Apps Test Engine's core files as well as updated questions and new tests are automatically downloaded from the central database. Centralized installation register allows to track all installations of In-Apps Test Engine. Furthermore, it allows answer tracking, identifies computers that have technical problems, and enables blocking of In-Apps Test Engine terminals.
- Centralized rights management offers a quick and convenient way to manage user identities.
- In-Apps Test Engine also supports multiple choice and hotspot questions, giving more flexibility in question formulation.

Currently, In-Apps Test Engine Testing module supports in application testing in MS Word 2007, MS Excel 2007 and MS PowerPoint 2007. Shortly, an ongoing active development will allow to expand the list of supported applications.

Offline testing mode allows testing in a case of the internet connection failures. Test results are automatically sent to central server and they are evaluated once the internet connection is restored.

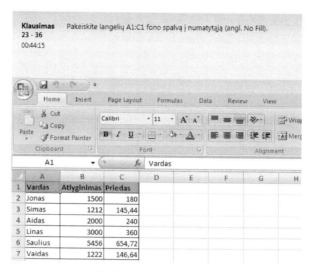

Fig. 3. InApps testing system

InApps Test Engine was developed with a multilingual support (see Fig. 3.).

5 Conclusions

For the high-level testing system there is the need to develop new theories and methods, that would enable to better assess the test-takers' knowledge. The proposed test design method has features of the automated test assembly as well as the adaptive test generation.

The typical ECDL testing system can be created by using a computer based adaptive testing theory. In this case, we can estimate students' knowledge more accurately, because the estimation is recalculated after every answered question, and the next question is given to the student according to how he had answered the previous question.

The use of the new innovative computer literacy test design method, increases test security and it could be claimed that questions are being generated for each individual test-taker. By using adaptive testing theory, the shortening of the test (up to a certain number) does not influence the assessment.

References

An official European Computer Driving Licence (ECDL). Available: http://www.ecdl.com. [viewed 2012 06 10].

Danieliene, R., Telesius, E. (2008). Analysis of Computer-Based ECDL Testing. In: Nunes, M. B., McPherson, M. (eds.) e-Learning 2008. IADIS Press, Amsterdam, pp. 243-246.

Danieliene, R. (2010). Research of intelligent computer literacy test design method: Doctoral Dissertation. Vilnius: Vilnius University, pp.195.

Guzmán, E., Conejo, R., & García-Hervás, E. (2005). An Authoring Environment for Adaptive Testing. In: Educational Technology & Society, vol. 8 (3), pp. 66-76.

Luecht, R. M. (2006). Operational Issues in Computer-Based Testing. In: Computer-Based Testing and the Internet. John Wiley & Sons, Ltd, pp. 91-115.

EMPATIC: Empowering Autonomous Learning through Information Competencies

Carol Priestley

MDR Partners, 2B Fitzgerald Rd, London, SW14 8HA, UK
carol.priestley@mdrprojects.com

Abstract: The EMPATIC project focused on promoting the effective exploitation of the results of the Lifelong Learning Programme (LLP) and also previous related programmes (at sectoral, regional, national and European levels) in the area of Information Literacy. The raison d'être was to encourage the best use of results, innovative processes and the exchange of good practices in the field covered by the LLP through four sectors: Schools, Higher Education, Vocational Education & Training and Adult Education & Lifelong Learning. Major results included a state of the art report Current State and Best Practices in Information Literacy, a strategic review of Information Literacy, identification of illustrative best practice cases and formulation of recommendations to policy makers. It is now important to build on the knowledge gained, the recommendations made and level of interest expressed through the project. LINQ2012 provides an important opportunity to further explore how information literacy is key to both innovation and quality, to outline a best way forward through collaboration with a large number of additional partners and to define an action plan.

Keywords: Information Literacy, Life Long Learning, Schools Sector, Higher Education, VET, Adult Education, Policy, Curriculum

1 Background

As the learning environment becomes more complex and the use of ICT based content and systems increases people need to understand the new information landscape and have confidence in navigating within it, at the same time as combining the information they acquire from different sources to achieve a balanced and coherent view. Information Literacy is increasingly an essential skill which underpins and transforms people's ability to be creative, to work effectively and to be entrepreneurial. Social networking, Web 2.0 and Second Life technologies have placed a new premium on the ability to assess, select, organise and communicate information effectively.

Information Literacy contributes to increased participation in Lifelong Learning by people of all ages because it gives them the skills they need to source, assess, organise and understand information and thus to learn. Equipping people with Information Literacy skills thus increases both their capability to learn and their confidence. It also leads to increased enjoyment of learning. Funded as a transversal project under EACEA's Lifelong Learning Programme (LLP) (2010-2012), EMPATIC sought to gather and prepare materials to influence practitioners and policy makers to enable them to recognise IL as an essential skill for all citizens and to stimulate the use and adoption of IL training across all learning sectors.

The ultimate goals of the project were to:

improve current perceptions among policy makers in Europe regarding the role, value and implementability of Information Literacy in learning;

- pave the way for piloting and eventual mainstreaming of information competencies in all levels of education and their integration in the reform of curriculum frameworks.

The 'core' objectives were to:

- draw together and valorise the results of previous Information Literacy initiatives and projects across the school, university, adult and vocational learning sectors;

- use this evidence to identify strategies that could influence policy makers' perceptions and actions to support a marked increase in piloting and mainstreaming of Information Literacy;

- identify new learning paradigms and prepare the way for strategic thinking on curriculum reform.

Considerable effort has been invested by practitioners in many parts of the world in defining and promoting Information Literacy (IL). In the USA Information Literacy has been a national policy issue since the establishment of the National Forum on IL in 1989. In European countries, by contrast, the IL issue has been pursued episodically and in a fragmented manner. EMPATIC therefore also encouraged and enabled a European dimension in systems and practices in the field of IL.

The project aimed to pave the way in collating, analysing, showcasing and disseminating best practice for the benefit of policy makers and practitioners, especially those with interest in lifelong learning programmes (including Erasmus, Comenius, Grundtvig, Leonardo). It involved a wide range of stakeholders in examining and discussing the best practice experiences and results of previous interventions with a view to drafting series of recommendations to be promoted to policy holders and decision makers.

2 Activities

The project embraced all 4 educational sectors: Schools, Higher Education, Vocational Education & Training and Adult Education & Lifelong Learning and involved 5 main implementing partners: the Istituto di Ricerca sull'Impresa e lo Sviluppo (CERIS), Italy; Jagiellonian University, Institute of Information and Library Science, Poland, Technical University of Crete, Greece, the Turkish Library Association (TKD), and MDR Partners, UK.

The main activities were grouped into:

- desk research, the aims of which were threefold:

- • to arrive at a practical definition of information literacy and an assessment of current thinking on its role in learner performance and learning outcomes at each level of education, taking into account the findings of LLP projects and other European initiatives;
- • to assess to what extent information literacy efforts are being employed within mainstream education;
- • identify best practices in school, higher education, adult and vocational educational bodies in formal and non formal settings.

- dissemination: the aim of which was to establish a web environment as a one-stop-shop Information Literacy portal providing interactive community building communication facilities and a basis for distribution of resources identified or created in the project.

- quality assurance and impact: development of a strategy to determine the ways in which project partners ensured outputs to be of suitable quality.

- strategic modeling, the aim of which was to draw on the results and analyses of the desk research to propound strategic models; standards & associated performance measures; and illustrative case studies for information literacy, which would subsequently be tested in the validation phase.

- validation: the models and case studies were validated and improved firstly through a series of sector workshops of invited policy makers and expert stakeholders who discussed and further defined major issues against a backdrop of the EMPATIC findings to date.

- resource development: included state of the art reports, the finalized case studies, and advocacy documents targeted to policy makers.

- exploitation: a strategy was developed to improve the spread of information literacy. Careful attention was paid to the context of the Lisbon strategy; the Education & Training programme 2010, the Bologna process for the higher education sector and the Copenhagen process for the vocational sector. Following the validification workshops a draft set of recommendation was developed which was refined through an international transversal workshop and an end of project conference.

EMPATIC paid special attention to developing partnerships and communication with potential stakeholders and target users. These included using professional and social communication and networking tools in addition to hosting of five international workshops and a final conference. Each partner brought a significant contribution in terms of subject matter and in implementation together with the involvement of their own professional networks both nationally and regionally It was therefore possible to build up a significant stakeholder database, involving members from 36 countries in Europe, and a total of 67 countries world-wide.

3 Results

As Information Literacy is such a key competence that underpins many, if not most, of the EU's most important objectives and strategies, including i2010, Education and Training 2010 and the Digital Agenda, considerable care and attention was given to the planning, preparation and dissemination of outcomes and results.

3.1 The major outputs from EMPATIC included:

- a report *Current State and Best Practices in Information Literacy*. In view of the aims as described in section 2 above, the report presents the state of the art in the area of information literacy, reflecting the most significant global challenges and developments in this domain. A concise presentation of the role information literacy plays within respect to lifelong learning is presented and illustrates how rich the concept of information literacy is and how the various points of view complement each other. Special attention was paid to the definitions and frameworks suggested by a number of bodies.

The report reaffirmed that Information Literacy is the capacity based on knowledge, skills and attitudes - as derived from the Alexandria Proclamation, then adopted by UNESCO's *Information for All Programme* – to successfully find, store & retrieve, analyze, evaluate and use information:

In the mentioned Alexandria Proclamation on Information Literacy and Lifelong Learning (UNESCO, 2005) it is perceived that:

> "Information Literacy (…) is crucial to the competitive advantage of individuals, enterprises (especially small and medium enterprises), regions and nations; provides the key to effective access, use and creation of content to support economic development, education, health and human services, and all other aspects of contemporary societies (…)".

> "Information Literacy lies at the core of lifelong learning. It empowers people in all walks of life to seek, evaluate, use and create information effectively to achieve their personal, social, occupational and educational goals. It is a basic human right in a digital world and promotes social inclusion of all nations."

Section 2 of the report provided data on the projects in the information literacy domain supported by the European Union, these activities cover the period 1994–2010 and include 79 projects. The section outlined a set of attributes identified for each project and used for initial analysis of the situation in Europe. These attributes include identification attributes (name of the initiative, acronym, URL, Leader institution, contacts); country of the coordinator if a multinational initiative; typology of the leading institution; classification of the kind of initiative; source of funding, main focus, target community, starting date and a description.

Even the initial analysis identified some essential specific features of the current situation in the EU support of information literacy initiatives. Information literacy projects are still mainly supported through national initiatives; the specialised funding programmes address them rather as an exception. This might mean that a serious debate on the priorities of some of the funding programmes in the EU is needed to position better the work in the information literacy domain;

Furthermore, the majority of initiatives had been centred on the concept of IL as a skill and is library-originated in kind. The IL policy dimension had been quite neglected. The report pulled together for the first time a descriptive list of 87 projects which the European Union and other bodies supported in this area between 1994 and 2010. The case studies that were finally selected therefore included where possible those where policy initiatives and recommendations.

Finally, the report synthesized the point of view taken by the EMPATIC project. Since as Section 1 of the report showed that there are multiple and not always converging points of view, this section illustrated and justified the EMPATIC framework of analysis identifying three dimensions of Information Literacy, each one supported by a number of arguments, and complementing each other: Information Literacy as a discipline of study; as a social objective; and as a cognitive acquisition of individuals. This theoretical background set the scene for the subsequent work on the policy recommendations which EMPATIC delivered.

A copy of the full report is available at http://empat-ic.eu/eng/Reports
- a strategic review of Information Literacy. The state of the art report concluded there were no ready tools or techniques for creating IL development strategies. The aim of the second outcome from EMPATIC was therefore to create a conceptual, generic and tentative framework for Information Literacy development, so that subsequent, more specific IL models can be developed. The two fundamental features of the framework were:
  - the model of IL development takes a strategic approach. This is based on the assumption that Information Literacy is critically important for well-being and success of today's individuals, societies and nations, so has to be a matter of an organized, planned and rational action on the European and national levels;
  - this is not a model of Information Literacy itself, but a strategy for IL development, mainly, but not only, by teaching/learning, in different contexts and on various levels.

A copy of the full report is available at http://empat-ic.eu/eng/Reports
- Illustrative Case Study Approaches: the 87 projects identified in the State of the Art Report were re-examined and evaluated in order to make a selection of 20 projects of good practice, five each of the four sectors: schools, HE, vocational education & training, and lifelong learning. These formed the basis of developed case studies to be produced and verified by each partner later in the project.

The full report is available from http://empat-ic.eu Reports and the Case Studies are available from http://empat-ic.eu/eng/Case-Studies
- reports from the four separate international workshops involving policy makers and other expert stakeholders to discuss and define the findings of EMPATIC in IL models as well as the case study approach and identification, for each of the 4 sectors. Copies of each report can be obtained from the relevant link to each event from http://empat-ic.eu/eng/EMPATIC-Events
- report on Finalised Information Literacy Case Studies: this report explains how and why the methodology of case studies and those examined in EMPATIC are relevant and important to each learning sector.

The most innovative best practice examples
The report also includes a set of links to key IL resources across Europe and worldwide. The report is available from http://empat-ic.eu/eng/Reports
- a set of promotional resources to support the exploitation and dissemination strategies of the project included the finalised case studies and a set of advocacy materials which campaigners can use to lobby for the inclusion of Information Literacy at each educational level.

- a series of Recommendations to policy makers also segmented by level of education, and also translated into Greek, Italian, Polish, and Turkish and are available for translation into other languages. The main purpose of the Recommendations was to stimulate action and the emulation of good practice at national level. Copies can be found from http://empat-ic.eu/eng/Recommendations
- an interactive web environment http://empat-ic.eu/ presenting all the above information in a structured way, the hosting of which was transferred to the European network for Information Literacy (EnIL) http://enil.ceris.cnr.it/Basili/EnIL/ from 1 April 2012.

3.2 Recommendations

The findings and conclusions from the project were verified using three main strategies:
- consultative workshops and a final conference
- mailings to the stakeholder and related databases
- through the EMPATIC and related websites.

Recommendations were prepared for each of the 4 sectors and can be found in detail from http://empat-ic.eu/eng/Findings-Recommendations. A number of recommendations applied to all sectors and can be summarised:

- Information Literacy is vital for the today's society in Europe and as such should be developed and promoted in different contexts and by various means;
- Information Literacy and its specialized fields must be promoted to society, decision makers, politicians and users;
- the strategy of IL development should encompass two main lines of action:
  - o IL awareness building among authorities and governments at national and European levels
  - o substantial, real work, "step by step", "project by project" awareness at a local level led by relevant individual institutions, organisations, etc.
- the identification of roles for multi-dimensional cooperation of different IL stakeholders is crucial;
- Information literacy curricula must be developed and integrated into official lifelong learning programmes, similar to the process already established for Computer Literacy;

- Social awareness of literacy should also be included within work culture and the way employers view it to prepare an informed, mobile work force and innovative economy within Europe.

4 The Future

The main purpose of the EMPATIC recommendations was to stimulate action. Throughout the lifetime of the project a number of aspects came to light that had not initially been established to work on. These included the increasingly transversal nature of IL in a world characterized by change, complexity and interdependence. Individuals today need a wide range of competencies to adapt to and be innovative in this continually changing, highly competitive and therefore challenging world.

Defining the key competencies, in other words transversal competencies, needed by today's individuals to improve how well prepared they are for life's challenges, as well as identify overarching goals for education systems and lifelong learning is necessary. Information literacy is closely and general related to the educational system and also particularly to the education process (teaching and learning). People learn more effectively if they are information literate. Education for information literacy should therefore be explicit and embedded. Related competences (critical thinking, digital & computer competences, communication skills, learning & research skills) are also based on information literacy and are crucial for life long learning.

The EMPATIC stakeholder base was envisaged to focus broadly on information specialists, educationalists and policy makers. Throughout the activity the importance of finding ways in which the three communities could work much more closely together was prevalent; however, it became very clear that many more stakeholders are key to the process; 'speaking' to members of any one community at a time has been a beginning but is not sufficient. The importance of increasing dialogue and implementation across communities as well as across the individual education sectors is imperative. Further work is required and as a first step it would be beneficial in future to bring these communities together. LINQ2012 provides an important opportunity not only to disseminate and discuss the outcomes, to further explore how information literacy is key to both innovation and quality, but also to outline a best way forward and develop a practical action plan through collaboration.

References

Andretta, S. (ed.). (2007). Change and Challenge. Information literacy for the 21st Century. Adelaide: Auslib Press

Barnard, L., *et al*. (2009). Measuring self-regulation in online and blended learning environments. *The Internet and Higher Education, 12*, 1-6

Basili, C. (2007). Theorems of Information Literacy. In: Proceedings of the Conference *"The Information Literacy Landscape"*, Belgrade, Serbia, 5th-7th October 2007

Basili, C. (ed.). (2011). Report on Current State and Best Practices in Information Literacy

Catts, R., & Lau, J. (2008), Towards Information Literacy Indicators. Paris: Unesco

Cisek, S., *et al* (2011). Illustrative Case Studies *[of Information Literacy]*, London, EMPATIC

Cisek, S & Prochnicka, M.(2012) Strategic Models in Information Literacy. London, EMPATIC

Corrall, S. (2008). Information literacy strategy development in higher education: An exploratory study. *International Journal of Information Management, 28*, 26-37

Eisenberg , M. (2008). Information Literacy: Essential Skills for the Information Age. *DESIDOC Journal of Library & Information Technology, 28* (2), 39-47

EMPATIC (2012) Report of European Meeting on Media & Inforamtion Litereracy Education (EMMILE) Milan. London: EMPATIC

EMPATIC & EMSOC (2012) Report of International Conference *Literacy, and Society, Culture, Media & Education.* Ghent University, 9-11 February, 2012. London: EMPATIC

Endrizzi, L. (2006). Les Dossiers d'actualité: Information literacy. *Lettre VST, 17*. INRP (Institut National de Recherche Pédagogique). Veille scientifique et technologique http://www.inrp.fr/vst/LettreVST/english/17-april-2006_en.php

Head, A.J. & Eisenberg, M.B. (December 1, 2009). *Lessons Learned: How College Students Seek Information in the Digital Age*. Project Information Literacy First Year Report with Student Survey Findings. University of Washington's

Information   School
http://projectinfolit.org/pdfs/PIL_Fall2009_finalv_YR1_12_2009v2.pdf

Head, A.J. (2007). Beyond Google: How Do Students Conduct Academic
Research?   *First*   *Monday,*   *12*(7)
http://www.uic.edu/htbin/cgiwrap/bin/ojs/index.php/fm/article/view/1998/187
3

Kelly, O., *et al.* (2009). Don't dilly dally on the way: Driving towards digital
information literacy capability. In: *Same places, different spaces. Proceedings
ascilite*   *Auckland*   *2009.*
http://www.ascilite.org.au/conferences/auckland09/procs/kelly-o.pdf

Krakowska, M (2012)   *MIL Experiences & Policy: The EMPATIC Project: the
Schools Sector* paper given European Meeting on Media and Information Literacy
Education in Libraries (EMMILE), 27 -29 February 2011, Milan, Italy

Kurbanoglu, S.S., Akkoyunlu, B. & Umay, A. (2006). Developing the information
literacy self-efficacy scale. *Journal of Documentation, 62*(6), 730-743

Lau, J. (2006), *Guidelines on Information Literacy for Lifelong learning.*
http://www.ifla.org/VII/s42/pub/IL-Guidelines2006.pdf

Liu, H., Chuang, H. & Huang, J. (2008). The correlation among web-based
learners' self-efficacy, learning strategies and outcomes. In: K. McFerrin *et al.*
(Eds.), *Proceedings of Society for Information Technology and Teacher Education
International Conference 2008* (pp. 3030-3034). Chesapeake, VA: AACE

Maybee, C. (2006). Undergraduate perceptions of information use: The basis
for creating usercentered student information literacy instruction. *The Journal of
Academic Librarianship, 32*(1), 79-85

McGuiness, C. (2006). What faculty think – exploring the barriers to
information literacy development in undergraduate education. *The Journal of
Academic Librarianship, 32*(6), 573-82

New Jersey Institute of Technology (NJIT). (2009). *Institute Information
Literacy Plan.* Newark, NJ. New Jersey Institute of Technology.
http://library.njit.edu/docs/njit-info-lit-plan-caa-approved-05-20-2009.pdf

Sharma, S., *et al.* (2007). Self-regulated learning and e-learning. In: H. Österle,
J. Schelp & R. Winter (Eds.), *Proceedings of the Fifteenth European Conference on
Information Systems* (pp. 383-394). St. Gallen: University of St. Gallen

Virkus, S. (2003). Information literacy in Europe: a literature review. Information Research, *8*(4), paper no. 159 http://informationr.net/ir/8-4/paper159.html

Webber, S., & Johnston, B. (2003). Information literacy in the United Kingdom: a critical review. In: Carla Basili (ed.), *Information literacy in Europe. A first insight into the state of the art of information literacy in the European Union* (pp. 258-283). Roma: Consiglio Nazionale delle Ricerche.

BILFAM - An Innovative Family Language Learning Model

Anca Cristina Colibaba, Elza Gheorghiu, Irina Gheorghiu

Gr.T.Popa University of Medicine and Pharmacy, EuroED Foundation str Florilor 1C Iasi
Romania
acolib@euroed.ro
EuroED Foundation str Florilor 1C Iasi Romania, V.Alecsandri College, Iași, Romania
elza.gheorghiu@gmail.com
Albert Ludwigs University Freiburg
irina_gheorghiu16@yahoo.com

Abstract: This article is a study of the Bilfam project. It highlights its results and aims at describing how an innovative methodology (developed by the psycholinguistic faculty from the Sapientia University in Rome) used in teaching foreign languages to very young learners was applied in Romania by the Euroed Foundation, Iasi, as part of a project funded by the European Union under the Lifelong Learning Programme: BILFAM (Bilingual Families). The model based on intergenerational family learning has shown that the affective relationship between the adult and children has improved the foreign language learning process. Scientific literature has found out that foreign language learning with very young learners in the context of informal education can develop bilingualism. Moreover, grandparents and parents with few foreign language competences can be very successful when involved in their children's foreign language acquisition, being given the necessary tools and strategies. The process shows a dramatic impact on participants' foreign language acquisition and will also create a positive attitude towards multilingualism.

Keywords: family language learning, bilingualism, The Narrative Format

The Bilfam project is focused on the educational model of intergenerational learning. It aims at two different target groups, which nonetheless have many things in common: children, who are at a critical time of language learning, and their parents, who need a good motivation to learn a foreign language, very often for instrumental reasons regarding work mobility, and who find it in their wish to support their children during the process of learning and practising a foreign language. The project encourages parents and grandparents to get involved in their children's foreign language acquisition by providing them with the necessary strategies and tools through face-to-face and online tuition. Grandparents and parents can make learning fun and engaging by creating the conditions for a really enriching learning experience. Being aware of the instrumental role foreign languages may play in their offspring's future, parents are willing to help their children learn a foreign language but they lack the confidence and tools to do so. Not only will the project help grandparents and parents teach their children the language but it will also encourage grandparents and parents to learn it.

The project involved 25 families per country (Italy, The UK, Slovakia, Spain and Romania). Each family was made up of at least one parent or grandparent and one or more children of three to six years old. The international group of the project was made up of 500 parents and 500 children.

The target languages chosen by the Romanian group were English and German. The adults were administered a language test at the beginning of the project which showed a low level of knowledge in the foreign language. The main criteria used in the selection of the parents were their interest in their children's linguistic performance and their own interest in language acquisition, which was considered to be essential in their future. The families were from different social strata but all of them had basic computer skills, had a computer and internet connection at home and were at least high school graduates.

The theoretical basis of the project is the Narrative Format methodology, which is based on the natural process of acquiring one's mother tongue within the family context. This method has been initiated by Prof Traute Taeschner of the Università Sapienza in Rome and has shown that the use of gestures, intonation, facial expressions and the affective relationship between adults and pupils is of great contribution to the foreign language learning process (Taeschner, T. 2004- p 4). The main aim of the method which involves a series of educational strategies, activities and materials is to recreate the conditions a child has when learning his mother tongue.

The method is partially based on Jerome Bruner's and Lev Vygotsky's findings. According to Jerome Bruner learning is an active, social process occurring in three stages: enactive (experiencing the concrete), iconic (representing mentally) and symbolic (using a symbolic system) during the interaction between the child and the adults (parents, teachers etc.). The adult has to adapt the information to be learned by the child into a format appropriate to the learner's current state of understanding. Bruner also draws attention to the spiral manner in which learning takes place so that new information is based on what children have already learned. He also highlights the importance of the child's interest in the material to be learned as the best stimulus to learning. Learning must be concerned with the experiences and contexts that make the child willing and able/ ready to learn (Bruner, J., 1983).

According to Lev Vygotsky human development is intertwined with learning from the first days of life. The quality of the social interaction (sensitive and warm human relationships established between caregivers and children), is the tool for fostering optimal development. These interactions are always mediated by language. Language is seen as an important factor in human development. He supported the idea that the learner's progress is in relation to the experience of the teacher and to the environment. The Vygotskian point of view also stresses the relationship between play, cognition and affective dimensions of development. Play helps the child develop his imagination, which represents a specifically human activity arising from action and play. Vygotsky also worked extensively on ideas about cognitive development, particularly the relationship between language and thinking. His writings emphasized the roles of historical, cultural, and social factors in cognition and argued that language was the most important symbolic tool provided by society (Vygotsky, L.S., 1978).

The theoretical teaching model behind the Narrative Format Methodology is based on mother tongue acquisition and the desire to recreate this in a family environment with a foreign language. Languages are learned through social interaction. Since languages are learnt most easily when two people (adult and child) interact in an excellent relationship, the project provides the families with the necessary tools and materials to make learning efficient and also facilitates good communication in the family.

Three key principles are at the basis of this method:

A. *Learning a foreign language should follow a similar pattern to acquiring a first language.* The child learns his mother tongue while sharing experiences with the adults around them. The formats, the repeated experiences, are therefore real-life situations that both parent and child share every day in a very emotional context which favours the development of non-verbal and verbal communication.

B. *Learning a foreign language should use interactive teaching/learning techniques, which follow the natural language acquisition processes and are enhanced by the relationship between children and adults.* According to this theory it is the emotional relationship between the child and the adult that stimulates communication and therefore learning. The child starts to speak and wants to speak because he likes the adult and wants to communicate with the person with whom he has established an emotional relationship. This happens in the first language and by analogy can happen in the second language too. (Gheorghiu I., Gheorghiu E., Colibaba S., 2012)

C. *Communicative skills are the basis for the teaching/ learning of the new language.*

Intentionality to speak with a person comes from a need to communicate which develops from daily activities, that is formats, in which people are engaged in a family context (such as feeding, changing nappies, taking naps etc.). The formats allow people to get to know each other, be able to anticipate and have expectations about the other person's behaviour, thus paving the way towards the intention to speak to each other. Formats create the best environment for good exchanges and thus good communication. On the other hand, formats are also essential when it comes to learning. They provide a reliable context against which words are related. The child experiences the words concretely and associates them with situations, objects, actions, tone of voice, facial expressions and gestures. Moreover, formats also provide the necessary repetitions one needs in order to retain things and use them spontaneously.

However, everyday situations used as formats become boring: this is a reason why the project uses stories as a challenging version. Stories fire children's imagination and this appeals to children because they go through their emotions. Imagination makes everything possible: it opens the door to the world of Bilfam stories about the wonderful adventures of Hocus and Lotus. The journey the children embark on turns them into little 'dinocrocs' who speak a new language. By acting out and role play children have first hand experience with Hocus's world and the new language. They assume all the roles of the stories, speaking all the parts in the dialogues and being active intellectually and emotionally all the time.

The stories related to the children's world are based on a problematic event which needs to be solved. Vocabulary and structures are simple at this level and are repeated several times through acting out, singing along and other engaging activities. Meaning is made clear through its context, body language and actions. The child experiences the language in a very participative and emotional way.

Parents or grandparents and children experienced the stories together in the magic world of Lotus and Hocus, where only the new language was spoken or understood. The key to success in learning within the family context was the parent-child relationship and the method used. The project made use of a variety of activities in order to reach its goal: meetings with parents, online tutoring, challenging activities meant to intellectually and emotionally amuse and engage participants as well as to enhance their motivation to learn.

The first face-to-face meetings with the parents concentrated on familiarising them with the project: its method, objectives, principles, innovative teaching strategies, activities and materials. The PPT with the project principles and objectives, Hocus and Lotus's model of learning a foreign language, the role of the adult as a magic teacher stirred our parents' interest. We highlighted the role that the parents can play in their children's learning a foreign language. The participants were also given the questionnaire and a flier with the project outline. They noticed the advantages of this method in learning a foreign language and they also highly appreciated the relationship developed between the child and the adult while doing the format. Some psychological aspects of the foreign language learning process as well as of bilingualism were also underlined. Theoretical aspects went hand in hand with practical issues: parents gained hands on experience in how to make a video, how to upload it on the platform or how to make a Voki.

Throughout the project parents and tutors communicated via the online project platform. Parents had access to a forum and activities to be carried out with their children at home, downloadable materials, instructions, how-to advice and the support of a tutor. The project encouraged exchanges of ideas on the site among parents as well as between parents and their tutors with a view to creating a community. Online communication progressed slowly at the beginning due to parents' lack of experience. In time, however, the platform became a useful means of communication, with everybody sharing ideas or finding support and help.

The parents were trained in the acting out of the formats. This was an important stage of the project. The formats were brought to life by children and parents alike, whenever the child wanted to do the activities. Everybody within the narrative format played all the characters, with extensive use of actions and body language.

The acting out of stories with the support of gestures and facial expressions encouraged language learning through active engagement. Parents even agreed that gestures often triggered the right words to use in real situations in the later stages when children started to narrate the stories.

The adult and the child participated together in all activities, against a relaxed environment. All participants in the project agreed that children felt safe as long as their emotional communication with the adult remained intact and strong. The parent's task was therefore to maintain the quality of the emotional communication with the children through eye contact, facial expressions, through warm and open body language and through gestures. It was noticed that any change in parents' attitude (lack of enthusiasm, tiredness, boredom) often put children off from doing the formats. Genuine emotional participation, pleasant atmosphere and good communication proved to be essential in accessing Hocus and Lotus's world. Repetition also helped children understand the story. There was no need for translation or explanations.

The activities suggested as part of the learning process were accessible on the project site and revealed gradually. The platform enabled families to carry out these activities according to their own learning pace. Singing the song while using gestures created a kind of mini-musical which allowed the child to listen to the story again and experience the story in the foreign language by singing. This new experience reinforced learning the new language through music and rhythm. (Gheorghiu I., Gheorghiu E., Colibaba S,. 2012)

The animated cartoons of the adventures of Hocus and Lotus made use of graphic and animation techniques and introduced other language learning principles such as the temporal sequencing of events and linguistic progression. Children were reported to be very fond of cartoons. Parents wrote that they often used cartoons as bedtime stories to put their children to bed.

The e-books of the adventures of Hocus and Lotus proved to be another way to listen to the stories accompanied by pictures. The e-books reinforced the vocabulary that the children started to learn. Some parents reported that e-books helped their children learn to read. (Gheorghiu I., Gheorghiu E., Colibaba S,. 2012)

The Hocus and Lotus Puppet theatre engaged children to participate in different ways according to their particular stage of development. It offered a challenging opportunity to repeat the story by creating the puppets and making puppet shows for the family and friends.

The Voki activity challenged children to create their own avatar (with an electronic or personal voice), which was sent to a friend or to another family in the project that was learning the same language. Some families uploaded it onto the project website. It was considered to be the most popular activity of the project.

The families were also encouraged to produce a new Hocus and Lotus story. Children were asked to organise pictures in sequence to tell a new story, by using the vocabulary and grammatical structures of the language they knew creatively in the new context.

The dinogame of the goose engaged both adults and little ones around the table. This time the game challenged children to use not only their language knowledge but also their knowledge of the characters and the stories.

These activities were launched by tutors who first presented them to the whole group. The tutors' main role was to motivate the participants and monitor their progress by supporting them and giving them the expected feedback. Feedback covered not only project learning materials and method but also online learning guidance. Tutors also facilitated the socialization of the learning group by commenting on their diary notes and inviting the other members of the community to do the same.

Spending time together and playing with Hocus and Lotus in English or German, daily or several times a week, had many positive effects on both children and adults. It led, as parents wrote in their Dino journals, to good communication and excellent family relationships; enhanced motivation and increased self-esteem.

The project offered an original opportunity to spend quality family time: by learning a foreign language together. The adult felt satisfied because he learned together with the child and motivated to act as he wished. The child also felt happy to share his learning experinces with his parents.

The model also gave bilingualism another dimension, which is in tune with EU main objectives because it best serves work mobility (Commission of the European Communities. White paper on education and training, 1995, p 47). It provided an innovative solution as regards bilingualism: for the first time parents were given a valid instrument to facilitate their children's acquisition of two languages. The project highlights that children can become bilingual if they are given enough input in the language and they have enough fun. Bilingual children can recognise their two languages and differentiate them from a very young age. Being bilingual does not necessarily mean having perfect knowledge of two languages. It means being able to communicate in two languages at different levels of competence. Children who learn two languages from birth or who learn them in succession when they already speak one language are bilingual. Adults who learn a foreign language well are also bilingual. A bilingual family is therefore one that has daily experiences in two languages, which is exactly what our project suggests.

The project materials raised participants' awareness about the cognitive advantages of bilingualism, as shown in parents' diaries. Bilingual children have an early awareness and knowledge of the words, structures and sounds of their languages; they often learn to read earlier than others; they are better at learning other languages and at switching tasks; they are better able to focus attention.

The disadvantages of bilingualism cannot be neglected but are outnumbered by its advantages and find adequate solutions in time. Some bilingual children start to speak a bit later than children who have learned one language. Bilingual children may initially have a reduced vocabulary in each of their languages, although their total vocabulary may be larger than the vocabulary of a monolingual child. Bilingual children sometimes mix both languages together (this often occurs when the child knows that s/he will be understood by the speaker because s/he is also bilingual (Pirchio, S., Taeschner, T., Sorace, A., Francese, G., Passiatore, Y. 2011- p 3).

In real situations there are usually two types of bilingual families: the family speak and understand a language and live in a society where another language is spoken and understood; some members of the family speak and understand a language and other members of the family speak and understand another language. In both cases the child's language learning is the responsibility of the family. There are also a few schools though which encourage bilingualism. This was the very objective of our project: for the first time, parents were given accredited tools to teach their children two languages at home and with friends and by doing so the family became a bilingual family.

The project also casts a new light on the role of motivation in learning a foreign language by adults and children, encouraging learning which involved different generations within a family. Learning relies on a good relationship which results in trust and good communication. This is entirely based on mutual affection between adult and child. Therefore, a relaxing warm learning atmosphere will stimulate motivation. Adults who are warm and open (e.g. returning eye contact when they are looked at) encourage children to communicate. This leads us to the conclusion that the child learns to speak a language if he likes the adult who uses that language.

The role that the affective relationship has in learning was illustrated by the project results and supported by parents' and children's feedback. What we noticed is that by the end of the first year the children were able to act out the formats with their families using all the sentence structures learned. They were also able to take single words, expressions and some simple nuclear sentences from the formats and apply them in new contexts.

Parents appreciated the stories as deeply rooted in their children's world, which made them easy to understand and retain. Children not only understood the meaning of the lines they heard but they also used them correctly in a real context whenever necessary. Parents said that it was a very efficient project not only because it was a challenging way to learn a new language but also because it enabled them to spend quality time with their children. Parents also wrote about the interactive platform which encouraged the exchange of ideas and provided support in finding solutions to problems. (http://www.bilfam.eu/).

Children were also very enthusiastic about their new friends: they liked the stories for different reasons. According to their parents' comments in their diaries, the stories appealed to the children because they were interesting and they also managed to learn English very quickly. Children also appreciated Hocus, the main character, because he looked like them and he was funny. Spending time with the family playing and learning together also ranked high in children's evaluation. They appreciated the variety of the activities and the element of surprise, which was a motivating ingredient throughout the whole intergenerational learning process. (http://www.bilfam.eu/)

The piloting of this model is being used by the Psycholinguistics Department of the University of Rome as an example of the way bilingualism works not only as a spontaneous but also as a guided phenomenon. The model underlines the role of emotions and feelings in learning foreign languages both by children and adults, as well as the role of motivation in learning foreign languages. The study highlights the effect of intergenerational learning and of the consolidation of learning through teaching and practice, the role of the narrative format and of play in learning. The prototype is classic but its application in the field of languages and particularly the implications of learning on both categories makes this model a remarkable and transferable one.

References

Bruner, J. (1983). Child's Talk: Learning to Use Language. New York: Norton;

Commission of the European Communities. (1995). White paper on education and training. Teaching and learning: Towards the learning society. Brussels: Commission of the European Communities;

Gheorghiu, I.; Gheorghiu, E.; Colibaba, S. (2012). Bilingualism and family language learning. In: Simpozion stiintific international, Iasi: Universitatea de stiinta si medicina;

Pirchio, S.; Taeschner, T.; Sorace, A.; Francese, G.; Passiatore, Y. (2011). Let's become a bilingual family! Roma: Dinocroc International Training Institute srl;

Taeschner, T. (2004). The magic teacher's kit. Roma: Dinocroc International Training Institute srl;

Vygotsky, L.S. (1978). Mind and society: The development of higher psychological processes. Cambridge, MA: Harvard University Press;

www.bilfam.eu (data on access: 08.08.2012).

NetBox: Community Learning Social Networks

Sarah Land

Meath Partnership, Unit 7, Kells Business Park, Cavan Road Kells, Co. Meath
sarah.land@meathpartnership.ie

Abstract: The main focus of the NetBox project is to support the development of local opportunities to provide greater access for learning and sharing of skills and resources in six rural communities across Europe, leading to stronger, proactive and socially inclusive rural communities. The NetBox project brings together a consortium of 9 partners from across Europe and is being piloted in 6 rural villages, namely; Oldcastle, Meath, Ireland; Wiveliscombe, Somerset, UK; Vale de Figueira & São Vicente do Paúl, Portugal; Gmina Ryki, Poland; Ştefan cel Mare, Romania and Kulautuva, Lithuania. The project consortium believe that it has identified an innovative, multi-faceted model for the development and provision of community education based on blending the best elements of two diverse tried and tested community development approaches and bringing them to life in bespoke social networking environments.

Keywords: Social and community networking; flexible online learning; targeted training opportunities; community needs and assets analysis.

1 Conceptualising the Project

1.1 Introduction and Background

With over 1.2 billion registered users worldwide (comScore, 2012, 2), if Facebook were a country it would be the second largest in the world, only in the wake of China. The growth of social networking is a global phenomenon. In a relatively short timeframe it has become an accepted part of everyday life. The willingness of people from all social and economic sectors to engage in these ubiquitous virtual communities continues and indeed is expanding. What is unequivocal is that Facebook and its other social networking counterparts have succeeded in creating new concepts of identity; new definitions of social. Nearly 1 in every 5 minutes spent online is spent using social networking sites (comScore, 2012, 2), with 250 million people also having access to social networking sites through their mobile devices (jeffbullas.com, 2012). The idea behind NetBox was to capitalise on the advances in these new technologies and on the ease by which people engage in social networking on a daily basis, to not only introduce a model of training which can be delivered using these ubiquitous online platforms, but also to re-invigorate the practice of community activation and community development in the 6 chosen rural communities across Europe.

In August 2007 there were 127.3 million social networking users in Europe, representing 56.4% of Europe's internet users (comScore, 2007). Estimates for 2012 suggest that up to 350 million Europeans are currently engaged in regular social networking actions. This represents over 73% of the total population of Europe. The total number of mobile social networking users in Europe reached 52 million in 2009. This represents 10.41% of the total population of Europe. A recent study by comScore of the EU5 (United Kingdom, Italy, Germany, France and Spain) has revealed that in 2012, in these countries this figure had risen to 45.2% of the EU5 population. With the internet and mobile devices becoming nearly omnipresent technologies and mobile internet penetration rising rapidly, it is now easier for more Europeans to use and access social networking sites. Mobile social networking is enabling users to be more engaged and interactive through location-based social networks and other activities, with over 190 million tweets published on Twitter every day by global users (jeffbullas.com, 2012).

Social networking is no longer a 'new' thing; it is now a part of who we are; what we do; how we see ourselves. The shift in mindsets that has been brought about by the success of social networking presents profound opportunities for governments, education service providers and community development organisations if they can harness the compliance of the general public toward social networking to create sustainable online service development and delivery networks. Taking advantage of the significant investments that have been made in developing social networking architectures and bringing the potential of social networking down to local community level is both a timely and cost-effective endeavour that education and other service providers need to consider.

1.2 Project Aims

The NetBox project aims *"to pilot and validate a model for educationally self-sufficient rural communities where traditional consumers of educational services can become producers of educational services and content"*. Through the use of the social media model, NetBox is working to develop an online learning community dedicated solely to the needs and uses of six individual rural communities across Europe. By this means, this social networking site will allow communities to identify learning needs and to find local providers and tutors who can deliver the required training. In this way, the aim of the NetBox project is to make rural communities self-sufficient in responding to the needs and demands that arise; allowing residents, businesses and local service providers to source solutions to problems locally. It is hoped that this new self-sufficiency will help to slow down local population decrease as generations of rural communities move to the larger more populace cities and centres in order to satisfy training needs or to find employment. Not only will NetBox seek to invert these demographic trends, but it will create a sense of community and ownership in the rural villages where the programme is being piloted, while also bringing the rural way-of-life into modern times, through the use of emerging technologies and up-skilling of residents.

2 Project Implementation

2.1 Building the model for project development

One of the key issues faced by the NetBox project consortium when it came to engaging with the local communities was deciding on the best way to implement the community consultation and auditing processes as outlined in the project proposal. Community development is a highly evolved practice in most Western EU Member States. There are a number of 'schools' of thought pertaining to the most appropriate community development methodologies and approaches. Two of the main competing approaches are:

- Asset Based Community Development (ABCD) – a concept that was first developed by Northwestern University, Illinois in the United States. ABCD considers local assets as the primary building blocks of sustainable community development. Building on the skills of local residents, the power of local associations, and the supportive functions of local institutions, ABCD draws upon existing community strengths to build stronger, more sustainable communities for the future. ABCD is regarded as being the best example of bottom-up community development work.
- Needs Based Community Development (NBCD) is perhaps the most widely used approach for supporting the development of sustainable communities. NBCD focuses on identifying the needs of groups at risk in disadvantaged communities and providing appropriate resources, supports and responses. NBCD is often criticised for being a top-down approach with little self-determination by communities involved.

There are a considerable volume of researches, evaluations and theses extolling the virtues of each approach as if it is essential to choose between the competing disciplines to achieve appropriate outcomes. However, there is a growing body of opinion that a mixed approach drawing on the best aspects of asset and needs based approaches produces the most sustainable and engaging results with communities and support agencies drawn equally into the process. What has not been addressed in any meaningful way is the potential impact of Web 2.0 technologies on the development and implementation of either or both community development approaches. This is the focus and the innovation behind the NetBox project.

However, trying to marry these two differing methodologies of community development together, while also incorporating the technological requirements of this project and transferring this knowledge to groups of local volunteers unversed in community development practices seemed impossible at one stage. This feat was only made possible by the development of an audit guide, induction programme and promotional materials which allowed project partners to raise awareness for the project, to recruit volunteers for the audit and to equip them with the necessary skills needed in order to undertake the community audit and get involved in NetBox.

In order to provide structure to the project, and as a means of measuring project progress, the project has been split into a series of phases: pre-development; development and exploitation and sustainability. Currently we are on the verge of beginning the development stage of the project with the majority of the research, consultation and community activation being completed in the first nine months of the project. An in-depth analysis of the tasks undertaken to date and those still to be completed in each project phase is as detailed below:

2.2 Pre-development:

The initial steps taken in this project phase were centred on community consultation. In the first months of the project, significant research was undertaken by each project partner. This research which has been collated and published by the Cypriot partner, CARDET, took the form of desk-based research, telephone interviewing and community consultation with local actors. The purpose of this report was to gauge the IT literacy of the local people and the capabilities of local IT infrastructure; to ascertain any previous audit experience of local communities groups; to provide a socio-economic profile of each rural community and also to identify best practice online learning resources and open-source resources which could be beneficial as additional supports to the NetBox communities. This research then influenced the supports that the consortium had to implement locally in order to involve all community members and to ensure the success of the NetBox project. The most significant tasks undertaken in this early phase were to engage with the local communities, recruit the volunteers and raise awareness for the project, both as a local development initiative, but also to make communities aware that this project is encouraging collaboration on a European level.

One of the first obstacles faced with the group in Oldcastle was that in order to get full use of the NetBox interface when it is developed, public computers would have to be provided and many of the residents would need up-skilling as they would not be considered computer literate. Therefore it was agreed from an early stage that there would be supports and bespoke training programmes available to these residents so that any skills deficits in this regard could be tackled. For example, under a previous Grundtvig project which Meath Partnership were the lead partner in, called *Connect in Laterlife,* a curriculum was developed for people over the age of 55 who wished to learn about social networking. This project established a social networking site, a dedicated online community for Older People in Europe, which can be found at www.connectinlaterlife.eu. Along with this social networking site, a full curriculum and suite of resources were similarly developed with the aim of helping Older People and socially disadvantaged groups to get online. These resources will be available to all partners in the consortium who are faced with similar skills deficits in their communities. In-roads are already being made in the community of Oldcastle, in Meath, Ireland to deliver this bespoke training to the first group of adult learners. This training is being provided in a dedicated NetBox office and training facility which is currently being set up by the local groups in Oldcastle in order to have a space where residents can gather information on the project, where questionnaires can be filled and where small events and training programmes can be delivered to local residents. The renovation of this office space and the purchase of computers and similar equipment is being financed through local fund-raising and a grant from Meath Partnership under the Rural Development Programme (LEADER).

Already in this community, augmenting levels of community collaboration are evident, with residents more determined to solve problems for themselves. Through this new attitude of cooperation, community members have identified a premises in the centre of Oldcastle to house their NetBox office, they have negotiated to lease this property for the duration of the project rent-free, and they have begun the application process for the public computers which they were lacking at the outset of this project. These computers when purchased will be housed in the NetBox office, free for all to use and to access.

This project phase has also been important for the community groups. During this time induction sessions were held at which capacity building was at the forefront for the local volunteers. The session coordinator, with the aid of the induction programme and audit guide, was able to equip all participants with the skills and competences necessary to undertake a comprehensive community asset and needs audit, while also drawing up a strategy of how this could be achieved. By adopting the method of participatory action research, volunteers have spent the summer months drafting questionnaires, and meeting with service providers, businesses and residents from their village to complete these questionnaires, and to analyse the data collected. In total, local researchers have surveyed at least 20% of residents, 50% of businesses and 33.3% of service providers in their local villages. This data has provided the research team and the project partners with a qualitative and quantitative overview of the needs and demands of these three community cohorts. The sample of residents, businesses and service providers surveyed are taken as a microcosm for the needs of all in the NetBox communities, and will be used and referenced continually for content acquisition, development and design for the learning social network platform.

2.3 Development:

Beginning with the completion of the community audit phase at the end of September, the first action in the development stage will be for partners to undertake further research to identify the most appropriate learning content to address the educational needs and harness the educational assets as reflected in the community audit report. As well as identifying the content for this online learning model, consortium-wide and country-specific resources will also be identified and developed to aid the learning of each local community.

While these are important steps in ensuring that content on the social networking site is relevant to local communities and address their needs, considering the level of consultation and development work the consortium has undergone, it is easy to overlook the fact that NetBox, while a community development project, is primarily a technology-based project. For this reason, the main deliverable from this project is the online learning social network. This is the key deliverable from the development phase. The consortium is expected to produce a pilot version of this platform by November 2012, with the final version of the site being launched in October 2013. To accompany this technology platform, an instructional DVD and manual will also be developed by the consortium and will be made available in August 2013 for dissemination to community groups. These groups will be involved in constant testing and consultation regarding the features and accessibility of this learning platform, until the final version is agreed. As well as housing an online collaborative zone, where residents, businesses and service providers can network and learn together, this site will also incorporate a language learning laboratory for all six communities.

As well as having a generic social network architecture behind the 'NetBox' portal, it is also important for the individual pilot communities to create a sense of ownership of their individual 'NetBoxes', and for this reason, and to encourage sustainability of the social networking site once the project development period has ceased, each community will train selected individuals on how to maintain the social media site. This information will be invaluable to the local communities chosen, and will help in a wider roll-out of the NetBox project in the regions of each project partner. NetBox has the potential to change the way that targeted community development and training opportunities are presented to local communities.

There is a sense in this project that communities are being given the opportunities to help and educate themselves; to develop their own communities as they see fit. This is being ensured through the constant community interaction and consultation with local groups, businesses, schools and residents. In order to achieve a point where the communities will take ownership of 'the NetBox' they need to be involved in the design of the platform, and the features which will be included on the site; the site has to be relevant to them. Not only will this site act as a tool where people can learn, and can network with each other both on a personal and professional level, it can also be used as an information point which will advertise local events, charities, business offers, etc. The NetBox project has the potential to add to the tapestry of the internet, by mapping these rural villages across Europe and giving them their own dedicated space on the World Wide Web.

The unique opportunities awarded to the NetBox communities are undeniable. Thanks to this pioneering learning portal, users will not only have the chance to create new learning opportunities, build on their own skills and assets, and enhance local community spirit; it also gives them an opportunity to promote their local towns and the assets it holds to a world-wide audience, boosting networking and tourism links across Europe. This was identified as a great motivation to local groups who have seen the level of tourism decline in their areas since the economic recession. The focus of this innovative project is seen locally as a complete revival of community development and education practices; a renewal of community spirit and vigour to direct one's own fate and to make things happen again in the community. The linking of these six communities will lead to European networks and collaborations developing from history projects with the young children attending primary school to social networking and online gaming with the Active Retirement Groups; the project opens the door to Europe for these rural communities who until now have felt remote, cut-off and forgotten.

Already NetBox has a presence online. The project website, which can be found at www.netboxproject.eu, was published in January 2012, and is available in 8 partner languages: English, Portuguese, Polish, Romanian, Lithuanian,

Finnish, German and Greek. This website contains information on the project, the partners involved and offers 'news items' which keep people updated on project progress. This website is updated regularly, and documents the significant milestones reached in the project to date.

When developing the idea for forming these Community Learning Social Networks, one of the key issues that were raised was how the consortium would mediate the transition of traditional consumers of education to those capable of delivering training and mentoring programmes. It was decided that the best model for this was a 'Train the Trainer' courseware, which would be delivered to the intended tutors through a blended learning approach. This will be facilitated through online tutorials, and face-to-face training events and study group sessions. This courseware will be called 'Induction to Pedagogy' and will be available to the first group of trainees from April 2013. Partners are aware that allowing this transition from training 'consumer' to 'provider' may in-turn produce quality control issues; however it has been agreed by the consortium that if and when these issues arise, a suitable framework will be devised in consultation with local tutors. The training programmes offered by these new tutors will then be monitored by each partner to ensure a high standard of training provision.

2.4 Exploitation and Sustainability

Similarly to the pre-development and development phases of the project, there are many steps involved in the exploitation and ensuring the sustainability of the NetBox project. However, it is worth noting that while this is the final project phase, the dissemination and exploitation of project results began at the very outset of the project. With the publication of promotional materials, a project pull-up display and a project leaflet, the aims and objectives of the project have been disseminated from very early on. The project website has been an important tool for this, as it not only offers information on the project in 8 European languages, but it provides the contact details for all local partners for those interested in getting involved in NetBox.

On-going activities in this phase include the quarterly publication of an online newsletter which is sent to a database of contacts for each of the 9 project partners, ensuring the wide dispersal of project aims, objectives and achievements to date. Furthermore, partners have held local dissemination workshops, with one held in February 2012, to engage with all groups at a local level, and a further workshop scheduled for April 2013. This second dissemination event will target specifically national actors and policy-makers in the six partner countries where NetBox is being piloted. At this event the community learning social network platform will be presented, along with the full suite of tools and supplementary resources, for feedback from these national stakeholders and revision by project partners. The supplementary resources to be developed include online web tutorials detailing how to maintain the site, and a series of video documentaries which will capture the experiences of local actors throughout the project cycle. Innoventum Oy, the Finnish partner, will develop the series of online tutorials to train partners in maintaining and updating the project website thereby ensuring that the website can be maintained in all partner languages after the project has ended. Both will be published online via the social networking platform.

As was previously mentioned, moderator training will be held in May 2013, and will provide training for at least six people from the six rural communities to be able to update and maintain the learning social network once the project development phase has concluded. This is a vital step in ensuring the sustainability of the NetBox site once the project funding period has ended. Further to this it is also expected that by October 2013, 100 users from the 6 villages will participate in educational programmes via the learning social network. This initial training, coupled with the projection that 20% of residents, 50% of business and 33.3% of service providers will register accounts on the site also by October 2013 should ensure the continued use of this innovative platform in the future.

There are also a number of additional measures proposed to support sustainability and exploitation. A business plan for the Community Learning Social Networks will be developed to sustain the networks into the future examining potential for corporate or statutory sponsorship. Each Local Management Group will enter at least one trans-national Online Twinning Agreement sustaining the potential for collaboration between residents, service providers and businesses. Service Level Agreements will be signed by service providers confirming their intention to utilise the new learning platforms created. It is expected that considerable exploitation can be achieved through this action as over time the Community Learning Social Networks will provide significant value-for-money to service providers encouraging them to support the establishment of new networks in other rural areas. In keeping with the social entrepreneur ethos of partners an IPR Agreement will confirm that access to all the tools and resources developed is available to potential future users on a free-of-change basis.

Project partners are keen to ensure that potential future users of the model are fully aware of what it is that the consortium did; why it did it; how it achieved its results. Therefore the final NetBox pack for distribution will include all documents, handbooks and technology architectures. This pack will be distributed to umbrella organisations to harness their potential to support exploitation through their vast networks in Member States.

Lastly, the final two deliverables under this project phase include the Project Summary document, and the Final Valorisation Conference. The Project Summary will comprise a concise overview of the development history of the project, the key target groups, the main aims and objectives and the methodology employed to achieve the project outputs. It will also contain case studies from each relevant partner country and it will be available in all partner languages. The Final Conference will be held in Poland in October 2013, and will be attended by up to 100 people. At this event all project outputs and tools will be launched and will be available for use. Project Summary and the Final Conference will act as the conclusive activities of an innovative project that has been well-planned, developed, delivered and disseminated, with the relevant training and expertise passed on to ensure the longevity and continuing success of NetBox in Europe.

3 Conclusion

The knowledge-intensive economy continues its rapid evolution placing significant premiums on higher skill-sets throughout the work-force. However, with 70% of those who will comprise the EU work-force in 2020 already finished their formal education the demand for new skills will continue to place additional pressure on providers of formal and informal education services.

Active take up of social computing has an impact on public services such as government, the health sector and education and training (Osimo, 2008; Ala-Mutka, 2008; Punie, 2008; Redecker, 2008, Cachia et al, 2007). Social computing tools are developing fast and continuously creating new communities around them. These new communities and technological platforms are important places for learning ICT and other skills, as they gather the knowledge of different users and motivate new people to learn (Ala-Mutka et al, 2008; Punie & Ala-Mutka, 2007). There is a need to develop sites for specific target groups that can easily be shared between Informal learners.

When it comes to education, the point is not anymore if technology platforms and online environments should be used, but rather how, where and for what activity. The project consortium believes that it has identified an innovative, multi-faceted model for the development and provision of community-based education, centred on blending the best elements of two diverse tried and tested community development approaches and bringing them to life in bespoke social networking environments.

Individually, none of the components of NetBox represent next generation innovation in the provision of educational services. Collectively, however, the merging of best practice from ABCD and NBCD approaches; the utilisation of accepted social networking norms and structures; and the provision of bespoke induction training and online learning resources represents a considerable new departure that can transform traditional consumers of educational services into producers of educational content and services. This project is currently working towards the development of a model for educationally self-sufficient communities where the educational needs of individuals and the community as a whole are satisfied by harnessing available skills and experiences within the community; where partnerships of individuals and institutions work together to develop local services and businesses; where older residents can support their younger counterparts; where experienced residents can mentor and support those embarking on new careers; where graduates can share their knowledge; where those who have been through the rigours of life can advise and support those on the threshold of independence. These innovations in education provision and delivery are the pioneering advances of the NetBox project.

As most rural communities are microcosms of society as a whole they contain all the instances of disadvantage, marginalisation and social exclusion that one regularly encounters throughout society. It is worth also stressing that these communities also contain most of the skills, knowledge and experience to address these issues. The major deficit inhibiting the realisation of self-sufficient communities is the lack of coherent strategies for engagement and mobilisation of resources. The approach proposed by NetBox has never been tried in any of the participating countries and represents a considerable innovation. As the project consortium and local communities work towards achieving these ambitious objectives the potential for exploitation of the model developed will be considerable.

Throughout Europe, access for all and equality of opportunity for all are accepted policy and philosophical benchmarks in education. Promoting the adoption and prioritizing the implementation, of non-discriminatory practices are high on education governance agendas. With 70% of all Europeans living in rural areas, it can be extrapolated that 70% of all aspiring learners also live in rural areas. While education providers in urban areas draw on significant population densities and attract large learner populations education providers in rural settings are required to provide services across much larger territories resulting in more limited resources available to people on the ground. So while educational policy and philosophy might promote equal access and opportunity in many cases these aspirations are not the deciding factor. The fact is that geography and demography discriminate, and access to educational services and supports in rural communities is significantly reduced when compared to their urban counterparts.

Partners are vastly experienced in their respective fields and are fully aware of the current status of adult education provision in their respective countries. Given the different stages of development between partner countries this project has also allowed for considerable opportunities for exchange of best practice leading to innovation at a local level. On entering this consortium all partners were of the opinion that more could be done to harness the potential of modern technologies to address some of the short-comings of traditional adult education provision and to reach a wider, more isolated rural population. The consortium agreed that there was a need for extensive innovation in this sector in order to achieve the desired self-sufficient community; however they did not see the need to create a new technology or new platform to pilot this project. Considering how adept people are to using social networking both on their computers and on the go through mobile devices, there was little sense in introducing a new platform to test this ambitious project on, when a perfectly suitable one, with which a large percentage of the population are already familiar, already exists.

The potential of NetBox is immeasurable. It not only has the ability to transform the model of community and adult education, it is challenging the traditional views that rural populations hold regarding further education. On the success of NetBox no longer will members of these communities believe that they must leave their towns and villages and either commute or move to a more populace area in order to satisfy their educational needs. While all required assets may not be found in the community, with this change in mindset and the encouragement of networking across the community, local people will be more prone to problem-solving and so will be more likely to seek resolutions to any issues they may have at a local level or through the networks which are being developed. The innovation behind this project cannot merely be measured through the marriage of new technologies with pioneering improvements in community education, but in the changes that it is evoking in the mindset of these rural communities; instilling confidence and restoring a sense of 'community' once again in these rural villages.

References

Ala-Mutka, Kirsti. (2008). Social Computing: Use and Impacts of Collaborative Content.

Ala-Mutka, Kirsti; Punie, Yves; Redecker, Christine. (2008). ICT for Learning, Innovation and Creativity. Policy Brief, pp.1-4

Ala-Mutka, Kirsti; Punie, Yves; Redecker, Christine. (2008). Digital Competence for Lifelong Learning. Policy Brief, pp.1-4

Bullas, Jeff. (2012). 20 Stunning Social Media Statistics Plus Infographic. Accessed at http://www.jeffbullas.com/2011/09/02/20-stunning-social-media-statistics/;

Cachia, Romina, et al. (2007). ICT, Social Capital and Cultural Diversity.

comScore. (2007). Social Networking Goes Global. Press Release, Accessed at http://www.comscore.com/Press_Events/Press_Releases/2007/07/Social_Networking_Goes_Global

comScore (2012). EU5 Map Usage via Smartphone Growing 7x Faster Than Classic Web. Accessed at

http://www.comscore.com/Press_Events/Press_Releases/2012/5/EU5_Map_Usage_via_Smartphone_Growing

comScore. (2012). It's a Social World: Top 10 Need-to-Knows About Social Networking and Where it is Headed. pp 4-69

comScore. (2012). 2012 Mobile Future in Focus. pp 44-47

Osimo, David. (2008). Web 2.0 in Government: Why and How?

Punie, Yves. (ed.) (2008). The Socio-economic Impact of Social Computing.

Short Papers

selected and approved after double-blind peer review
by the Scientific Programme Committee

Language e-Learning Tools for Vocations

Monika Nowakowska-Twaróg

Globalnet sp. z o.o. Poland, 20/18a Ratajczaka Street
monika@globalnet.com.pl

Abstract: The goal of the presented project "Language e-learning tool for vocations- share the standards" is to develop innovation with respect to the vocational language learning and to introduce standardization in the vocational language learning. Products developed in the course of that project are language courses and e-learning solutions. The project aims at working out an effective model for teaching vocational languages, along with the tools and techniques to facilitate the process (an e-learning tool). These vocational language courses are based on Common European Framework of Reference for Languages and are related to the Language Competence Framework of Reference for the Vocations. They introduce and work out standardization in the vocational language learning. Several vocations (cook, psychologist, footwear worker, graphic designer) and several languages have been taken into account. Also those less known and less frequently used languages in order to support and promote language diversity in the European Union. The project presented has been funded with support from the European Commission under the Lifelong Learning Programme Leonardo da Vinci. The base for the project realization is the cooperation between language teachers involved in the project and the industry experts. The language tests writers and language teachers aren't familiar with the industry jargon and they need constant exposure to that language and to the documentation of that profession as well as frequent contact with its users.

1 Background

The general idea of lifelong learning is to make the process coherent and cohesive, which means that citizens may combine and build on their learning from school to university, and all this learning should be recognised and identified in the same way in all Member States. Recognition in all EU countries is crucial when the European citizenship and free movement within the EU are concerned. There are some institutions in the EU that coordinate and help to assess the learners' qualifications on the basis of diplomas and certificates they possess. One of them is The European Credit Transfer System, which ensures transparency, manages the recognition of the studies and diplomas, and creates an Open European area of education and training where students and teachers can move without obstacles.

The Commission's Action Plan for skills and mobility called for instruments supporting the transparency and transferability of qualifications to be developed and strengthened to facilitate mobility within and between sectors.[15] The EU also called for action to increase transparency in vocational education and training, through the implementation and rationalisation of information tools and networks, including the integration of existing instruments into one single framework.[16] This framework for the transparency of qualifications and competences (Europass) should consist in a portfolio of documents with a common brand name and a common logo, supported by adequate information systems and promoted through sustained promotional action at European and national level.

A number of instruments have been developed in recent years, both at the Community and at the international level, to help European citizens to recognize better their qualifications and competences when looking for a job or for admission to a learning scheme. These include the following: the common European format for curricula vitae (CVs); the Diploma Supplement recommended by the Convention on the Recognition of Qualifications concerning Higher Education in the European Region; the Europass Training on the promotion of European pathways in work-linked training, including apprenticeship; the Certificate Supplement and the European Language Portfolio developed by the Council of Europe.

The European Commission has regarded language learning and teaching as a priority for over 30 years. Every European citizen should be able to communicate in at least two foreign languages in addition to his/her mother tongue. This is the objective the European Union is striving for. The Common European Framework of Reference for Languages (CEF) is a document which describes in a comprehensive manner the competences necessary for communication, the related knowledge and skills, and the situations and domains of communication. The CEF defines levels of language proficiency in different aspects and provides a detailed description of each language level and accompanying skills. The main

---

[15] Cf. Recommendation of the European Parliament and of the Council of 18 December (2006: 1).

[16] Cf. The Council Resolution of 19 December 2002 on the promotion of enhanced European cooperation in vocational education and training (2002).

aim of the CEF is to achieve greater unity among the EU members. Language learning in Member States should be compatible with the CEF's assumptions which provide a basis for the mutual recognition of language qualifications, thus facilitating educational and occupational mobility. The CEF is being increasingly used in the reforms of national curricula and by international consortia for the comparison of language certificates. The European Union Council's Resolution (Nov 2001) recommended the use of this Council of Europe instrument in setting up systems of validation of language competences.

2 Goals of the project

The project is striving for creation the vocational language courses that follow the aforementioned ideas. Specific goals are, inter alia, the followings:

- to develop professional skills of teachers
- to make students more competitive
- to enable the employees who would like to work in various European countries to obtain transparent and standardised language competence certification for their specific vocational field
- to help organisations such as employment agencies, labour offices and employers' organisations to evaluate the language proficiency of foreign workers who are seeking employment
- to teach European vocational languages online: Italian, English, Greek, Polish, Portuguese
- to improve the accessibility to lifelong learning for vocations by presenting the status of vocational learners in partnership countries, difficulties they encounter, and by presenting joint solutions
- to provide vocational learners with tools to improve their knowledge and competence in order to avoid their social exclusion and help them enter and re-enter the job market
- to facilitate the cooperation between partners' organizations by organizing partnership meetings, with the aim of setting up closer partnerships and implement the project
- to improve existing pedagogical approaches to lifelong learning in order to include more vocational learners into this process by developing teaching materials, methods and techniques.

3 The origin of the project

The project is based on the LCCTV project whose main product is the Manual containing (1) the LCCTV Methodology for Designing Employment-Specific Language Tests, (2) the Language Competence Framework of Reference for the Vocations (LCFRV), and (3) several Appendices illustrating the implementation of the Methodology and the Framework. There are several Manual Translations: Bulgarian, German, Spanish, Turkish. Additionally, some sample language testing material has been produced in line with the LCCTV Methodology and Framework for the vocational fields of Construction and Seafaring. The second major result of the project is a two-level course book, *English for Mariners*, providing sector-specific vocational language learning material at basic and intermediate level.

This is an innovative multilateral project. The innovative nature of the project lies in the form of support, i.e. it relates to an approach that has not previously been used in Poland, Greece, Italy and Portugal in the area of vocational language learning and standardization of vocational language learning. The project is also innovative in that it combines these specific trainings with modern ICT technologies. Local trainings so far have been addressing training problems of the general audience, not of particular vocations (in the partnership countries).

All the courses are designed for learners with at least A2 level of foreign language knowledge, the courses will be correlated with the Commmon European Framework. They cover A2 and go towards B1. The language courses (student books) provide approximately 60 hours of core teaching material. The textbooks contain a balanced quantity of grammar, pronunciation with an emphasis put on vocational vocabulary. They equip students with skills necessary to get them speak the foreign language with confidence. The course book is for young adults and adults who want to learn to communicate effectively. Based on communicative approach, it combines different methodologies in order to make learning and teaching easier. In the process of the creation of the course many aspects will be taken into consideration: target groups (characteristics, age, education, social context), their knowledge of the foreign language, their attitudes, motivation.

The content of the textbooks, that is topics, grammar, vocabulary, functions, skills etc., should reflect the overall aims of the course. Apart from that, topics are related to users' interests and the content is meaningful for them. The teacher may adapt the content of the book so that the topics are more personalized and of interest for the course participants. The textbook includes topics that are especially motivating for students, such as those connected with the target language country and culture as well as humorous elements.

The compiled courses are translated and transformed into partners' languages and are adjusted to the conditions of the particular countries. The aim of the project is also to promote less known languages (Polish, Greek), to translate courses into those languages with the aim of teaching people those languages. Next, the language courses are transformed into e-learning courses, to create a virtual school with students, teachers and different professions, to make this e-learning platform and vocational language courses more available, acceptable, with an interesting layout and graphic design in order to keep the teachers' and students' attention through the whole course.

The e-learning platform structure consists of content and assessment, with media content (simulations, demos, audio, graphics) and testing script (navigation, links, user volume).The e-learning platform is created with the aim of being constantly developed (content and structure development), so that it can benefit from the most up to date pedagogical approaches to e-learning. It is made in a way that the potential user can easily move through it, learn, practice language skills, self-test and observe his /her progress. The structure of the platform is easily accessible with an assumption that the audience has no previous experience with a similar application.

There will be several updates to this application, the updates will not require training from users.

Innovative Life Long Learning for Construction Personnel across EU

Paweł O. Nowak, Jacek P. Zawistowski

Warsaw University of Technology, Civil Engineering Faculty
Armii Ludowej 16, 00-637 Warsaw, Poland
p.nowak@il.pw.edu.pl, jz@il.pw.edu.pl

Abstract: Paper presents assumptions, goals and results of the Leonardo da Vinci (LdV) projects. The main task of the projects was to deepen and improve Directive's ideas, which lead to creation of proper European system of comparison, certification and mutual recognition of managerial qualifications in construction, as well as increasing of learning quality by creation of the innovative training tools (for example augmented reality).

Keywords: education, distance learning, management, innovation, training quality.

1 Introduction

Authors are members of research teams for several EU funded projects connected with education of construction personnel in Europe. This paper presents the following projects: A) - LdV CLOEMC I, II, III projects (No: PL/06/B/P/PP/174014; 2009-1-PL1-LEO05-05016; 2011-1-PL1-LEO05-19888) titled: "Common Learning Outcomes for European Managers in Construction" related to the creation of the Construction Managers Library, for better recognition of managerial qualification in construction industry; B) - LdV MAIN.CON project (No: 2010-1-ES1-LEO05-20930), titled: "Augmented Reality Applied to Machinery Maintenance from Construction Sector" related to the creation of innovative system facilitating construction machinery maintenance, with use of the basis for augmented reality; C) - LdV TRAIN-TO-CAP project (No: 2010-1-PL1-LEO05-11469), titled: "Strengthening of European Union funds absorption capacity for infrastructure construction projects" related to the creation of blended learning courses at internet platform, courses related to risk management in construction; D) - LdV SHANIME project (No: 2011-1-TR1-LEO05-27941), titled: "Preventing Accidents in Construction – Health and Safety

Multimedia Animated Learning" related to the courses and materials which increase the safety in construction.

2 Leonardo da Vinci CLOEMC project

Project is based on European Directive nr 89/48/EWG on regulated professions in respect to scope of recognition, maintain of high standard in professional disciplines, promotion and certification of qualifications by international associations and organizations – also from construction sector. General works on the project were started in 1998 with recognition of educational system within construction industry in Poland and other European Countries. The main task of the project is to deepen and improve ideas mentioned in the directive, which will lead to creation of European system of comparison, certification and mutual recognition of managerial qualifications in construction. In order to fully take advantage from results of previous LdV funded Project, there is a necessity to create set of manuals, as a follow-up activity. The manuals will allow process of standardization in EU countries of certification process of engineers applying for the title of EurBE (European Building Expert). The EurBE title was developed by AEEBC (The Association of European Building Surveyors & Construction Experts, with headquarter in Brussels, Belgium). AEEBC associates management in construction related associations from numerous European countries (Belgium, Denmark, Finland, France, Germany, Ireland, Italy, The Netherlands, Poland, Spain, Sweden, United Kingdom, http://aeebc.org/). Department of Construction Engineering and Management, Warsaw University of Technology, Faculty of Civil Engineering was the promoter of the project, and list of Partners can be found here: www.leonardo.il.pw.edu.pl. First set of manuals was created (in CLOEMC I), called Construction Manager Library (CML), consisting of 7 books, available at the Polish bookstores: M1 - Project Management, M2 - Human Resources Management, M3 - Strategic Collaborative Working/Partnering in Construction, M4 - Business Management in Construction Enterprises, M5 - Facilities Management in Construction, M6 - Economy and Financial Management in Construction, M7 - Construction Management. The set of books was highly graded by external experts and representatives of the construction industry. Second set of manuals was created for CML in CLOEMC II project, consisting of: M8 - Risk Management in Construction, M9 – Processes Management and Lean Construction, M10 - Computer Methods in Management of Construction Projects, M11 - PPP projects in Construction, M12 - Value Management in Construction, M13 - Best Practice in Construction Projects. New Manuals (in CLOEMC III) for CML will be ready in the late 2013 (this new project, related to the soft elements of management): M14 - Due-diligence in Construction, M15 - Motivation and Psychology Aspects in Construction Industry, M16 - Professionalism and Ethics in Construction, M17 - Sustainability in Construction, M18 - Health and Safety in Construction, M19 - Pathology in Construction. Set of manuals will be used also for teaching purposes, carried out in English language for students in many European countries. That will allow increase of mobility among students going on scholarships in Erasmus programs; self-education by CPD of construction industry personnel; facilitation of the process of standardization (in all 17 countries associated in AEEBC, and other also) of certification process of engineers applying for the title of EurBE.

3 Leonardo da Vinci MAIN.CON project

MAIN.CON project Promoter is the Labour Foundation for the Construction Sector, Spain, list od other Partners can be found here: www.mainconproject.eu. The aim of the Leonardo da Vinci MAIN.COM project is to design and apply a training system in basic machinery maintenance using a new technology called augmented reality (combination of reality and virtual reality). This system will improve the basic skills of machinery operators related with a safe maintenance of their machines and not only with their operation. MAIN.CON project consist of several general tasks related to the analysis of construction earthworks machinery, than creation of a map of basic skills in machinery maintenance, and finally development of the software and hardware based on Augmented Reality for maintenance training. All products of the project were tested and evaluated. Full, usable version of the Augmented Reality system for machines operators should be ready at the end of the year 2012.

4 Leonardo da Vinci Train to Cap (TTC) project

Full title of the LdV project, realized by Polish Association of Construction Industry Employers (PZPB) and Warsaw University of Technology is: "Strengthening of European Union funds absorption capacity for infrastructure construction projects". Full list of Partners and additional information can be found here: www.traintocap.eu. The main problem being tackled is to increase EU funds absorption in infrastructure construction projects in EU Members Countries and countries entering the Union. The aims of the project are to: minimize problems connected with disputes and claims in infrastructure construction projects; increase transparency of procedures in risk management and claims processes and; increase the access to trainings throughout MOODLE in informal vocational education. Foreseen Project's products are as follows: training manual concerning risk management, training manual concerning claims and disputes management, two training courses for each of manuals with use of MOODLE platform (Multi Object Oriented Dynamic Learning Environment), manual for tutors with methodology of the courses.

5 Leonardo da Vinci SHANIME Project

Another important project for education of EU construction managers is LdV project titled: "Preventing Accidents in Construction – Health and Safety Multimedia   Animated   Learning"   (2011-1-TR1-LEO05-27941, www.css.anadolu.edu.tr/shanime).   According   to   International   Labour Organization data, annually 1.2 million people lose their life because of occupational illnesses and industrial accidents. The construction industry is one of the most risky sectors for industrial accidents and occupational illnesses all over the world. According to statistics, the accident rates in this industry are one of the highest across all over the industries. To prevent accidents, construction workers must be well educated about health & safety. However, the majority of health and safety trainings given to construction workers are theoretical trainings. Since the majority of the construction workers have a low education level, it becomes difficult for them to learn the concepts of health & safety with this kind of trainings. Therefore, the animations that will be prepared in this project are highly vital for the contribution to health and safety trainings in construction industry. Learning by animations has been used in several areas. Animations have the potential to make trainings more attractive and enjoyable, and can significantly facilitate learning. Thus, a more effective tool will be performed for health & safety trainings with these animations. The animations that show construction accidents can be used in health and safety trainings in construction industries for reducing accidents causing death and major injuries. SHANIME aims to prepare animations that show construction accidents. These animations can be used in health and safety trainings in construction industries to minimize accidents causing death and major injuries. Learning the health and safety concepts with theoretical trainings are quite difficult for these low educated workers. Animations have the potential to make trainings more attractive and enjoyable, and can significantly facilitate learning. Furthermore, the products of this project can be a guide for other industries such as manufacturing and mining in which accidents are also a major problem.

6 Summary

Leonardo da Vinci program facilitates education of the construction personnel, leading for development of the modern learning techniques, increasing availability and accessibility of the training and raising the quality of education.

References

Minasowicz, A., Nowak P. Final report. Development of New Type of Studies and Courses in the Field of Management in Construction for Engineers According to the Requirements of European Union, Warsaw, Manchester, Porto, 2002-2010.

WP II Report. Recognition of needs and creation of professional training in the area of management of infrastructure construction projects, Leonardo da Vinci Project number PL/04/B/P/PP/-174 417, 2005.

LDV MAIN.CON Leonardo da Vinci project (No: 2010-1-ES1-LEO05-20930), titled: "Augmented Reality Applied to Machinery Maintenance from Construction Sector" draft working materials, Warsaw, Madrid, 2011.

Project Presentations

selected and approved after Open Call for Presentations

AGRICOM: Transfer of the Water Competences Model to AGRIcultural COMpetences

Main goal of the project AGRICOM is the transfer and population of the WACOM Water Competence Model (WCM) from the Water Sector to the Agricultural Sector.

Main objectives of AGRICOM are identifying and analysing targeted needs and competences that are required by the labour market for specific use cases and jobs from several fields of the agricultural sector, transferring and adapting the generic WACOM competence model towards the AGRICOM competence model (ACM) allowing more agricultural use cases, pilot testing the ACM to the jobs specialisations related to agricultural uses of water resources (irrigation, hydroponics, etc).

Main target groups of the project are representatives in vocational education and training in the agricultural sector and in particular in the fields of irrigation and hydroponics.

AGRICOM introduces the competence modelling to the agricultural sector to strengthen the transparency and comparability of VET opportunities through the transfer of WCM and the adaptation of ECVET and EQF. AGRICOM establishes the first competence model for Hydroponics and Irrigation Management to be applied and validated for the management of Irrigation Management and subsequently be transferred to other fields of the water sector as well as to other branches.

The presentation, the sharing and re-use of skills and competence information is an important and necessary step towards outcome-based education and training and is most important for learning innovations and quality today.

More information about the AGRICOM project is at:
www.agriculture-competence.eu/

AMaP: Age Management in Practice

The Age Management in Practice (AMaP) project is a collaborative partnership funded by the Leonardo da Vinci Lifelong Learning Programme. The project aims to address the challenge around access to, and participation in, Continuing Vocational Education and Training (CVET) among older workers aged 50+, and to increase awareness of the European Qualification Framework (EQF). The project also considers the challenge of an ageing workforce through the lens of employers, seeking current views and attitudes towards older workers and promotes the implementation of age management practices.

Main target groups of the project are Older Workers; Employers; Policy Makers.

Given the ageing challenge, more consideration should be given to widening learning and career opportunity. To achieve this, a quality model is required for engaging and supporting older workers in making the most of lifelong learning and understanding the value of VET. This is the key purpose of the AMaP project.

Main outcomes of the project are development of a learner engagement model for older workers aged 50+ and improvement of knowledge and awareness among older workers of the European Qualification Framework (EQF). Furthermore, carry out an employer's survey to measure awareness of the ageing workforce and attitudes towards older workers as well as organising seminars for employers on age management and the creation of a DVD of employer views.

Innovation and quality related to learning programmes for older workers that allow them to continue working and contributing to the European economy longer and later in life.

ARISTOTELE: Personalised Learning & Collaborative Working Environments Fostering Social Creativity and Innovations inside the Organisations

Aim and objectives of the project:

ARISTOTELE aims at enhancing learning and training of the workers within their organisations through the support of the emergence of competences and creativity. In particular, the objective of the ARISTOTELE project is to impact on the following five areas:

- Learning and Training by improving learning and training processes tailored to knowledge worker needs and expectations
- Human Resource Management by supporting Human Resource development, team formation, allocation, recruitment
- Collaboration by improving collaboration among workers using social approach and sharing knowledge
- Knowledge Management by improving the knowledge management practices
- Innovation by fostering innovation process

Main target groups of the project

The target groups of the ARISTOTELE project are medium and large enterprises

How does your project contribute to learning innovations and/or learning quality?

A key point of ARISTOTELE project is a new way to conceive the relation among knowledge flows, the organization learning objectives, and creativity by:

- combining adaptive learning strategies with "non-adaptive" emergent competence change.

- combining personalised experiential learning and vicarious learning, based on serendipitous exploitation of someone else's knowledge, made available via the social network.

- providing a methodological and technological support for self-organizing acquisition, processing and sharing of new information and knowledge with peers, via the Personal Work Learning Environment (PWLE).

What are your main outcomes?

The main outcomes of ARISTOTELE project are:

- Ontological models for representing enterprise assets, worker's competences and preferences, and the didactical approaches.

- Methodologies for: automatic extraction and alignment of knowledge; creation of innovation factories; decision support to human resource management; automatic generation of learning experience;

- Tools implementing the methodologies and the ARISTOTELE platform integrating such tools.

A short quote: What is most important for learning innovations and quality today?

Supporting collaborative learning using personalisation and adaptive learning experiences.

More information about the ARISTOTELE project is at:
http://www.aristotele-ip.eu/

DECIDE-IT

The goal of DECIDE-IT is to create an innovative, easily used teaching methodology that improves learners' capabilities when they are forced to take decisions in conditions of stress.

Main target group of the project is the business world interested in the final product of the project. Narrowing the focus, we will concentrate our efforts towards the involvement of such professionals that could benefit from the use of our product:

- Managers who act as main characters in communicational and decision making processes;
- Corporate executives who have to deal with complex situations under stressful conditions.

By designing a multiplayer role game aimed at training hard decision making skills within an educational strategy that will be experience-based, simulating stressful situations without exposing learners to the risks they might involve. To this end the project will adopt a blended approach, mixing classical training with tutor-supervised virtual role-playing in an online 2D environment.

The main project outcomes is a tight coupling between the designed game and the adopted methodology so to create an effective blended approach easily customizable an adaptable to the various learning needs. The project will take an existing multiplayer online serious game (DREAD-ED) originally designed to train personnel involved in the management of natural and industrial disasters, and adapt it for use in management training.

Providing learners with an experience the most similar to the real working contexts they face everyday so to guarantee a high grade learning opportunity.

More information about the DECIDE-IT project is at http://www.decide-it.eu/

eLiS: E-Learning in Studienbereichen[17] / E-Learning across campus

E-Learning offers are differently spread across university. In several disciplines, interactive tasks are available in electronic form, while others stick to learning management systems for file and data deposition only. Widespread implementation of E-Learning requires harmonized activities on different levels:

- technical development: A central goal of eLiS is the combination of existing educational platforms and tools as well as basic IT services to a consistent system. The E-Learning platform (moodle), the campus management system (based on HIS), along with storage, email, library applications and other campus services are integrated to a consistent, personal learning environment (PLE). It supports core processes in teaching and learning in a transparent and intuitive manner. This PLE is extended by additional components, e.g. an e-portfolio solution and social community tools.

- content development: In collaboration with media and data centres of the university, high quality teaching and learning material is produced and offered. Dedicated staff with high expertise in didactical and technical issues of media production is provided. Thus, sustainable content is created, enabling teachers and students to focus on their endeavour for knowledge and to maintain their campus routines.

- organizational development: Various processes and organizational structures for identification, design and use of E-Learning content and methods are proposed.

eLiS provides E-Learning coordinators in all faculties. They identify existing needs and elaborate valid methods, considering local players, topics, workflows and

---

[17] could be translated to English as: E-Learning across campus

structures. Thus, E-Learning can be established in an interdisciplinary and subject-specific manner. Cultural changes are initialized within the faculties.

These activities are accompanied by systematic quality management. It is based on a structured analysis of requirements. For this purpose, a web-based interface for all members of the university was established. They can describe so-called user stories, along with acceptance criteria that make requested parameters measurable to be compliant. This is followed by field tests of developed offers with relevant target groups and institutions, as well as in continuous evaluations throughout their use.

Main target groups of the project are learners (by improving the quality of educational offers, especially in overloaded disciplines) and teachers (especially those interested in E-Learning who did not yet feel ready to implement own offers).

This project contributes to learning innovations and learning quality using

- systematic approach to combine activities on different levels: development of IT-infrastructure, organizational structure, and content,
- conceptual integration of quality management (from requirements analysis to evaluation) throughout development process.

The main outcomes of this project are:

- local E-Learning coordinators exploiting the special needs and adjusting support mechanisms to the culture of single disciplines
- central support teams and training for various aspects of E-Learning: didactics, media production, and IT
- compilation of "lighthouse projects" and dissemination across campus, informing and motivating other teachers
- web-based tool for crowd-sourcing of system requirements, largely involving students, teachers, and staff
- prototype of personal learning environment to be completed within next years

eLiS consortium's answer on the question, what is most important for learning innovations and quality today, is: Innovation is unbounded creativity. Quality assurance is structure and rules. The challenge is to integrate both.

EnEf: Energy Efficiency in the Building Sector, a Sustainable Future

EnEf project (Energy Efficiency in the Building Sector, a sustainable future) aims at improving energy efficiency in buildings alleviating the lack of knowledge of entrepreneurs and managers of the building industry. Specific objective is to build up new methodologies and training modules concerning energy efficiency in buildings, delivered through an interactive e-learning platform and enriched by a simulation tool.

Direct target group are European SMEs active in the building sector and particularly micro enterprises, directly involved in the development and validation of the training system.

The project intends to be innovative in the way the training is delivered: the coordinator uses the new-coined word "VISEDUCATION", a matching of traditional education and visual interactive elements that makes learning faster, more attractive, and memorization of contents more effective. The innovation in learning is assured by the interplay of:

- an e-learning platform providing flexible learning modules and test for self-evaluation

- a 3D simulation tool linked to the contents and giving instant feedback about the efficiency of energy-saving measures in a building that the learner can modify interactively.

Main outcomes of the project is the complete training system, made of 7 modules, 7 tests and a simulation tool, all accessible by visiting project website (www.enef-project.eu), which also provides in downloadable format the developed dissemination materials.

The most important thing for learning innovation toady is the development of training system as close to the learners needs as possible and to make learning more attractive and effective by using innovative tools as did in EnEf.

E-VIWO: Education in a Virtual World

The objectives of E-VIWO are to plan, create and implement a Second Life learning environment where students can gain skills necessary for both their academic courses and for employability e.g. programming skills, entrepreneurship, marketing and language skills in a multicultural environment.

Concrete aims and objectives are to learn how to

- move around and how to communicate in SL
- communicate in English in a multicultural virtual environment in SL
- program in 3D
- meet with experts on a variety of topics
- study in an English-speaking workshop

Main target groups of the project are students and teachers focusing on computing and language training.

Teachers from all partners have developed and shared teaching materials within this environment. E-VIWO is a pedagogical learning platform used during lessons. The students have implemented entrepreneurial thinking and companies are involved in the Virtual Fair activities.

The feedback has shown that SL is a great learning environment for Language learning. The same goes for improving communication and presentation skills. The environment also provides a multicultural environment. The partners have also together developed and shared teaching materials, environments and resources within this virtual world.

Creating courses in a virtual environment is a creative way of teaching and learning is most important for learning innovations and quality today.

More information about the eVIWO project is at http://eviwo.com/

GINCO: Grundtvig International Network of Course Organisers

GINCO is a Grundtvig network, funded with support of the LLP Programme of the European Commission and aims to create a European wide network of adult education organisations actually running Grundtvig courses or willing to do so in the future. The aim of the network is to share expertise, to collect, create and share useful material and to enhance communication and cooperation in order to improve the quality of Grundtvig courses, to enlarge the scope of provision and to improve the visibility and success of professional development of educators.

Main target groups of the project are adult education organisations organising international in-service training (IST) courses or organisations running national IST courses and willing to 'go international', curriculum developers and policy makers interested in professional development of adult trainers.

By raising the quality of in-service training of adult educators GINCO wants to raise the quality of AE itself. Quality in adult education provision and delivery, appropriate ICT use, validation of informal learning outcomes, a European scope, intercultural awareness, networking skills and competence driven teaching and learning are elements contributing to the innovation and quality raise of adult education. European in-service training courses, as developed in the Grundtvig programme, can be a model for innovative solutions in these priority areas. They can help create a European area of adult education and be a driver for innovation and the transfer of knowledge and expertise. GINCO strives to enhance and improve this role of Grundtvig courses in a European innovation policy.

The main outcomes of the project are: the network itself and useful material to raise the quality of international courses, to validate the learning outcomes and to enlarge the provision.

Most important for learning innovations and quality in in-service training is: self-evaluation, appropriate ICT-use, a competence oriented approach and validation of learning outcomes.

Info: www.ginconet.eu, www.sealll.eu, www.vilma-eu.org.

LoO: Improving Intercultural Dialogue: Exploring the Legacy of Oppression

This project intends to compare the adult educational approaches and packages of a range of institutions working with oppressed groups across Europe, bringing together, an NGO working with Roma groups in Slovakia; a Museum educating around Roma exclusion in the Czech Republic; a Foundation in Germany working with disabled people facing prejudice and discrimination; an NGO providing training around anti-discrimination and inclusion in the UK; along with a specialist in EU policy and partnership working in Belgium. Through this diverse partnership, we will attempt to isolate the similarities, differences and salient principles in the experience of oppression and the effects of this 'legacy' on social exclusion and intercultural dialogue, especially intercultural communication and learning.

Along with promoting the objectives of the '2010: European Year for Combating Poverty and Social Exclusion' this project aims to challenge the underlying negative stereotypes and stigma attached to poverty and social exclusion. The project will provide a framework for the development of adult educational materials, focusing on competencies, reflection benchmarks and practical tools in order to improve the impact and effectiveness of intercultural dialogue. The project approach will be both inter- and trans-disciplinary.

The main target groups of the project are oppressive and oppressed people everywhere. By focusing on what emotional learning blocks the process of oppression can initiate and using the findings of our explorations to overcome these obstacles. The main outcomes of this project are a framework outlining methodologies to engage, teach and boundary students, a website containing all project notes, presentations and research, newsletters, leaflets and a best practice dissemination event to present results.

It is most important for learning innovations and quality today to address the topic of competence and skills development in lifelong learning because what prevented people from developing these skills and competencies was their being historically categorised as inferior.

ODS: Open Discovery Space

ODS addresses various challenges that face the eLearning environment in the European context. ODS will fulfil three principal objectives. Firstly, it will empower stakeholders through a single, integrated access point for eLearning resources from dispersed educational repositories. Secondly, it engages stakeholders in the production of meaningful educational activities by using a social-network style multilingual portal, offering eLearning resources as well as services for the production of educational activities. Thirdly, it will assess the impact of the new educational activities, which could serve as a prototype to be adopted by stakeholders in school education.

Main target groups of the project are students, teachers, parents and policy makers.

ODS joins a high number of European e-Learning portals from different countries by providing a single platform with fully transparent access to all the portals' educational resources in order particularly, to ease the teachers' and learners' search for educational resources that are appropriate for each ones current requirements. Further on, ODS builds up local and over-regional communities in order to support the information/knowledge exchange between the stakeholder groups.

There are several important aspects that still need to be considered. From perspective of the ODS consortium, one major challenge they have to face in the next years is fostering the international exchange of educational resources and programs. Providing educational programs for international audiences is a key to foster international exchange and understanding. In a truly globalized world, achieving skills related to international exchange and understanding needs to start earlier than with the professional life. However, many barriers yet need to be overcome.

More information about the ODS project is at http://opendiscoveryspace.eu/

Opening Up the Natural History Heritage
for Europeana

OpenUp!: Opening Up the Natural History Heritage for Europeana

Although clearly within the scope of EUROPEANA as part of the scientific and cultural heritage, multimedia objects from the natural history domain are still dramatically underrepresented. This project aims to close this gap. It will initially make available over 1 million high quality images, movies, animal sound files, and natural history artwork from 23 institutions in 12 European countries.

The primary target groups are scientists, academics and new content providers, and education sector, although the wider audience may be quite variable.
High quality data with clear CC licences can be very valuable for the educational.

We are currently running an extensive survey to help determine requirements and receive feedback from lectors and students from several European countries.

- 585 662 objects from NH collections accessible on Europeana at the moment.
- newsletters, leaflets, posters, the project website and BLE virtual exhibition adaptation.
- developing the (ABCD)EFG standards for paleontological and geological content on Europeana.
- creation of the BioCASe Monitor tool.
- Documentation of usage and transformation of the metadata for the Europeana ESE schema.

We believe the most important for learning innovation and quality is to provide high quality data, including multimedia objects and metadata with open access and clear copyright statement; to show via case studies, virtual exhibitions and publications how these data can be effectively used; to provide open source or limited copyright technologies and tools which are able to work with these data and are adaptable for the educational sector. All these features need to be developed according to actual requirements from teachers and students in countries all over the world.
OpenUp! website is http://www.open-up.eu

PUMO: Educational Support for PUpils on the MOve

The aim of the project is to develop a system (teacher training course and know-how) to enable pupils away from their home country to maintain their progress in homeland specific subject areas and to monitor their progress in other subjects to ensure that they can re-integrate with their original cohort when they return home.

Main target groups of the project are beneficiaries are pupils living (temporarily) abroad. The PUMO training course will be used primarily by teachers where some pupils leave temporarily to move abroad. The course and know-how will also be used by organisations (public and private) planning to start offering online learning lessons and teach mother tongue and homeland specific studies.
Educational publishers/schools of the "paper age" provide(d) pupils and teachers' resources, which are "written in stone". Learners accommodate(d) themselves to the study material. In the future, publishers/schools will endeavor to develop services for learning teams of pupils and teachers providing rich and appropriate information, services and collaborative learning events to enable learners to construct their own knowledge. Learning solutions developed by PUMO project work to make this change happen. PUMO outcomes will not only help its primary target group, pupils living abroad, but same methodology can be used in other learning situations.

Main outcomes of this project are teacher training course, know-how and a social network of teachers and pupils, which enables pupils away from their home country to maintain their progress in mother tongue and also other homeland specific subject areas

In the "paper era" quality assessment mostly paid attention to correctness of learning materials and knowledge pupils/students gained. Today and in the future more attention is/will be paid on skills how to collect information, think critically and how to use knowledge gained during the learning process.

quality
certification for VET

Q-Cert-VET: Quality Certification of Vocational Education and Training

Q-Cert-Vet is the European research project for the quality certification (Q-Cert) of vocational education and training (VET) and is co-funded by the European Commission. The European initiative Q-Cert-VET develops a new quality standard and supports a related certification scheme for the vocational education and training (VET) sector in Portugal.

The project Q-Cert-VET has developed and published a national quality standard (NP 4512:2012) and initiates the development of required tools for professional quality certification. The reference framework QPL (short for Quality Platform Learning), developed in Germany, provided the basis for the new quality standard and related instruments and tools for the certification scheme, including the first training course for lead auditors. A strong desire from the Q-Cert-VET consortium members goes beyond a national quality standard: the evaluated and optimized quality certification standard NP 4512:2012 will be submitted to the European standardization CEN TC 353 to become an official European Norm (EN) for Quality and Certification in vocational education and training.

The consortium of Q-Cert-VET is coordinated and led by Center for Research and Innovation in Business Sciences and Information Systems (CIICESI). It includes eight partners from four countries: Germany, Luxembourg, Portugal, and Romania. The University of Duisburg-Essen, Germany, one of the Q-Cert-VET project partners and the project co-coordinator, is author and auditor of QPL and providing long-term expertise in learning quality.

More information about Q-Cert-VET is available online at
http://edu-certification.eu/

QUEST for Quality for Students: Towards a Genuine Student Centered Quality Concept

The project QUEST for quality for students aims to identify the true European student viewpoint on quality and the ways to enhance it through a European student survey. Furthermore in QUEST, we stress that students should also be able to control the sources of Information based on which they make their choices, thus we have also Included this aspect of transparency. The survey is complemented by desk research and exercises that compare views of students and match it with already existing tools like quality assurance.

The main outcome of QUEST will be a Student Quality Concept that draws from research and will propose a truly student centered and innovative approach to improving quality and making it visible and which would enshrine students' views. The main innovation of the project, being the survey, will change perceptions of policy makers and will contribute strongly to building a common European Higher Education Area by promoting availability of new modes of information and more evidence based policy making.

The main target group consists of students and in particular student representatives in national and local student unions and ESU student quality assurance experts' pool. The secondary group is leadership and academic staff, in particular individuals working on quality assurance at higher education institutions.

The most important for learning innovations and quality is to ensure students' involvement in the development of the studies and HE systems as such, ownership and being heard increases motivation and the quality of the learning experience.

More information about the QUEST for quality for students project is at
http://www.esu-online.org/projects/current/quest/

SimBase: Simulation Based Learning and Training

SimBase brings together public authorities, some of the leading healthcare simulation centres in Europe, technology providers and healthcare trainers to collaboratively promote the implementation of ICT-enhanced simulation training techniques in healthcare courses around Europe. To do so, requires that decision makers in the lifelong learning and public health sectors take decisions to adopt cutting edge technologies and pedagogies, and make significant investment in their application. Thus, the project will provide a rationale and methodology for such policymakers to be able to make and implement decisions in this area. To this end, an impact assessment model, made up of indicators for training effectiveness and indicators for contribution to public health priorities, has been developed. The model will further benchmark the ICT-enhanced approaches against more traditional training approaches to quantify their value added.

The project will run four pilots involving the introduction of ICT-enhanced simulation into healthcare courses, in each case:

- using the model to create an implementation strategy at the institutional/course level,
- running a course with integrate technology enhanced simulation
- comparing the impact of the course against projected results (validating the model) and against traditional approaches

Based on these experiences, SimBase will also produce a Policy-Roadmap for decision-makers wishing to adopt the project approach, together with an implementation guide. To maximise impact and widen adoption further, it will actively seek out new partners through networking the activities, with the aim of signing memoranda of understanding with new organisations so as to develop partnerships.

More information about the project SIMBASE is at
http://www.simbase.co/

VOA3R: Virtual Open Access Agriculture & Aquaculture Repository: Sharing Scientific and Scholarly Research related to Agriculture, Food, and Environment.

The general objective of the project is to improve the spread of European agriculture and aquaculture research results by using an innovative approach to sharing open access research products.
The target end user communities are:
- Researchers/academics,
- Practitioners and
- Students

Open access to scientific/scholarly content removes the access barriers related to copyright retention to the outcomes of research. The VOA3R platform deploys an advanced, community-focused integrated service for the retrieval of relevant open content and data that includes explicit models of the scholarly methods and procedures used and of the practical tasks targeted by applied research which represent a principal information need expression for practitioners.The main outcome of VOA3R is a Virtual Open Access Agriculture & Aquaculture Repository for Sharing Scientific and Scholarly Research related to Agriculture, Food, and Environment.

The VOA3R platform will offer innovative and semantic interfaces and services that enable researchers to:
- formulate their information needs in terms of elements of the scientific methods established in their field (variables, techniques, assessment methods, kinds of objects of interest, etc.) combined with topical descriptions as expressed in metadata ;
- browse concepts and topics using graphical representation ;
- experiment an alternative publishing process ;
- use social functions/criteria like ratings, public reviews, social tagging.

Open access to scientific/scholarly content removes the access barriers related to copyright retention to the outcomes of research is most important for learning innovations and quality today!

More information about the VOA3R project is at
http://voa3r.eu/

Author Index

all authors in alphabetic order

Author Index

Albert, Dietrich

Department of Psychology,
University of Graz,
Austria
dietrich.albert@uni-graz.at

Prof. Dr. Dietrich Albert graduated from the University of Göttingen (Germany) with a degree in psychology. He received his Dr.rer.nat. and his postdoctoral degree (Habilitation in Psychology) from the University of Marburg/Lahn (Germany). He was Professor of general experimental psychology at the University of Heidelberg (Germany). Currently he is professor of psychology at University of Graz, senior scientist at TUGraz, and key researcher at the Know-Centre. His research topics cover several areas in experimental and cognitive psychology; his actual research focus is on knowledge and competence structures, their applications, and empirical research, and their integration with theories of motivation and emotion. Currently he is the Chair of the Board of Trustees of the Centre for Psychological Information and Documentation (ZPID), Germany, and a member of several scientific advisory boards. Relevant projects: Dietrich Albert's expertise in European R&D projects is documented by several IST/IT projects since FP5 including iClass, ELEKTRA, Target, ROLE.

Berthold, Marcel

Knowledge Management Institute,
Graz University of Technology,
Austria
marcel.berthold@tugraz.at

Marcel Berthold completed his Diploma in Psychology at the University of Graz, Austria. Since 2007, he has been working at a company that researches and develops computer-based assessment tools in the field of self-regulated learning. Since 2010 he is researcher at the Cognitive Science Section and is working European projects on technology enhanced learning. His main research interests include learning styles and techniques, self-regulated learning, and evaluation of technology-enhance learning.

Colibaba, Anca Cristina

Gr.T.Popa University Of Medicine and Pharmacy, EuroED
Foundation
Romania
acolib@euroed.ro

Anca Cristina Colibaba has over 30 years of experience in language education, especially English. She is the President of the EuroEd Foundation, Iasi, Romania, having a wide experience in managing and coordinating transnational projects in the field of linguistic education and training, adult education and LLL. She has been a project coordinator of over 25 (EU) projects implemented locally, nationally or trans-nationally by the EuroEd Foundation. She has an international diploma in educational management and she also works as a professor at Gr.T.Popa University of Medicine and Pharmacy, Iasi, the oldest university city of Romania, being the Chair of the foreign languages department.

Dahn, Ingo

Knowledge Media Institute,
University of Koblenz-Landau,
Germany
ingo.dahn@uni-koblenz.de

Dr. Ingo Dahn, the CEO of the Knowledge Media Institute, has a habitation in Mathematics from Humboldt University Berlin. Being trained as a specialist in Mathematical Logic, he moved in 1998 from Humboldt University Berlin to the Artificial Intelligence Group at the University in Koblenz. He has developed Slicing Book Technology which used AI methods for the semantic search and aggregation of legacy data. Dr. Dahn served 2007-2011 as a member of the Technical Advisory Board of the IMS Global Learning Consortium. He is a member of the Editorial Board of the International Journal of Technology, Instruction Cognition and Learning.

Danielienė, Renata

Information Technologies Institute,
Lithuania
renata@ecdl.lt

Renata Danielienė is Information Systems Manager of Information Technologies Institute, as well as a lecturer at the Vilnius University, where she teaches courses in Computer Design. She has more than 11 years of experience in system design, development and management. Renata Danielienė also has experience in children security and safety on Internet, IT training and testing service providing, ECDL courseware development at the Information Technologies Institute. 2002 – 2004 Renata Danielienė worked in some Leonardo da Vinci projects, where she was as co-author of educational material. 2010 – 2012 she worked in Leonardo Transfer of Innovation project e-GUARDIAN, where she was co-author of e-GUARDIAN programme and e-GUARDIAN tests. Renata Danielienė holds doctor degree in Informatics, she is the co-author of 3 books in computer literacy and has publications in IT.

Dujardin, Anne-Florence

Sheffield Hallam University,
Centre for Education and Inclusion Research,
UK
a-f.dujardin@shu.ac.uk

Designing and supporting e-learning have been the focus of Florence's career in Higher Education. Over the last 16 years, she has taught and supervised mature students enrolled on an online Master's Programme in Professional Communication. To design learning experiences with a range of software applications, including social media, she has built on insights gained during her previous career in software training and communication consultancy. Florence has a BA and MA in English Literature from the Sorbonne-Paris IV, and a MEd from the University of Cambridge. Her current PhD research focuses on the educational use of social media.

Engel-Vermette, Sebastian

University of Duisburg-Essen, Campus Essen
Information Systems for Production and Operations
Management
Germany
sebastian.vermette@icb.uni-due.de

Sebastian Engel-Vermette is a post-graduate research assistant for third-party projects at the department of Information Systems for Production and Operations Management at the University of Duisburg-Essen. His responsibilities include communications and marketing for the projects and conferences with which the department is involved. His research interests as a MA student include migration and societal integration concepts and discourse within Europe, especially in Germany.

Gheorghiu, Elza

EuroED Foundation
Romania
elza.gheorghiu@gmail.com

Elza Gheorghiu is a trainer and a teacher at EuroEd Foundation, British Council and Vasile Alecsandri College, Iasi, Romania. She coordinates international educational projects. Her field of interest covers work with innovative educational web 2.0 methodologies in training/teaching and non-formal education. Target group for her teaching/training are young learners and adults. A special area of intervention is training special needs children and their teachers for foreign language communication.

Gheorghiu, Irina

Albert Ludwigs University Freiburg
Germany
irina_gheorghiu16@yahoo.com

Irina Gheorghiu is a PhD student in German literature at the Albert Ludwigs University Freiburg, Germany. She received her M.A. in European Literatures and cultures from the Albert Ludwigs University Freiburg, Germany. Currently she is doing research in cultural and collective memory applied to German and Romanian literature. She has also been involved in national and international projects.

Goeman, Katie

Hogeschool-Universiteit Brussel, Faculty of Economics and Management, Educational Research and Development, Brussels,
Belgium
Katie.Goeman@hubrussel.be

Katie Goeman obtained a PhD in Social Sciences at the Free University of Brussels (VUB, Belgium). In November 2009 she was appointed Assistant Professor and Project Leader for Educational Innovation at the faculty of Economics and Management of the Hogeschool-Universiteit Brussel. She coordinates the implementation of innovations in business education e.g. blended learning for mature students, and is responsible for carrying out research projects involving the investigation of ICT applications for educational purposes. These studies are related to implementation issues for online, distance or blended teaching and learning, the monitoring and quality assurance of such initiatives, as well as educational design scenarios for mobile learning, multicampus education and so forth. Other specialties include: multimethod user research and policy analysis, practice-based studies and train the trainers.

Hirata, Kenji

Toyo University
Department of Social Psychology
skillmgt@gmail.com

Bachelor by Waseda University. Ph.D. in Decision Science and Technology, Tokyo Institute of Technology (2002). After he worked in Japanese mayor management consulting firm, he was an associate professor at Sanno University and Toyo

University. Now he is founder of Institute Expert Science. He was an editor of "ISO/IEC 19796-3 Quality Management, Assurance and Metrics: Method and Metrics" 2009, and "Data Specification for Competency Semantics" by the society HR mark-up language. Dr. Hirata is several Japan national skills standard committee members, and delegation of ISO/IEC Japan national body. He got awards by Japan society of information processing, and HR-XML consortium.

Kameas, Achilles

Hellenic Open University, Greece
kameas@eap.gr

Achilles D. Kameas received his Engineering Diploma (in 1989) and his Ph.D. (in 1995) from the Department of Computer Engineering and Informatics, Univ. of Patras, Greece. Since 2003, he is an Assistant Professor with the Hellenic Open University (HOU), where he teaches software design and engineering. Since 2007 he is Director of the e-Comet Lab with HOU (http://eeyem.eap.gr). He has participated as researcher / group leader / co-ordinator in several EU R&D projects in IST/ICT (including eGadgets, Astra, Atraco, etc.) and LLP frameworks (including TIPS, PIN, CompAAL, SONETOR, etc.), has published over 100 journal articles, conference papers and book chapters, authored and co-edited more than 10 five books and conference proceedings. His current research interests include applications of ICT in education, semantic modeling and ontology matching.

Kiefel, Andreas

Knowledge Media Institute,
University of Koblenz-Landau,
Germany
andreas.kiefel@uni-koblenz.de

Andreas Kiefel has studied computer science at the University of Koblenz-Landau. After graduation (Dipl.-Inf.) he worked in public service responsible for software modelling and development. He joined the Knowledge Media Institute (IWM,

University Koblenz-Landau) in 2009, working for the EU Responsive Open Learning Environments project.

Kosulnikov, Yury A.

Moscow State Technological University "STANKIN",
Information System Department, 1,
Russia
iourik@stankin.ru

Yury Kosulnikov received his physics teacher diploma at the Moscow State Pedagogical University and worked for 30 years in the design and implementation of information systems in various industries in Russia and other countries (Hungary, Finland). For 12 years he has been working as a lecturer of the Department "Information Systems", Moscow State Technological University, where he developed three multimedia lecture course "Design of Information Systems", "Enterprise Information Systems" and "Global information resources and networks." In recent years, he took part in the development of international and national standards for information technology and the application of information technology in education. He is the executive secretary of the Russian Technical Committee 461 on standardization of information technology in education, and also works as an expert in two subcommittees of ISO/IEC JTC1: SC 32 and SC 36.

Lachmann, Pablo

Knowledge Media Institute,
University of Koblenz-Landau,
Germany
pablo.lachmann@uni-koblenz.de

Pablo Lachmann studied adult education (Pädagogik, Erwachsenenbildung / Weiterbildung) and received a M.A. (Dipl.-Päd.) at the University Koblenz-Landau by mid of 2009. After graduation he managed a project developing a training concept for usage of outdoor handheld devices for forestry workers. He also worked for various research projects as a student assiciate and acquired experiences in evaluation of E-learning in the field of academic teaching.

Currently he's contributing to the psycho-pedagogical foundation and to the modelling of data- and process models in the EU Responsive Open Learning Environments (ROLE) project.

Land, Sarah

Meath Partnership,
Ireland
sarah.land@meathpartnership.ie

Sarah Land has a Bachelor Degree in English and History, and has been working in Meath Partnership since May 2009. She provides administrative support to the European Project team within Meath Partnership, focusing on quality management aspects insuring the successful implementation of projects in the agreed timeframe. She is currently studying for her Master of Science degree in Development Studies in University College Dublin.

Laughton, Simone

University of Toronto Mississauga Library,
Canada
simone.laughton@utoronto.ca

Bachelor of Science and a Master of Information Studies from the University of Toronto (2003). She is currently completing an M.A. in the accessibility of e-tests at the Ontario Institute for Studies in Education/U. of T. Simone is an Instructional Technology Liaison Librarian at the University of Toronto Mississauga, where she explores the use of different technologies to assist with information literacy assessments. Her research interests include the development of information technology competencies at the undergraduate and graduate levels, the effective use of multimedia in teaching and learning, and collaborative work on the development of online assessment tools. She is vice chair of the Canadian Advisory Committee for ISO/IE JTC1 SC36.

Lohr, Manfred

BG/BRG Schwechat,
Austria
manfred.lohr@gmail.com

After graduating from the high school in Bruck/Leitha in 1976 Manfred Lohr studied Mathematics and Physics at the University of Vienna. He finished his studies with the degree of Magister rerum naturalis in 1981. In 1981 he began to work as a teacher of Mathematics and Physics and since 1988 he has also been a teacher of Computer Science at the BG/BRG Schwechat.

Since 1997 he has been participating as teacher and project coordinator in many European projects in the field of eLearning and the use of modern technologies in education. In 2003 he started a cooperating with the Austrian Ministry of Education in order to share his experience gained in European projects with schools in Austria.

In 2001 Manfred Lohr took over the coordinator of information and computer technologies at the BG/BRG Schwechat. Since 2005 in his position of an eLearning coordinator he has been responsible for the pedagogical concept of the learning management system Moodle at the BG/BRG Schwechat as well as the eLearning teacher training.

Mahood, Ed

DEKRA Akademie GmbH,
Germany
ed.mahood@dekra.com

Mohsin, M. Naeem

G.C University Faisalabad, Pakistan
mnmohsin71@gmail.com

Dr. Muhammad Naeem Mohsin has been is a director in Directorate of Distance learning Education at G. C. University Faisalabad Pakistan. He has completed his Post Doctorate from University of Vienna, Austria. He is an internationally renowned researcher and highly respected groundcover and soils educationist. He has a wealth of experience working with innovative projects with national and international organizations.

He is the author of more than twenty research paper at international level and presented research papers at international conferences. He is the author of four books at national and international level. His area of interest is Computer application in teacher education, assessment, distance learning and Special Education. He has received merit scholarship, Higher Education Commission (HEC) Pakistan Research Fellowship Award and Training Award from PELI, USA.

Najjar, Jad

Eummena, Leuven, Belgium
Computer Science Department, AL-Quds University, Jerusalem, Palestine
jnajjar@eummena.org

Dr. Jad Najjar Holds a PhD in Computer Engineering from the Katholieke Universiteit Leuven (Belgium) on learning technologies, standards, applications and user experience. He serves as expert and work package leader in EU projects and standards bodies in learning technologies, competences and metadata.

Dr. Najjar is also a part-time assistant professor at AL-Quds University (Jerusalem). He supervises several master thesis students in their work and teachs courses on Human Computer Interaction (HCI), Multimedia and Learning Technologies.

Negri, Michael

FOM Hochschule,
Germany
michael.negri@bcw-gruppe.de

Nowak, Paweł O.

Warsaw University of Technology, Civil Engineering Faculty
Poland
p.nowak@il.pw.edu.pl

Paul Olaf Nowak, PhD. MSc. Eng., FCIOB, EURBE (European Building Expert). Vice Dean for Faculty Development, Faculty of Civil Engineering, Warsaw University of Technology, Poland; Researcher at Division of Construction Engineering and Management at the Faculty; Lecturer of construction and project management, building law, contract conditions, construction organization and technology; Member of Polish Association of Building Managers. Researcher and promoter of numerous EU funded projects in the area of education in construction development – increasing quality, introduction of new educational tools, comparison of managerial qualifications of construction engineers across EU.

Nowakowska-Twaróg, Monika

Globalnet sp. z o.o.
Poland
monika@globalnet.com.pl

Monika Nowakowska-Twaróg is director of the Language School, responsible for the European projects, especially for the language learning, MSc in Economics department International economic and political relations, a bachelor degree in English Teaching Methodology. She worked as a English Teaches for 3 years. She has been responsible for the European projects for 6 years, especially foreign language projects for particular groups of people, seniors, employees 45+, vocational language courses - police officers, psychologists. She has 6 years of experience in international projects management within the framework of the EU Programme such as: Grundtvig, LEONARDO DA VINCI.

Nussbaumer, Alexander

Knowledge Management Institute,
Graz University of Technology,
Austria
alexander.nussbaumer@tugraz.at

Alexander Nussbaumer received a M.Sc. (Dipl.-Ing.) in Telematics (Computer Technics) from Graz University of Technology, Austria, and has gained experience in industry as software developer in Web-based and virtual reality applications. From 2006 to 2011 he was member of the interdisciplinary team of the Cognitive Science Section of the Department of Psychology at the University of Graz and since 2009 he has been member of the (same) Cognitive Science Section of the Knowledge Management Institute at the Graz University of Technology, Austria. In the context of these affiliations he has been participating in several EC-funded TEL projects (e.g. iClass, GRAPPLE, and ROLE), where he was involved in modelling and implementing competence-based knowledge representation models and their applications for learning purposes in an adaptive and self-directed learning context.

Pozdneev, Boris M.

Moscow State Technological University "STANKIN", Information System Department,
Russia
bmp@stankin.ru

Boris M. Pozdneev graduated from the Moscow Institute of Technology «STANKIN». He received engineer for metal forming diploma. He is now a doctor of technical sciences, professor and the chair of "Information Systems" department and provost for IT of the University «STANKIN». In 2004, due to initiative of prof. B. M. Pozdneev Technical Committee for Standardization (TC 461) "Information and Communication Technologies in Education" has been established. It is a national committee which he heads as a chairman. TC 461 has the functions of a permanent national body to ISO / IEC JTC1 SC 36 "Information technology for learning, education and training." Pozdneev as head of the national delegation of Russia provided the Russian participation in the plenary meetings of the SC 36 from 2006 to 2012. He participated in the development of international standards for terminology and quality of e-learning. He published more than 50 scientific papers on standardization and certification in the areas of information technology and the use of IT in education.

Priestley, Carol

MDR Partners,
UK

carol.priestley@mdrprojects.com

Carol Priestley was Manager for EMPATIC (EMPowering Autonomous learning Through Information Competencies). Her particular interest is that all people are able to access, utilize and contribute information, ideas and knowledge necessary to support sustainable and equitable development. Carol has a keen interest in Information Literacy and worked for many years in collaboration with the UNESCO Media & Information Literacy training programs and activities. She is a member of the European Conference of Information Literacy (ECIL).

Psochios, Yiannis

Agro-Know Technologies, Athens,
Greece
psochios@agroknow.gr

Yannis Psochios has a lifetime involvement with the food and beverages sector where he has worked for years, also holding a specialization degree on their management and logistics. He has long working experience supporting SMEs that operate in the agricultural, food, beverages and tourism sectors in rural areas like Epirus and Crete, Greece. Yannis has a particular interest in the way that ICT and Web technologies can be applied in real-life situations and this lead him to co-found Agro-Know Technologies in 2008. For a long period of time he has been serving as the Managing Director of Agro-Know getting involved in to the administration & coordination of its participation in EU projects related to enhancement of Vocational education and Training in Agriculture and other related thematic areas.

Richter, Natalja

University of Duisburg-Essen, Campus Essen
Information Systems for Production and Operations
Management
Germany
natalja.richter@icb.uni-due.de

Natalja Richter is a Scientific Assistant at the University of Duisburg-Essen (UDE). She studied Business Information Systems at the UDE obtaining her B. Sc. Dagree in 2012. Since October 2010 she is working at the UDE in the Department "Information Systems for Production and Operation Management" (WIP).

Rodriguez Toquero, Xenia

University of Duisburg-Essen, Campus Essen
Information Systems for Production and Operations
Management
Germany
Xenia.Rodriguez@icb.uni-due.de

Xenia Rodriguez Toquero is Finance- and Project Manager, working at the University of Duisburg-Essen, Campus Essen. Before managing the WACOM (Water Competences Model) Project and supporting the eCOTOOL (eCompetences Tools) Project she studied Business Economics (Bachelor of Science) at the University of Duisburg-Essen, Campus Essen (2011). Her research interests are E-Learning, Competence- and HR-Management with regard to cultural and international Challenges as well as the Corporate Governance Debate (Master Studies at the University of Wuppertal since 2012).

Seta, Kazuhisa

Collage of Sustainable System Sciences,
Osaka Prefecture University
seta@mi.s.osakafu-u.ac.jp

He received the Ph.D. from Osaka University in 1998. He is currently a professor in the Collage of Sustainable System Sciences, Osaka Prefecture University. His research interests include software engineering, intelligent tutoring systems, human resource management and ontological engineering. He is a member of JSAI, IEICE, IPSJ and JSiSE.

Shamarina-Heidenreich, Tatiana

University of Duisburg-Essen, Campus Essen
Information Systems for Production and Operations Management
Germany
tatiana.shamarina-heidenreich@icb.uni-due.de

Tatiana Shamarina-Heidenreich is Scientific Researcher at the University of Duisburg-Essen (UDE). She studied Business Information Systems at the UDE obtaining her Diploma in 2010 and Education and Linguistics at the Barnaul State Pedagogical University (Russian Federation) receiving her Diploma in 1998. Since February 2011 she is working in the fields of Lifelong Learning at the UDE in the Department "Information Systems for Production and Operation Management" (WIP). She has got a strong background and expertise in evaluation and in leading, coordinating and contributing to research projects (ARISTOTELE, OERtest, SIMBASE, Q-Cert-VET). Currently she is responsible for the research activities in the ARISTOTELE, Q-Cert-VET and SIMBASE projects.

Song, Ju Youn

University of Luxembourg,
Campus Walferdange
jun.song@uni.lu

Ju Youn Song is a researcher within a research group "The Dynamics in Interaction, Communication and Activity research group" (DICA lab). She graduated from a trilingual master program Learning and Development in Multicultural and Multilingual Contexts at the University of Luxembourg.
Within her current research fields, she is very much engaged in the topic of web 2.0 language learning communities socialization and development of language competences through multimodal interaction. Ju youn worked of the European

network "Language learning and social media: 6 key dialogues" and is currently working as a researcher of "Improving web strategies and maximizing social media presence of LLP projects" under the LLP of the European Commission at the University of Luxembourg.

Stoitsis, Giannis

Agro-Know Technologies,
Athens,
Greece
stoitsis@agroknow.gr

Giannis Stoitsis received the Diploma of Electrical and Computer Engineering from the Aristotle University of Thessaloniki in 2002, and the M.Sc. and Ph.D. degree in Biomedical Engineering from the University of Patras in 2004 and 2007, respectively. Currently Giannis is serving as the Managing Director of Agro-Know and is largely responsible for designing, setting up, supporting and refining complex processes that can efficiently be integrated in the management and coordination of large EU initiatives. He is also responsible for guiding the research & development activities of the group that are related to Semantic Web and Bioinformatics applications for agricultural and Biodiversity applications.

Stracke, Christian M.

University of Duisburg-Essen, Campus Essen
Information Systems for Production and Operations Management
Germany
christian.stracke@icb.uni-due.de

Christian M. Stracke is Coordinator of European and international research and cooperation at the University of Duisburg-Essen (see: www.wip.uni-due.de) and Adjunct Professor for E-Learning at the Korean National Open University (see: www.knou.ac.kr/engknou2/). He is leading the Team for E-Learning and Competence Development managing international, European, and national consortia and research projects, amongst others the largest project for Quality and Standards in E-Learning (see: www.qed-info.de), QLET (see: www.qualitydevelopment.eu/) and many European projects (e.g. ARISTOTELE,

ODS, VOA3R, Q-Cert-VET, AGRICOM). He has founded and established eLC, the European Institute for Learning, Innovation and Cooperation (see: www.elc-institute.org). And he is co-initiator and Member of the Executive Committee of the German E-Learning Association D-ELAN (see: www.d-elan.net) and elected speaker of the SIG "International E-Learning".As an internationally recognized researcher his main working fields are competence modelling, technology enhanced learning, quality management and evaluation as well as standardisation in these fields. He is elected officer at the international (ISO-Convener for SC36) and European (Chair of CEN/TC 353) Standardisation Committees for TEL. He has published numerous articles and book chapters and is an invited speaker and PC member at many international conferences. As senior consultant and project manager he has gained extensive experience in leading projects and in consulting and supporting enterprises and public organisations to develop long-term policies and to implement and improve technology enhanced learning. Christian M. Stracke is the Co-Author of several standards for technology-enhanced learning and for competencies in HR with long-term experiences in their adaptation, application, and implementation within enterprises as well as research projects.

Sutyagin, Maxim

Gazprom Corporate Institute, Moscow, Russia
M.Sutiagin@institute.gazprom.ru

Maxim Sutyagin graduated from the Moscow Institute of Technology «STANKIN». He received engineer for metal forming diploma. He is now a candidate of technical sciences, chief of the IT Department at the Gazprom Corporate Institute. In 2004, he took part together with prof. B. Pozdneev in creation of Technical Committee for Standardization (TC 461) "Information and Communication Technologies in Education". Now he is a deputy secretary of the Committee. He participated in several sessions of ISO / IEC JTC1 SC 36 in the frame of activities of Russian delegation. He participated in the development of international standards for terminology and quality of e-learning. He published more than 30 scientific papers on IT, standardization and certification in the areas of information technology and the use of IT in education.

Telešius, Eugenijus

Information Technologies Institute,
K. Petrausko 26, LT-44156 Kaunas,
Lithuania
et@ecdl.lt

Dr. Eugenijus Telesius is mathematician by education and has spent all his active life in the Lithuanian IT industry. He is active member of the Lithuanian Computer Society, Country Representative in IFIP and IT STAR association. Currently he is Managing Director of Information Technologies Institute, CEO of ECDL Lithuania. He also deals as project manager with EC funded projects at the Information Technologies Institute. Eugenijus was associated professor at various Universities in Lithuania, he holds a doctorate in Computer Science, and also is a co-author of 17 books in computer literacy and a lot of publications in IT.

Thanopoulos, Charalampos

Agro-Know Technologies, Athens,
Greece
cthanopoulo@agroknow.gr

Charalampos Thanopoulos has a diploma in Crop Science, Specialization in Vegetable Crop Production, a M.Sc. in Modern Systems of Crop Science, Plant protection and Landscape architecture (Specialization in Plant Physiology of Vegetables) and a Ph.D. in pre- / post-harvest physiology of vegetables, all from the Laboratory of Vegetable Production of the Agricultural University of Athens, Greece.
He is involved as an associate researcher for Agro-Know Technologies, Greek Research & Technology Network and Laboratory of Vegetable Production of the Agricultural University of Athens in several EU projects in the framework of vocational education and training in agricultural topics and linking agricultural educational resources of open access repositories.

Hua-Hui Tseng (曾華惠)

Tainan University of Technology, Music Department
Taiwan
t50005@mail.tut.edu.tw

Tseng, Hua-Hui is professor of Graduate School of Music, Department of Music, the Tainan University of Technology (TUT), Director of Library of TUT, Gender Equality Education Committee Member, TUT. Most previous positions: Dean of the College of Fine and Applied Arts of the Tainan University of Technology (TUT), Dean of the Cluster of Fine and Applied Arts of the Tainan Woman's College of Arts and Technology (TWCAT), Tainan; Dean of the Graduate School of Music and Music Department of TWCAT, Tainan, Taiwan. In 2011: Second Annual life-long learning model Award from the Ministry of Education, Taiwan in recognition of distinguished achievements in social service.

van Laer, Stijn

Katholieke Universiteit Leuven,
Media & Learning Unit, Heverlee, Belgium
stijn.vanlaer@dml.kuleuven.be

Zawistowski, Jacek P.

Warsaw University of Technology, Civil Engineering Faculty
Poland
jz@il.pw.edu.pl

Zourou, Katerina

Web2learn,
Greece,
katerinazourou@gmail.com

Katerina Zourou is a post-doctoral researcher in the field of computer supported collaborative language learning at the University of Luxembourg. She co-edited a journal special issue (Alsic) "Social media and language learning: (r)evolution"? with F. Demaizière, and a book for Palgrave, "Social networking and language education", with M.-N. Lamy. Her research interests involve the role of computer tools in foreign language education as well as telecollaborative practices online. She is the initiator and project leader of two EC-funded projets, the network "Language learning and social media" (2010-2012) and the project "Improving Internet strategies and maximizing social media presence of LLP projects" (2012-2013).

http://www.learning-innovations.eu

LINQ 2012 Programme Committee

Conference Chair   Christian M. Stracke

Conference Managers   Tatiana Shamarina-Heidenreich

Xenia Rodriguez

Natalja Richter

Conference Communication   Sebastian Engel-Vermette

**Members of the Scientific
Programme Committee:**

Albert, Dietrich (Austria)

Amiel, Tel (Brazil)

Anido Rifón, Luis (Spain)

Bø, Ingeborg (Norway)

Collett, Mike (UK)

Conole, Grainne (UK)

Downes, Stephen (USA)

Glidden, Julia (UK)

Hatzakis, Ilias (Greece)

Hoel, Tore (Norway)

Junge, Kerstin (UK)

Kastis, Nikitas (Greece)

Koskinen, Tapio (Finland)

Kwak, Duk Hoon (Korea)

Le Hénaff, Diane (France)

Mason, Jon (Australia)

Moreira Teixeira, António (Portugal)

Nakabayashi, Kiyoshi (Japan)

Nussbaumer, Alexander (Austria)

Øverby, Erlend (Norway)

Pawlowski, Jan (Finland)

Ramfos, Antonis (Greece)

Reimers, Christian (Austria)

Ritrovato, Pierluigi (Italy)

Rodriguez Artacho, Miguel (Spain)

Salerno, Saverio (Italy)

Salvador, Sánchez Alonso (Spain)

Schumann, Sabine (Spain)

Sgouropoulou, Cleo (Greece)

Shon, Jin Gon (Korea)

Sicilia, Miguel-Angel (Spain)

Sotiriou, Sofoklis (Greece)

Specht, Marcus (NL)

Szucs, András (Hungary)

Thammetar, Thapanee (Thailand)

White, Nancy (USA)

Wolpers, Martin (NL)

Zhiting, Zhu (China)

Zistler, Elisabeth (Austria)

Ausgewählte Literatur für die Bereiche

Betriebswirtschaft	Qualitätsmanagement
Electronic Business	Wandlungsfähigkeit
Unternehmensführung	Wirtschaftsinformatik
und Organisation	Wissensmanagement

Betriebswirtschaft

8315	Nyhuis, Peter (Hrsg.)	Wandlungsfähige Produktionssysteme	468 S.	978-3-942183-15-4
8318	Gronau, Norbert	Störungsmanagement (Productivity Management 3/2010)	66 S.	978-3-942183-18-5
8323	Gronau, N.; Eggert, S.; Fohrholz, C. (Hrsg.)	Software as a Service, Cloud Computing und Mobile Technologien	380 S.	978-3-942183-23-9
8328	Gronau, Norbert	Effizienz durch ERP (ERP Management 1/2011)	82 S.	978-3-942183-28-4
8339	Gronau, Norbert; Meier, Horst; Bahrs, Julian (Hrsg.)	Handbuch gegen Produktpiraterie – Prävention von Produktpiraterie durch Technologie, Organisation und Wissensflussmanagement	248 S.	978-3-942183-39-0
8340	Gronau, Norbert	Anpassungsfähigkeit und Flexibilität (ERP Management 2/2011)	66 S.	978-3-942183-40-6
8342	Gronau, Norbert	Erfolgsfaktor Personal (Industrie Management 4/2011)	82 S.	978-3-942183-42-0
8349	Gronau, Norbert	Kostenreduktion durch ERP (ERP Management 3/2011)	66 S.	978-3-942183-49-9
8358	Soelberg, Christian	Wissenskapital als Instrument der strategischen Unternehmensführung	233 S.	978-3-942183-58-1

Electronic Business

77115	Gronau, Norbert; Benger, Alf	JXTA Workshop: Potenziale, Konzepte, Anwendungen	122 S.	978-3-936771-15-2
77136	Scholz-Reiter, Bernd	Digital Engineering (Industrie Management 2/2005)	66 S.	978-3-936771-36-7
77138	Gronau, Norbert	Interoperabilität (Industrie Management 4/2005)	66 S.	978-3-936771-38-1
77151	Gronau, Norbert	Geschäftsprozessmanagement (ERP Management 3/2005)	66 S.	978-3-936771-51-0
77171	Gronau, Norbert	Mobile Technologien (PPS Management 2/2006)	66 S.	978-3-936771-71-8
77183	Scholz-Reiter, Bernd	Industrial Engineering (Industrie Management 5/2006)	66 S.	978-3-936771-83-1
1919	Scholz-Reiter, Bernd (Hrsg.); Höhns, Hartmut	Konzeption einer adaptiven Auftragskoordination im Rahmen des Supply Chain Managements	250 S.	978-3-940019-19-6
1975	Gronau, Norbert	Prozessmanagement (ERP Management 2/2009)	66 S.	978-3-940019-75-2
1984	Gronau, Norbert	ERP-Integration (ERP Management 3/2009)	66 S.	978-3-940019-84-4
1995	Gronau (Hrsg.)/Stein/ Röchert-Voigt/u.a.	E-Government-Anwendungen	264 S.	978-3-940019-95-0
8308	Nösekabel, Holger	Mobile Education, 2. Auflage	366 S.	978-3-942183-08-6
0314	Fohrholz, Corinna	Business Software für Apple-Plattformen (iSuccess 1/2010)	66 S.	978-3-942183-14-7
8316	Amt24 e.V.; Tanja Röchert-Voigt; Denise Berg	Web 2.0 in der öffentlichen Verwaltung	92 S.	978-3-942183-16-1
8325	Gronau, Norbert	Lizenzmodelle für ERP-Systeme (ERP Management 4/2010)	66 S.	978-3-942183-25-3
8327	Gronau, Norbert	Mobiles Arbeiten und Sicherheit (iSuccess 1/2011)	66 S.	978-3-942183-27-7
8347	Flach, Guntram; Schultz, Jürgen (Hrsg.)	6. Rostocker eGovernment-Forum 2011 – Nachhaltiges eGovernment: Herausforderung und Notwendigkeit	82 S.	978-3-942183-47-5
8353	Stracke, Christian M.	Competence Modelling for Human Resources Development and European Policies	168 S.	978-3-942183-53-6
8354	Gronau, N., Fohrholz, C.	Wirtschaftliche Geschäftsprozesse durch mobile ERP-Systeme	287 S.	978-3-942183-54-3

GITO

Betriebswirtschaft
Electronic Business
Unternehmensführung
und Organisation

Qualitätsmanagement
Wandlungsfähigkeit
Wirtschaftsinformatik
Wissensmanagement

Qualitätsmanagement

8324	Scholz-Reiter, Bernd	Prozessmanagement (Productivity Management 4/2010)	66 S.	978-3-942183-24-6
8331	Scholz-Reiter, Bernd	Industrial Automation (Productivity Management 2/2011)	46 S.	978-3-942183-31-4
8342	Gronau, Norbert	Erfolgsfaktor Personal (Industrie Management 4/2011)	82 S.	978-3-942183-42-0
8345	Bentele, Markus; Gronau, Norbert; Schütt, Peter; Weber, Mathias (Hrsg.)	KnowTech - Unternehmenswissen als Erfolgsfaktor mobilisieren!	610 S.	978-3-942183-45-1
8353	Stracke, Christian M.	Competence Modelling for Human Resources Development and European Policies	168 S.	978-3-942183-53-6

Unternehmensführung und Organisation

77109	Scholz-Reiter, Bernd	Prozessorientierte Fertigung (PPS Management 4/2003)	82 S.	978-3-936771-09-1
77116	Bichler, Martin; Holtmann, Carsten	Coordination and Agent Technology in Value Networks	112 S.	978-3-936771-16-9
77119	Krallmann, Herrmann; Scholz-Reiter, Bernd; Gronau, Norbert	Prozessgestaltung (Industrie Management 1/2004)	82 S.	978-3-936771-19-0
77121	Gronau, Norbert	Wandlungsfähigkeit (Industrie Management 2/2004)	82 S.	978-3-936771-21-3
77135	Gronau, Norbert	Unternehmensarchitekturen (ERP Management 1/2005)	66 S.	978-3-936771-35-0
77137	Gronau, Norbert	Innovationsmanagement (Industrie Management 3/2005)	66 S.	978-3-936771-37-4
77143	Scholz-Reiter, Bernd	PPS und Controlling (PPS Management 4/2005)	66 S.	978-3-936771-43-5
77158	Kern, Eva-Maria	Verteilte Produktentwicklung - Rahmenkonzept und Vorgehensweise zur organisatorischen Gestaltung	230 S.	978-3-936771-58-9
77163	Scholz-Reiter, Bernd	Szenario Produktion 2020 (Industrie Management 1/2006)	66 S.	978-3-936771-63-3
77169	Gronau, Norbert	Kooperationsnetzwerke (Industrie Management 3/2006)	82 S.	978-3-936771-69-5
77174	Aier, Stephan; Schönherr, Marten (Hrsg.)	Enterprise Application Integration – Serviceorientierung und nachhaltige Architekturen (2. Auflage)	428 S.	978-3-936771-74-9
77176	Aier, Stephan; Schönherr, Marten	Enterprise Application Integration - Flexibilisierung komplexer Unternehmensarchitekturen (2. Auflage)	274 S.	978-3-936771-76-3
77177	Gronau, Norbert	Fabrikcontrolling (Industrie Management 4/2006)	66 S.	978-3-936771-77-0
77184	Gronau, Norbert	Business Intelligence (ERP Management 3/2006)	66 S.	978-3-936771-84-8
77193	Scholz-Reiter, Bernd	Globalisierung und Produktion (Industrie Management 1/2007)	82 S.	978-3-936771-93-0
77196	Benger, Alf	Gestaltung von Wertschöpfungsnetzwerken	180 S.	978-3-936771-96-1
77198	Gronau, Norbert (Hrsg.)	4. Konferenz Professionelles Wissensmanagement – Erfahrungen und Visionen, Band 1 / D	446 S.	978-3-936771-98-5
77199	Gronau, Norbert (Ed.)	4th Conference on Professional Knowledge Management – Experiences and Visions, Band 2 / E	392 S.	978-3-936771-99-2
1902	Gronau, Norbert	Personalmanagement (ERP Management 1/2007)	66 S.	978-3-940019-02-8
1905	Gronau, Norbert	Beschäftigungssicherung (Industrie Management 2/2007)	82 S.	978-3-940019-05-9

Ausgewählte Literatur
für die Bereiche

GITO

Betriebswirtschaft	Qualitätsmanagement
Electronic Business	Wandlungsfähigkeit
Unternehmensführung	Wirtschaftsinformatik
und Organisation	Wissensmanagement

Nr.	Autor	Titel	Umfang	ISBN
1915	Gronau, Norbert (Hrsg.); Bahrs, Julian; Schmid, Simone; Müller, Claudia; Fröming, Jane	Wissensmanagement in der Praxis – Ergebnisse einer empirischen Untersuchung	102 S.	978-3-940019-15-8
1916	Gronau, Norbert	Industrielles Informationsmanagement (Industrie Management 4/2007)	66 S.	978-3-940019-16-5
1917	Scholz-Reiter, Bernd (Hrsg.), Gavirey, Sylvie	Dezentrale Veränderungen in Produktionsunternehmen – Potenziale und Grenzen lokaler Maßnahmen für organisatorisches Lernen	186 S.	978-3-940019-17-2
1921	Gronau, Norbert	Outsourcing (ERP Management 3/2007)	64 S.	978-3-940019-21-9
1930	Gronau, Norbert	Wettbewerbsfähigkeit (Industrie Management 2/2008)	82 S.	978-3-940019-30-1
1931	Gronau, Norbert	China (Industrie Management 1/2008)	66 S.	978-3-940019-31-8
1934	Bichler, Martin; Hess, Thomas; Krcmar, Helmut; Lechner, Ulrike; Matthes, Florian; Picot, Arnold; Speitkamp, Benjamin; Wolf, Petra (Hrsg.)	Multikonferenz Wirtschaftsinformatik 2008	444 S.	978-3-940019-34-9
1936	Kuster, Jürgen	Providing Decision Support in the Operative Management of Process Disruptions	118 S.	978-3-940019-36-3
1937	Müller, Claudia	Graphentheoretische Analyse der Evolution von Wiki-basierten Netzwerken für selbstorganisiertes Wissensmanagement	288 S.	978-3-940019-37-0
1938	Großmann, Uwe; Kawalek, Jürgen; Sieck, Jürgen (Hrsg.)	Information, Kommunikation und Arbeitsprozessoptimierung mit Mobilen Systemen – Zahlen, Ergebnisse und Perspektiven zum IKAROS-Projekt	222 S.	978-3-940019-38-7
1944	Gronau, Norbert (Hrsg.)	Wettbewerbsfähigkeit durch Arbeits- und Betriebsorganisation	302 S.	978-3-940019-44-8
1949	Scholz-Reiter, Bernd (Hrsg.)	Technologiegetriebene Veränderungen der Arbeitswelt	328 S.	978-3-940019-49-3
1952	Scholz-Reiter, Bernd	Industrielle Dienstleistung (Industrie Management 5/2008)	82 S.	978-3-940019-52-3
1955	Gronau, Norbert; Eggert, Sandy (Hrsg.)	Beratung, Service und Vertrieb für ERP-Anbieter	258 S.	978-3-940019-55-4
1956	Strickmann, Jan	Analysemethoden zur Bewertung von Entwicklungsprojekten. Ein integriertes semantisches Modell von Projekt- und Produktdaten zur Bewertung der Entwicklungsleistung im Projektcontrolling	194 S.	978-3-940019-56-1
1957	Gronau, Norbert	Produktpiraterie (Industrie Management 6/2008)	66 S.	978-3-940019-57-8
1962	Rohloff, Michael	Integrierte Gestaltung von Unternehmensorganisation und IT	377 S.	978-3-940019-62-2
1966	Gronau, Norbert	Internationalisierung im Mittelstand (ERP Management 1/2009)	66 S.	978-3-940019-66-0
1967	Felden, Carsten	Energiewirtschaftliche Fragestellungen aus betrieblicher und ingenieurwissenschaftlicher Sicht	120 S.	978-3-940019-67-7
1972	Scholz-Reiter, Bernd	Schlanke Produktionssysteme (PPS Management 2/2009)	66 S.	978-3-940019-72-1
1974	Scholz-Reiter, Bernd	Selbstorganisation (Industrie Management 3/2009)	66 S.	978-3-940019-74-5
1975	Gronau, Norbert	Prozessmanagement (ERP Management 2/2009)	66 S.	978-3-940019-75-2
1979	Gronau, Norbert	Strategisches Management (Industrie Management 4/2009)	66 S.	978-3-940019-79-0
1980	Schenk, Michael	Digital Engineering - Herausforderung für die Arbeits- und Betriebsorganisation	400 S.	978-3-940019-80-6

Ausgewählte Literatur für die Bereiche

GITO

Betriebswirtschaft
Electronic Business
Unternehmensführung
und Organisation

Qualitätsmanagement
Wandlungsfähigkeit
Wirtschaftsinformatik
Wissensmanagement

Nr.	Autor	Titel	Seiten	ISBN
1989	Gronau, Norbert	Indien (Industrie Management 6/2009)	66 S.	978-3-940019-89-9
1994	Gronau, Norbert	Prozessorientiertes Wissensmanagement (Industrie Management 1/2010)	66 S.	978-3-940019-94-3
1995	Gronau (Hrsg.)/Stein/ Röchert-Voigt/u.a.	E-Government-Anwendungen	264 S.	978-3-940019-95-0
1996	Gronau, Norbert	ERP-Architekturen (ERP Management 1/2010)	66 S.	978-3-940019-96-7
1997	Gronau, Norbert	Factory Automation (Productivity Management 1/2010)	66 S.	978-3-940019-97-4
1998	Schröpfer, Christian	Das SOA-Management-Framework - Ein ganzheitliches, integriertes Konzept für die Governance Serviceorientierter Architekturen	360 S.	978-3-940019-98-1
8305	Scholz-Reiter, Bernd	Digital Engineering (Industrie Management 2/2010)	82 S.	978-3-942183-05-5
8306	Gronau, Norbert	Digital Factory (Productivity Management 1a/2010)	46 S.	978-3-942183-06-2
8307	Gronau, N.; Lindemann, M.	Einführung in das Informationsmanagement (2., überarbeitete Auflage)	236 S.	978-3-942183-07-9
8308	Nösekabel, Holger	Mobile Education, 2. Auflage	366 S.	978-3-942183-08-6
8309	Gronau, Norbert	Open Source (Industrie Management 3/2010)	66 S.	978-3-942183-09-3
8310	Gronau, Norbert; Lindemann, Marcus	Einführung in das Produktionsmanagement (2., überarbeitete Auflage)	272 S.	978-3-942183-10-9
8311	Gronau, Norbert	Business Intelligence mit ERP-Systemen (ERP Management 2/2010)	66 S.	978-3-942183-11-6
8312	Scholz-Reiter, Bernd	Kopplung MES - ERP (Productivity Management 2/2010)	66 S.	978-3-942183-12-3
8313	Gronau, Norbert	Qualitätsmanagement (Industrie Management 4/2010)	82 S.	978-3-942183-13-0
8314	Fohrholz, Corinna	Business Software für Apple-Plattformen (iSuccess 1/2010)	66 S.	978-3-942183-14-7
8315	Nyhuis, Peter (Hrsg.)	Wandlungsfähige Produktionssysteme	468 S.	978-3-942183-15-4
8316	Amt24 e.V.; Tanja Röchert-Voigt; Denise Berg	Web 2.0 in der öffentlichen Verwaltung	92 S.	978-3-942183-16-1
8317	Scholz-Reiter, Bernd	Globale Logistik (Industrie Management 5/2010)	66 S.	978-3-942183-17-8
8318	Gronau, Norbert	Störungsmanagement (Productivity Management 3/2010)	66 S.	978-3-942183-18-5
8319	Gronau, Norbert	ERP-Auswahl und -Einführung (ERP Management 3/2010)	66 S.	978-3-942183-19-2
8322	Flach, G.; Schultz, J. (Hrsg.)	5. Rostocker eGovernment-Forum 2010 – Wissensbasiertes eGovernment: Erschließung und Nutzung von Verwaltungswissen	78 S.	978-3-942183-22-2
8323	Gronau, N.; Eggert, S.; Fohrholz, C. (Hrsg.)	Software as a Service, Cloud Computing und Mobile Technologien	380 S.	978-3-942183-23-9
8325	Gronau, Norbert	Lizenzmodelle für ERP-Systeme (ERP Management 4/2010)	66 S.	978-3-942183-25-3
8326	Scholz-Reiter, Bernd	Autonome Systeme (Industrie Management 1/2011)	66 S.	978-3-942183-26-0
8327	Gronau, Norbert	Mobiles Arbeiten und Sicherheit (iSuccess 1/2011)	66 S.	978-3-942183-27-7
8328	Gronau, Norbert	Effizienz durch ERP (ERP Management 1/2011)	82 S.	978-3-942183-28-4
8330	Scholz-Reiter, Bernd	Brasilien (Industrie Management 2/2011)	82 S.	978-3-942183-30-7
8332	Bill, R., Flach, G., Klammer, U., Lerche, T. (Hrsg.)	GeoForum MV 2011 – Geodateninfrastrukturen: Drehscheibe für Wirtschaft und Verwaltung	181 S.	978-3-942183-32-1
8334	Heine, Moreen	Transfer von E-Government-Lösungen – Wirkungen und Strategien	178 S.	978-3-942183-34-5

GITO

Betriebswirtschaft
Electronic Business
Unternehmensführung
und Organisation

Qualitätsmanagement
Wandlungsfähigkeit
Wirtschaftsinformatik
Wissensmanagement

8339	Gronau, Norbert; Meier, Horst; Bahrs, Julian (Hrsg.)	Handbuch gegen Produktpiraterie – Prävention von Produktpiraterie durch Technologie, Organisation und Wissensflussmanagement	248 S.	978-3-942183-39-0
8342	Gronau, Norbert	Erfolgsfaktor Personal (Industrie Management 4/2011)	82 S.	978-3-942183-42-0
8345	Bentele, Markus; Gronau, Norbert; Schütt, Peter; Weber, Mathias (Hrsg.)	KnowTech - Unternehmenswissen als Erfolgsfaktor mobilisieren!	610 S.	978-3-942183-45-1
8353	Stracke, Christian M.	Competence Modelling for Human Resources Development and European Policies	168 S.	978-3-942183-53-6
8355	Gronau, Norbert	ERP-Strategien (ERP Management 4/2011)	66 S.	978-3-942183-56-0
8358	Soelberg, Christian	Wissenskapital als Instrument der strategischen Unternehmensführung	233 S.	978-3-942183-58-1

Wandlungsfähigkeit

7716O	Gronau, Norbert	Wandlungsfähige Informationssystemarchitekturen – Nachhaltigkeit bei organisatorischem Wandel (2. Auflage)	324 S.	978-3-936771-60-2
77178	Gronau, Norbert (Hrsg.); Andresen, Katja	Design and Use Patterns of Adaptability in Enterprise Systems	147 S.	978-3-936771-78-7
1904	Gronau, Norbert; Lämmer, Anne; Andresen, Katja (Hrsg.)	Wandlungsfähige ERP-Systeme – Entwicklung, Auswahl und Methode (2. Auflage)	182 S.	978-3-940019-04-2
1971	Frazzon, Enzo Morosini	Sustainability and Effectiveness in Global Logistic Systems	179 S.	978-3-940019-71-4
1974	Scholz-Reiter, Bernd	Selbstorganisation (Industrie Management 3/2009)	66 S.	978-3-940019-74-5
1984	Gronau, Norbert	ERP-Integration (ERP Management 3/2009)	66 S.	978-3-940019-84-4
1992	Broy, M., Gronau, N., Wildemann, H.	Gestaltung interorganisationaler Software-Entwicklung – Herausforderungen durch Wandlungsfähigkeit und Wiederverwendung	352 S.	978-3-940019-92-9
8300	Tanja Röchert-Voigt, Moreen Stein, Edzard Weber	Wandlungsfähige Schutzstrukturen - Handlungsleitfaden	20 S.	978-3-942183-00-0
8302	Tanja Röchert-Voigt, Moreen Stein, Edzard Weber	Wandlungsfähige Schutzstrukturen – theoretische Grundlagen und praktische Anwendungen - Handlungsleitfaden	54 S.	978-3-942183-02-4
8303	Eggert, Sandy	Wandlungsfähigkeit von Enterprise Content Management – Gestaltung wandlungsfähiger ECM-Prozesse unter Verwendung kartographischer Methoden	292 S.	978-3-942183-03-1
8305	Scholz-Reiter, Bernd	Digital Engineering (Industrie Management 2/2010)	82 S.	978-3-942183-05-5
8309	Gronau, Norbert	Open Source (Industrie Management 3/2010)	66 S.	978-3-942183-09-3
8313	Gronau, Norbert	Qualitätsmanagement (Industrie Management 4/2010)	82 S.	978-3-942183-13-0
8315	Nyhuis, Peter (Hrsg.)	Wandlungsfähige Produktionssysteme	468 S.	978-3-942183-15-4
8316	Amt24 e.V.; Tanja Röchert-Voigt; Denise Berg	Web 2.0 in der öffentlichen Verwaltung	92 S.	978-3-942183-16-1
8326	Scholz-Reiter, Bernd	Autonome Systeme (Industrie Management 1/2011)	66 S.	978-3-942183-26-0
8328	Gronau, Norbert	Effizienz durch ERP (ERP Management 1/2011)	82 S.	978-3-942183-28-4
8330	Scholz-Reiter, Bernd	Brasilien (Industrie Management 2/2011)	82 S.	978-3-942183-30-7

Ausgewählte Literatur
für die Bereiche

GITO

Betriebswirtschaft	Qualitätsmanagement
Electronic Business	Wandlungsfähigkeit
Unternehmensführung	Wirtschaftsinformatik
und Organisation	Wissensmanagement

Ausgewählte Literatur
für die Bereiche

GITO

Betriebswirtschaft
Electronic Business
Unternehmensführung
und Organisation

Qualitätsmanagement
Wandlungsfähigkeit
Wirtschaftsinformatik
Wissensmanagement

1904	Gronau, Norbert; Lämmer, Anne; Andresen, Katja (Hrsg.)	Wandlungsfähige ERP-Systeme – Entwicklung, Auswahl und Methode (2. Auflage)	182 S.	978-3-940019-04-2
1906	Steffens, Ulrike; Addicks, Jan Stefan; Streekmann, Niels (Hrsg.)	MDD, SOA und IT-Management (MSI 2007) Workshop, Oldenburg, April 2007	82 S.	978-3-940019-06-6
1907	Schmid, Simone; Rölske, Tilman	Qualifizierung und Support von ERP-Systemen – Ergebnisse einer empirischen Untersuchung	76 S.	978-3-940019-07-3
1908	Michael A. Herzog (Hrsg.)	Content Engineering - Konzepte, Technologien und Anwendungen in der Medienproduktion	180 S.	978-3-940019-08-0
1911	Freund, Tessen	Software Engineering durch Modellierung wissensintensiver Entwicklungsprozesse	316 S.	978-3-940019-11-0
1912	Gronau, Norbert	ERP-Systeme für die öffentliche Verwaltung (ERP Management 2/2007)	66 S.	978-3-940019-12-7
1913	Gronau, Norbert; Stein, Moreen (Hrsg.)	ERP-Systeme in der öffentlichen Verwaltung	266 S.	978-3-940019-13-4
1916	Gronau, Norbert	Industrielles Informationsmanagement (Industrie Management 4/2007)	66 S.	978-3-940019-16-5
1918	Dietrich, Jens	Nutzung von Modellierungssprachen und -methodologien standardisierter B2B-Architekturen für die Integration unternehmensinterner Geschäftsprozesse	294 S.	978-3-940019-18-9
1921	Gronau, Norbert	Outsourcing (ERP Management 3/2007)	64 S.	978-3-940019-21-9
1926	Müller-Birn, Claudia; Gronau, Norbert (Hrsg.)	Analyse sozialer Netzwerke und Social Software – Grundlagen und Anwendungsbeispiele	326 S.	978-3-940019-26-4
1927	Gronau, Norbert	ERP-Systeme im Dienstleistungssektor (ERP Management 4/2007)	66 S.	978-3-940019-27-1
1928	Gronau, Norbert	Serviceorientierte Architekturen (ERP Management 1/2008)	66 S.	978-3-940019-28-8
1929	Appelrath, H.-Jürgen; Felden, Carsten; Uslar, Mathias (Hrsg.)	IT in der Energiewirtschaft: Track Proceedings der MKWI 2008	54 S.	978-3-940019-29-5
1931	Gronau, Norbert	China (Industrie Management 1/2008)	66 S.	978-3-940019-31-8
1934	Bichler, Martin; Hess, Thomas; Krcmar, Helmut; Lechner, Ulrike; Matthes, Florian; Picot, Arnold; Speitkamp, Benjamin; Wolf, Petra (Hrsg.)	Multikonferenz Wirtschaftsinformatik 2008	444 S.	978-3-940019-34-9
1936	Kuster, Jürgen	Providing Decision Support in the Operative Management of Process Disruptions	118 S.	978-3-940019-36-3
1937	Müller, Claudia	Graphentheoretische Analyse der Evolution von Wiki-basierten Netzwerken für selbstorganisiertes Wissensmanagement	288 S.	978-3-940019-37-0
1938	Großmann, Uwe; Kawalek, Jürgen; Sieck, Jürgen (Hrsg.)	Information, Kommunikation und Arbeitsprozessoptimierung mit Mobilen Systemen – Zahlen, Ergebnisse und Perspektiven zum IKAROS-Projekt	222 S.	978-3-940019-38-7
1942	Gronau, Norbert	Business Performance Management (ERP Management 2/2008)	66 S.	978-3-940019-42-4
1948	Steffens, Ulrike; Addicks, Jan Stefan; Streekmann, Niels (Hrsg.)	MDD, SOA und IT-Management (MSI 2008) – Workshop, Oldenburg, Sept. 2008	108 S.	978-3-940019-48-6

GITO

Betriebswirtschaft
Electronic Business
Unternehmensführung
und Organisation

Qualitätsmanagement
Wandlungsfähigkeit
Wirtschaftsinformatik
Wissensmanagement

Nr.	Autor	Titel	Umfang	ISBN
1958	Herzog, Michael A. (Hrsg.)	Prozessgestaltung in der Medienproduktion. Neue Geschäftsmodelle und Technologien für Mobile Portale und HD Broadcast	198 S.	978-3-940019-58-5
1960	Gronau, Norbert; Gäbler, Andreas	Einführung in die Wirtschaftsinformatik, Band 1 (2. durchgesehene Auflage 2010)	318 S.	978-3-940019-60-8
1962	Rohloff, Michael	Integrierte Gestaltung von Unternehmensorganisation und IT	377 S.	978-3-940019-62-2
1963	Gronau, Norbert; Gäbler, Andreas	Einführung in die Wirtschaftsinformatik, Band 2 (2. durchgesehene Auflage 2010)	286 S.	978-3-940019-63-9
1967	Felden, Carsten	Energiewirtschaftliche Fragestellungen aus betrieblicher und ingenieurwissenschaftlicher Sicht	120 S.	978-3-940019-67-7
1978	Offermann, Philipp	Eine Methode zur Konzeption betrieblicher Software mit einer Serviceorientierten Architektur	236 S.	978-3-940019-78-3
1981	Ulrike Steffens, Jan Stefan Addicks, Matthias Postina, Niels Streekmann (Eds.)	MDD, SOA und IT-Management (MSI 2009) – Workshop, Oldenburg, October 2009	99 S.	978-3-940019-81-3
1985	Fröming, Jane	Ein Konzept zur Simulation wissensintensiver Aktivitäten in Geschäftsprozessen	346 S.	978-3-940019-85-1
1987	Gronau, Norbert; Eggert, Sandy (Hrsg.)	Architekturen, Geschäftsmodelle und Marketingstrategien für ERP-Anbieter	258 S.	978-3-940019-87-5
1990	Michael H. Breitner, Karsten Sohns, Christine Voigtländer	Perspektiven des Lebenslangen Lernens – dynamische Bildungsnetzwerke, Geschäftsmodelle, Trends	328 S.	978-3-940019-90-5
1991	Gronau, Norbert	Usability (ERP Management 4/2009)	66 S.	978-3-940019-91-2
1992	Broy, M., Gronau, N., Wildemann, H.	Gestaltung interorganisationaler Software-Entwicklung – Herausforderungen durch Wandlungsfähigkeit und Wiederverwendung	352 S.	978-3-940019-92-9
1994	Gronau, Norbert	Prozessorientiertes Wissensmanagement (Industrie Management 1/2010)	66 S.	978-3-940019-94-3
1995	Gronau (Hrsg.)/Stein/ Röchert-Voigt/u.a.	E-Government-Anwendungen	264 S.	978-3-940019-95-0
1996	Gronau, Norbert	ERP-Architekturen (ERP Management 1/2010)	66 S.	978-3-940019-96-7
8303	Eggert, Sandy	Wandlungsfähigkeit von Enterprise Content Management - Gestaltung wandlungsfähiger ECM-Prozesse unter Verwendung kartographischer Methoden	292 S.	978-3-942183-03-1
8304	Sultanow, Eldar	Zusammenarbeit in verteilten Projekten - Dekomposition, Barrieren und Lösungen im Kontext der Webentwicklung	134 S.	978-3-942183-04-8
8307	Gronau, N.; Lindemann, M.	Einführung in das Informationsmanagement (2., überarbeitete Auflage)	236 S.	978-3-942183-07-9
8309	Gronau, Norbert	Open Source (Industrie Management 3/2010)	66 S.	978-3-942183-09-3
8310	Gronau, Norbert; Lindemann, Marcus	Einführung in das Produktionsmanagement (2., überarbeitete Auflage)	272 S.	978-3-942183-10-9
8314	Fohrholz, Corinna	Business Software für Apple-Plattformen (iSuccess 1/2010)	66 S.	978-3-942183-14-7
8316	Amt24 e.V.; Tanja Röchert-Voigt; Denise Berg	Web 2.0 in der öffentlichen Verwaltung	92 S.	978-3-942183-16-1
8320	Hasselbring, Wilhelm (Hrsg.)	Betriebliche Informationssysteme: Grid-basierte Integration und Orchestrierung	498 S.	978-3-942183-20-8
8322	Flach, G.; Schultz, J. (Hrsg.)	5. Rostocker eGovernment-Forum 2010 – Wissensbasiertes eGovernment: Erschließung und Nutzung von Verwaltungswissen	78 S.	978-3-942183-22-2
8323	Gronau, N.; Eggert, S.; Fohrholz, C. (Hrsg.)	Software as a Service, Cloud Computing und Mobile Technologien	380 S.	978-3-942183-23-9

Ausgewählte Literatur für die Bereiche

Betriebswirtschaft
Electronic Business
Unternehmensführung
und Organisation

Qualitätsmanagement
Wandlungsfähigkeit
Wirtschaftsinformatik
Wissensmanagement

GITO

8327	Gronau, Norbert	Mobiles Arbeiten und Sicherheit (iSuccess 1/2011)	66 S.	978-3-942183-27-7
8333	Krallmann, Hermann; Levina, Olga; Schulz, Marcel	Chronik des Fachgebiets Systemanalyse und EDV	130 S.	978-3-942183-33-8
8334	Heine, Moreen	Transfer von E-Government-Lösungen – Wirkungen und Strategien	178 S.	978-3-942183-34-5
8336	Hölzl, Ribe-Baumann, Brückner (Ed.)	Joint Workshop of the German Research Training Groups in Computer Science	242 S.	978-3-942183-36-9
8340	Gronau, Norbert	Anpassungsfähigkeit und Flexibilität (ERP Management 2/2011)	66 S.	978-3-942183-40-6
8343	Kretzer, Michael (Hrsg.)	Spannungsfelder des Software-Engineering im Medizin- und Pharmaumfeld	112 S.	978-3-942183-43-7
8347	Flach, Guntram; Schultz, Jürgen (Hrsg.)	6. Rostocker eGovernment-Forum 2011 – Nachhaltiges eGovernment: Herausforderung und Notwendigkeit	82 S.	978-3-942183-47-5
8354	Gronau, N., Fohrholz, C.	Wirtschaftliche Geschäftsprozesse durch mobile ERP-Systeme	287 S.	978-3-942183-54-3
8355	Gronau, Norbert	ERP-Strategien (ERP Management 4/2011)	66 S.	978-3-942183-55-0
8358	Soelberg, Christian	Wissenskapital als Instrument der strategischen Unternehmensführung	233 S.	978-3-942183-58-1

Wissensmanagement

77104	Gronau, Norbert	Wissensmanagement (Industrie Management 3/2003)	82 S.	978-3-936771-04-6
77114	Gronau, Norbert	Wissensmanagement: Potenziale - Konzepte - Werkzeuge	364 S.	978-3-936771-14-5
77131	Gronau, Norbert; Petkoff, Boris; Schildhauer, Thomas	Wissensmanagement - Wandel, Wertschöpfung, Wachstum	442 S.	978-3-936771-31-2
77132	Neumann, Nadine	Modellierung eines prozessorientierten Wissensmanagementkonzeptes im Innovationsprozess	442 S.	978-3-936771-32-9
77133	Gronau, Norbert	Produktionsfaktor Wissen (Industrie Management 1/2005)	66 S.	978-3-936771-33-6
77147	Gronau, Norbert; Schmid, Simone	Wissensmanagement im Betrieb komplexer ERP-Systeme	312 S.	978-3-936771-47-3
77152	Gronau, Norbert	Enterprise Content Management (ERP Management 4/2005)	66 S.	978-3-936771-52-7
77153	Gronau, Norbert (Hrsg.); Bahrs, Julian; Schmid, Simone	Anwendungen und Systeme für das Wissensmanagement – Ein aktueller Überblick (2. Auflage)	312 S.	978-3-936771-53-4
77159	Hahn, Axel; Grauer, Manfred	Informations- und Wissensdrehscheibe Produktdatenmanagement	74 S.	978-3-936771-59-6
77170	Gronau, Norbert	Support von ERP Systemen (ERP Management 2/2006)	66 S.	978-3-936771-70-1
77180	Gronau, Norbert; Hasselbring, Wilhelm (Hrsg.)	M-WISE: Modellierung wissensintensiver Prozesse im Software Engineering	540 S.	978-3-936771-80-0
77186	Gronau, Norbert; Fröming, Jane; Schmid, Simone (Hrsg.)	Kompetenzmanagement in der Praxis – Schulung, Staffing und Anreizsysteme	232 S.	978-3-936771-86-2
77192	Kratzke, Nane	Modellbasierte Analyse interorganisationaler Wissensflüsse	222 S.	978-3-936771-92-3
77198	Gronau, Norbert (Hrsg.)	4. Konferenz Professionelles Wissensmanagement – Erfahrungen und Visionen, Band 1 / D	446 S.	978-3-936771-98-5
77199	Gronau, Norbert (Ed.)	4th Conference on Professional Knowledge Management – Experiences and Visions, Band 2 / E	392 S.	978-3-936771-99-2

Ausgewählte Literatur für die Bereiche

GITO

Betriebswirtschaft
Electronic Business
Unternehmensführung
und Organisation

Qualitätsmanagement
Wandlungsfähigkeit
Wirtschaftsinformatik
Wissensmanagement

1907	Schmid, Simone; Rüsike,Tilman	Qualifizierung und Support von ERP-Systemen – Ergebnisse einer empirischen Untersuchung	76 S.	978-3-940019-07-3
1908	Michael A. Herzog (Hrsg.)	Content Engineering - Konzepte, Technologien und Anwendungen in der Medienproduktion	180 S.	978-3-940019-08-0
1914	Gronau, Norbert (Hrsg.); Uslar, Mathias	Potenziale des Skill Management: Stand, Anforderungen und Ausblicke für KMU (2. Auflage)	126 S.	978-3-940019-14-1
1915	Gronau, Norbert (Hrsg.); Bahrs, Julian; Schmid, Simone; Müller, Claudia; Fröming, Jane	Wissensmanagement in der Praxis – Ergebnisse einer empirischen Untersuchung	102 S.	978-3-940019-15-8
1917	Scholz-Reiter, Bernd (Hrsg.); Gavirey, Sylvie	Dezentrale Veränderungen in Produktionsunternehmen – Potenziale und Grenzen lokaler Maßnahmen für organisatorisches Lernen	186 S.	978-3-940019-17-2
1926	Müller-Birn, Claudia; Gronau, Norbert (Hrsg.)	Analyse sozialer Netzwerke und Social Software – Grundlagen und Anwendungsbeispiele	326 S.	978-3-940019-26-4
1937	Müller, Claudia	Graphentheoretische Analyse der Evolution von Wiki-basierten Netzwerken für selbstorganisiertes Wissensmanagement	288 S.	978-3-940019-37-0
1957	Gronau, Norbert	Produktpiraterie (Industrie Management 6/2008)	66 S.	978-3-940019-57-8
1958	Herzog, Michael A. (Hrsg.)	Prozessgestaltung in der Medienproduktion. Neue Geschäftsmodelle und Technologien für Mobile Portale und HD Broadcast	198 S.	978-3-940019-58-5
1977	Gronau, Norbert (Hrsg.); Bahrs, Julian; Vladova, Gergana	Anwendungen und Systeme für das Wissensmanagement – Ein aktueller Überblick (3. Auflage)	372 S.	978-3-940019-77-6
1985	Fröming, Jane	Ein Konzept zur Simulation wissensintensiver Aktivitäten in Geschäftsprozessen	346 S.	978-3-940019-85-1
1990	Michael H. Breitner, Karsten Sohns, Christine Voigtländer	Perspektiven des Lebenslangen Lernens – dynamische Bildungsnetzwerke, Geschäftsmodelle, Trends	328 S.	978-3-940019-90-5
1993	Schmidt, Benedikt	Wettbewerbsvorteile im SAP-Outsourcing durch Wissensmanagement - Methoden zur effizienten Gestaltung des Übergangs ins Application Management	289 S.	978-3-940019-93-6
1994	Gronau, Norbert	Prozessorientiertes Wissensmanagement (Industrie Management 1/2010)	66 S.	978-3-940019-94-3
8304	Sultanow, Eldar	Zusammenarbeit in verteilten Projekten - Dekomposition, Barrieren und Lösungen im Kontext der Webentwicklung	134 S.	978-3-942183-04-8
8305	Scholz-Reiter, Bernd	Digital Engineering (Industrie Management 2/2010)	82 S.	978-3-942183-05-5
8308	Nösekabel, Holger	Mobile Education, 2. Auflage	366 S.	978-3-942183-08-6
8322	Flach, G.; Schultz, J. (Hrsg.)	5. Rostocker eGovernment-Forum 2010 – Wissensbasiertes eGovernment: Erschließung und Nutzung von Verwaltungswissen	78 S.	978-3-942183-22-2
8332	Bill, R., Flach, G., Klammer, U., Lerche, T. (Hrsg.)	GeoForum MV 2011 – Geodateninfrastrukturen: Drehscheibe für Wirtschaft und Verwaltung	181 S.	978-3-942183-32-1
8334	Heine, Moreen	Transfer von E-Government-Lösungen – Wirkungen und Strategien	178 S.	978-3-942183-34-5
8339	Gronau, Norbert; Meier, Horst; Bahrs, Julian (Hrsg.)	Handbuch gegen Produktpiraterie – Prävention von Produktpiraterie durch Technologie, Organisation und Wissensflussmanagement	248 S.	978-3-942183-39-0
8342	Gronau, Norbert	Erfolgsfaktor Personal (Industrie Management 4/2011)	82 S.	978-3-942183-42-0

Ausgewählte Literatur
für die Bereiche

GITO

Betriebswirtschaft
Electronic Business
Unternehmensführung
und Organisation

Qualitätsmanagement
Wandlungsfähigkeit
Wirtschaftsinformatik
Wissensmanagement

8345	Bentele, Markus; Gronau, Norbert; Schütt, Peter; Weber, Mathias (Hrsg.)	KnowTech - Unternehmenswissen als Erfolgsfaktor mobilisieren!	610 S.	978-3-942183-45-1
8347	Flach, Guntram; Schultz, Jürgen (Hrsg.)	6. Rostocker eGovernment-Forum 2011 – Nachhaltiges eGovernment: Herausforderung und Notwendigkeit	82 S.	978-3-942183-47-5
8351	Spath, Dieter (Hrsg.)	Wissensarbeit – Zwischen strengen Prozessen und kreativem Spielraum	494 S.	978-3-942183-51-2
8352	Gronau, Norbert (Hrsg.)	Modeling and Analyzing knowledge intensive business processes with KMDL – Comprehensive insights into theory and practice	522 S.	978-3-942183-52-9
8358	Soelberg, Christian	Wissenskapital als Instrument der strategischen Unternehmensführung	233 S.	978-3-942183-58-1